$4.95

D0893910

By Kenya
Possessed

Studies in
Imperialism
Robin W. Winks
Editor

The Correspondence
of Norman Leys
and J. H. Oldham
1918–1926

BY
KENYA
POSSESSED

Edited and
with an
Introduction by
John W. Cell

The University
of Chicago Press
Chicago
and London

BENEDICTINE UNIVERSITY LIBRARY
IN THE KINDLON HALL OF LEARNING
5700 COLLEGE ROAD
LISLE, IL 60532-0900

DT
433.575
.L487

The University of Chicago Press, Chicago 60637
The University of Chicago Press, Ltd., London

© 1976 by the University of Chicago
All rights reserved. Published 1976. Printed in the
United States of America

JOHN W. CELL is associate professor of history at
Duke University where he has taught since 1962. He
is the author of *British Colonial Administration in
the Mid-Nineteenth Century: The Policy Making
Process*.

Library of Congress Cataloging in Publication Data
Leys, Norman Maclean.
    By Kenya possessed.

    (Studies in imperialism)
    Includes index.
    1. Kenya—Politics and government.   2. Oldham,
Joseph Houldsworth, 1874–1969.   3. Leys, Norman Maclean.
I. Oldham, Joseph Houldsworth, 1874–1969.   II. Cell, John Whitson.
III. Title.
DT433.575.L48 1976   320.9'676'203   75-27894
ISBN 0-226-09971-7

Contents

Series Editor's Preface

The single greatest need in imperial studies today is for a systematic exploration of the intellectual history of imperialism. We know a good bit—but not enough—about the intellectual (or, perhaps more properly, antiintellectual) origins of thinking about race. We know a good bit—but again not enough—about the changing meanings accorded to the word *imperialism* by different generations, from the time when one could declare pride in being called imperialist to the time in which the word is automatically and emotionally denigratory. We know less—and far from enough—about the ways in which the actual experience of imperialism, the experiment in the field as it were, changed the attitudes of the imperialists. Certainly there exists no overall intellectual history of the British colonial system.

The present book is an important start in this direction. While its focus is on Africa, the issues raised by J. H. Oldham and Norman Leys between 1918 and 1926 are precisely those with which the historian of imperialism must now wrestle. This was the first generation of imperial administrators to be deeply influenced by the findings of the more sophisticated of the anthropologists. This was the period by which the Boer War, and World War I, had taken any romantic bloom left on the role of the imperialist, and that role had simply become the role of the bureaucrat in the field. This was the period, extending through the interwar years, in which the first stirrings of reaction against the notion of indirect rule had led some few of the British administrators to think in terms of a more limited future in Africa. A variety of questions were being asked: about the nature of Christian missions in the empire; about the continued applicability of the teachings of the New Testament to that empire; about justifying compulsory labor; about the problem of bringing fundamental change to racially stratified societies. Norman Leys, as a medical doctor and

Christian socialist, and J. H. Oldham, as a Christian reformer and secretary of the International Missionary Council, canvassed these and similar kinds of questions in a lengthy, rich correspondence during the crucial immediate post-World War I years.

Dr. Cell has drawn upon this correspondence to open the door wider upon the intellectual preoccupations of the imperialists of the time. Norman Leys' radicalism was incisive, thoughtful, never doctrinaire. Oldham's responses, while based on a tradition he respected, were never mere echoes of earlier positions. Between them, as this correspondence shows, they asked the questions that needed to be asked at a time when too few were doing so. One often learns most about people from the questions they ask, from their preoccupations and worries, and such is the case here. As Dr. Cell's introduction makes clear, the Leys-Oldham correspondence helps make possible that intellectual history of the British Empire which he, and others, are now writing.

ROBIN W. WINKS

Acknowledgments

Most of the correspondence between Dr. Norman Leys and Dr. Joseph H. Oldham, 1918–1926, is found in the archives of the Council of British Missionary Societies at Edinburgh House in London, and I thank Miss Marjorie Ellmer, the archivist, for permission to edit it. I also thank Mr. A. J. van der Bent, archivist of the World Council of Churches in Geneva for allowing me to use materials from the records of the International Missionary Council. Professor Arnold Toynbee, executor of the estate of Professor Gilbert Murray, allowed me to quote from Leys' early correspondence with Murray from Africa, contained in the Murray papers at the Bodleian Library, Oxford. And I gratefully acknowledge the cooperation and assistance of Norman Leys' family: Duncan Leys, his half-brother; Professor Colin Leys, his nephew and a distinguished Africanist; and above all his daughter, Mrs. Agnes Avery, who told me much about her father and who read my introduction critically and sympathetically. Mrs. Dorothy Sapp typed the manuscript superbly, and I thank her. Last I thank my colleague, Gerald Hartwig, and my wife, Gillian Cell.

I have included virtually all the Oldham-Leys correspondence, omitting only routine exchanges. Mr. van der Bent also permitted me to include several Oldham letters to other individuals, notably Randall Davidson, the archbishop, which are extremely pertinent. Unless otherwise indicated the source may be assumed to be the main collection at Edinburgh House (Oldham papers, Box 247).

In the introduction I have tried to explain the several contexts the correspondence addresses: the politics of a settlement colony in British Africa between the wars; the role of Christianity in a racially stratified society; and the intellectual climate concerning African issues which Leys and Oldham represented and which, in their different ways, they tried to change.

J. H. Oldham

Introduction

Introduction

The correspondence between Dr. Norman Leys and Dr. Joseph H. Oldham, 1918–1926, centers on Kenya. Both were important figures in the Kenya debate, Leys as publicist and agitator, Oldham as the organizer of disparate factions for concerted action. Their interchange therefore constitutes a valuable record of the calculations of what may be broadly defined as the British humanitarian lobby in an era of crucial importance in the history of East Africa. But Leys and Oldham were unusually thoughtful as well as committed and influential, and their correspondence is not parochial. It ranges widely over the ultimate issues raised by British imperialism and European settlement in Africa: over how to maintain the integrity of African societies at a time of rapid transition when they must change to survive; over the question of race as a real or ephemeral determinant of human differences; over the nature of Christianity and its proper relationship to cultural interaction and conflict.

Although their relationship was at times a fruitful collaboration, Oldham and Leys were never personally close. Primarily their discourse was a confrontation, comparable in many ways to the collision during World War II between Margery Perham and Elspeth Huxley.[1] Both collections, while centering on the problems of Kenya, provide evidence of how the British approached the "dilemmas of trusteeship"[2] in a period when colonialism still seemed to be invincible.

Kenya became the central test case of British colonial trusteeship through a process of elimination. West Africa and the Sudan had no settlers. Mineral interests and plantation industries might cause commercial exploitation but not the far more destructive competition for land, grass, water, and living space that has marked the history of settlement colonies. Uganda too had few settlers, a well-organized indigenous kingdom, and a flourishing cotton export trade. The administration of Tanganyika, the former German

colony, had to be defended periodically before the
Mandates Commission of the League of Nations as
being in the interests of the Africans themselves, giving the governor considerable leverage in his dealings
with commercial and settler interests.[3] For both humanitarians and settlers Kenya was thus the key to
East Africa. Uganda and Tanganyika would pose
insuperable problems only if Kenya were "lost" first.
In British Central Africa, in what are now Zambia
and Malawi, local white interests were not yet strong
enough to challenge the administration as they were to
do in the 1950s. South Africa and Rhodesia, where
the domination of African majorities by white minorities was far more complete than in Kenya, were constitutionally protected, South Africa by her independent membership in the Commonwealth, Rhodesia
by the concession of responsible government in 1923.[4]
Often warned by local liberals that their intervention
only made things more difficult, British critics of
southern Africa recognized their impotence. Thus,
partly by design but largely by default, Kenya became
the test case, the pass which must be defended at all
costs, the one colony where British humanitarians
could hope to exercise a decisive influence.

Such a position of notoriety would have surprised
the founders of the East Africa Protectorate. Zanzibar's northern hinterland had always been an undeveloped and unpromising backwater. The Arabs had
bypassed the region in their trade in ivory and slaves
which had centered on the Great Lakes region. The
first Europeans to move systematically into the interior, Sir William Mackinnon's Imperial British East
Africa Company, had concerned themselves principally with developing trade with the Baganda.[5] Passing through on his way to Buganda, Frederick Lugard
had remarked upon the industriousness and efficiency
of the Kikuyu peasant farmers, as well as upon the
inviting beauty of highland areas climatically suitable
for European settlement.[6] But the protectorate's early

years under the Foreign Office did nothing to lift the country from its traditional obscurity. Administered by officials possessing diplomatic but not proconsular experience, who remained in Zanzibar and had only a skeletal staff in the interior, British East Africa was meant to be managed with a minimum of expense and involvement.[7] Involvement there was—including the defeat in 1896 of the Mazrui rebellion and a succession of punitive expeditions. In East Africa as elsewhere the truism persisted that the man on the spot was likely to prove more aggressive than his superiors in Whitehall.

The completion by 1901 of the Uganda Railway was a turning point. Not that it made the East Africa Protectorate itself any more promising. That indeed was the problem. Somehow the place must be made to produce enough revenue to enable the railroad to pay its way. Colonial Office experts would later come to believe that the best course lay after all in developing the agricultural production of Africans on their own land for export.[8] That however would have been a painfully slow process even among the sedentary Kikuyu or Kavirondo, let alone among the pastoral Nandi or Masai. Governor Sir Charles Eliot chose a shortcut.[9] From 1903 British and South African settlers began to enter the allegedly empty "white highlands."[10] In brief this white colony centered on Nairobi suffered the usual fate of new European settlements overseas: lack of capital, shortage of labor, extreme dearness of imported goods, and difficulty in creating an industry that would pay. The shortcut proved to be painfully long. By the 1930s, while the African export economies of the Gold Coast, Southern Nigeria, Uganda, and even Tanganyika were progressing, Kenya remained backward. The Colonial Office was already coming to believe that their backing of European settlement in East Africa had been a profound mistake.

Kenya's basic economic problem, as Norman Leys

argued, was not land but labor (see below, p. 175). There *was* enough land for colonization without necessarily displacing Africans. But the country was so sparsely populated that a labor shortage existed even in "native" areas. Each European employer merely tied up an increasing number of people who were barely able to maintain themselves even in good years. Had Europeans been using surplus population, as the jute plantations can be said to have done in Bengal, they might have been economically beneficial. Competing as they did for labor already in critically short supply, they were adding little if anything to the overall output.

Kenya settlers naturally saw matters quite differently. They alone made Africans productive. An emigrant to Canada or Australia returned to the Empire only the product of his own labor. In East Africa the settler could unleash the latent productivity of a thousand Africans.[11] Without his capital and organization those Africans would continue to produce only for the immediate needs of their primitive economy. The problem was not too many settlers but too few. Great Britain should increase the stake. The colony needed more capital and improved communications. In the years after the first world war the colonial and imperial governments responded. Land was made available to retired officers. Large transport loans were raised under guarantee of the imperial treasury. By various means male Africans of agricultural tribes were induced to work on European farms.

The number of Europeans in Kenya remained small (less than seventeen thousand by 1931)[12] and their economic position weak. What is difficult to explain is how such a tiny group can have sustained so complicated and so vehement a political atmosphere.[13] Contemporaries wondered about the effects on the European temperament of the combination of high altitude and tropical sun. The various movements, associations, campaigns, and controversies this population sustained is almost incredible. The settlers' vision matched their organizational enthusiasm. They aimed to acquire self-government and political domination over the two million Africans of Kenya and, if the closer union movement of the years up to 1931 had succeeded, over those of Uganda and Tanganyika as well.

These goals were grand indeed. In retrospect the settlers may appear to have had little chance of attaining them. Economically they never really made a go of it, and the depression of the 1930s increased their difficulties. The Colonial Office grew disillusioned. Closer union was defeated with surprising ease.[14] Kenya's whites were on the defensive, first against the Indians (who outnumbered them six to one in the years after World War I), then from the early 1950s against African nationalism. It is even possible to wonder whether the almost single-minded attention that was devoted to Kenya was necessary. Might not the friends of Africans have spread their energies, doing more about Rhodesia?

To contemporaries the conclusion of the Kenya struggle by no means appeared foregone. Dame Margery Perham recalls the mood of a desperate rearguard action. Among the pronative faction Oldham was not alone in believing that within perhaps a generation nothing could prevent the Europeans from achieving responsible government or East Africa from becoming a "white dominion." Time looked to be on the side of the settlers. How could their ultimate political domination possibly be prevented? In such a view the most likely strategy might well have been to hope to educate the whites to use their power responsibly. The chances for a more favorable verdict must have seemed slim indeed.

Among the champions of Africans in Kenya none was so devoted as Norman Leys. By Kenya he was possessed. It was the overriding center of his existence, "my one job" as he explained to Oldham "that may redeem my life from failure." His home and surgery at Brailsford near Derby became the nerve center of an intense, unceasing publicity campaign. There he pored over colonial blue books and the East African press. He carried on a huge correspondence with colonial officials, missionaries, fellow agitators, and African politicians. His destruction of this material by fire, however characteristic it may have been of one who thought himself in no way extraordinary, is a loss to African scholarship. Leys infuriated settlers and embarrassed governments. The Colonial Office tried to ignore him but could not quite succeed. For Norman Leys was simply Britain's leading expert on Kenya.

Leys was born in Liverpool in 1875, the son of a Scottish barrister. After his mother died giving birth to his brother Kenneth, the children were sent to live with their paternal grandparents. The family situation was further complicated by his father's conversion to Catholicism, a traumatic event for a strict Presbyterian family that led to a celebrated court case for custody of the children. The father won the suit, but the family spirited the boys off to America to be reared by aunts, from whence they returned only in time for Norman to enter the University of Glasgow. Although he graduated in medicine in 1901, specializing in obstetrics, he studied Greek literature under Gilbert Murray, with whom he formed a close personal attachment that was to last for the rest of his life. Lacking the means to enter medical practice in the United Kingdom, he decided upon a career overseas, "the general idea being," he told Murray,

that a man ought to do what most needs doing. And what I imagine the black and yellow people need most is not so much treatment for dyspepsia or rheumatism as something to make them stand up to the circumstances of the new civilization that is coming to them.[15]

After a year of further study at the Liverpool School

of Tropical Medicine he went out in 1902 to the port
of Chinde in Portuguese East Africa to begin a career
that would take him to Nyasaland (1904), to the East
Africa Protectorate (1908), and back to Nyasaland
(1913), before a lung disease later diagnosed as tuberculosis ended it in 1918.

The minor official in the technical departments of a
colonial administration, moving about frequently and
writing papers that were incorporated into the reports
of superiors, ordinarily left few traces. Leys left as
many as most. His only publication from this period is
a compilation of anthropometrical statistics from
African patients who passed through his surgery, a
publication of no interest to the student of the evolution of his attitudes.[16] Were it not, indeed, for his
long and continuous correspondence with Murray the
period in his life before he settled in Brailsford in
1918 would be virtually a closed book.

No man possessing the attitudes of opposition to all
forms of colonialism that we associate with *Kenya*
could have survived for fifteen years as a member of
the British colonial service. (Leys' initial posting in
Portugese East Africa was of course outside the colonial service.) The young man settled down to his medical practice, to the very serious program of reading
that was to make him such a broadly educated man,
and to learn about this strange corner of the world.
His early letters reveal the sensitivity, the systematic
thinking, and the poetic grasp of concreteness that
would later characterize his books. Fortunately for his
sanity—for in these early years he had little practical
alternative to life in Africa—his attitudes toward race
and colonialism evolved only gradually.

Leys came to Chinde prepared to "think well" of
the Portuguese, but his resolve encountered difficulty
from the start. Their administration was rife with
vice and corruption. That they had deteriorated as a
people he had no doubt, and he pondered the effects
of the "black blood" in their veins. They treated Afri-

cans like so much livestock. So did the British, except
that they treated neither animals nor natives with
such "callous cruelty." To the servile attitude of the
Portuguese houseboy he, a "child of democracy,"
preferred the "mission boys" from Livingstonia in
Nyasaland: "Even a little education is a magical
thing."[17] He had come already convinced that education would be the fundamental cure for the problems
that beset non-Western peoples. He meant to cure not
just their bodies but their minds and spirits. Yet he
wondered how the white man should relate to Africans.
Most of his compatriots, British and Portuguese alike,
took concubines. That practice horrified him:

As a man who tries to treat nobody as his inferior, I
am met with one difficulty at the outset. If black and
white are to be social equals there will be mixed mar-
riages. I can give no good reason but I regard them
with horror. Half castes are such a miserable pitiable
crew. And to me the indisputable equality of the man
and woman are [sic] essential to the sacrosanct nature
of marriage.[18]

Leys' first letters from Africa thus reveal a fundamental ambivalence that was to continue.

After leave in 1904 Leys went to Nyasaland as a
member of the colonial medical service. He had expected a new world under British administration,
albeit that of a chartered company. But the differences were ones of degree. He felt a greater sense of
responsibility. "One can't live long in Africa," he con-
fided, "without taking sides." When he appealed to
a high-court judge against a magistrate's illegal action, he was told of worse injustices supported from
on high:

If I ever come to first hand knowledge of one of these
I think I'll make the thing public if I can learn how to.
The great thing the Commissioner and his party dread
is a question in Parliament with a public inquiry to
follow. The threat of it always humbles them. Given

a good case the thing would be to find an M.P. I could
act anonymously any time through the Aborigines
Protection Society. But I wouldn't like to. To speak
out and push the thing home would mean leaving the
Administration. That wouldn't matter much except
for the pension. But really, the fact is that neither the
British people nor their representatives have any control at all over their dependencies. And nobody in the
Colonial Office cares for a little Protectorate like
this.[19]

By the summer of 1905 Leys had come to see that
there were inherent evils in the colonial system and
that only public exposure could correct them. Already
he was thinking of a test case.

The ambivalence however continued. By 1908, now
stationed at Nakuru in the East Africa Protectorate,
Leys could accompany a punitive expedition against
the Kisii, write a humorous circular letter back to his
friends, and confess the ambiguity of his feelings.[20]
Vividly he described the comically tortuous procession
of porters, "the real heroes of Africa," weaving their
way in single file; the burning of huts and rounding
up of livestock that provided most of the opportunities
for "heroism"; the popping off of Maxim guns at the
few Africans who showed active hostility; the inflated
counts of the dead, whom no one ever saw; and the
ludicrously low casualty rate of the expedition—four,
all accidental. "Punitive expeditions," he concluded,
"are abominable things." The innocent suffered
along with the "guilty":

All this I not only admit but wish to insist on. But I
wish also to ask the question what else could have
been done? Granted the existence of British East
Africa, to do nothing would have been as unjust as
to do what we did.

Even at home the innocent, for instance the families
of criminals, often suffered under the law. In Africa
justice was blinder. The Africans who had refused to

pay their taxes, or the individual who had sunk a
spear into a district officer's back, might or might not
have been punished. There was no way of telling.
Even so, civilization and law were preferable to barbarism and anarchy. Although by now at heart a critic
of the colonial system in practice, Leys was still ready
in the last resort to defend the use of force to maintain
it. This ambiguity he never overcame.

In 1910 came the test case, the celebrated move of
the Masai. A mere five years after their reserve (already in effect partitioned) had been guaranteed by
treaty, the administration of Sir Percy Girouard began to urge the northern section to move their great
herds of cattle from the Laikipia area, which was
desired by settlers. They would rejoin the rest of their
tribe in a reserve to be extended to the south. The
controversy revolved around whether the new region
was equal, mainly in water resources, to the area that
was being given up, and whether the government was
bringing pressure upon the northern Masai. To com-
plicate the situation the "paramount chief," Lenana,
came to favor the move as a means of reasserting his
authority. In 1911 he even made it his deathbed wish.[21]
First to Murray (who sent a copy of his letter minus the
signature to the Colonial Office),[22] then to the future
Labour prime minister Ramsay MacDonald, who
asked embarrassing questions of secretary of state Sir
Lewis Harcourt,[23] Leys charged that the government
of the East Africa Protectorate was acting unjustly
and breaking its solemn word.

This complicated affair ultimately caused the resignation of Sir Percy Girouard, an unsuccessful court
action by the Masai, and in 1913 Leys' own dismissal
from the service of the East Africa Protectorate. My
concern is Leys' attitudes and the extent of his role.
Toward the Masai themselves he was ambiguous.
Given their vast herds which they never sold or culled,
given their military age-grade system, there was no

escaping the fact that the Masai *were* (and are) a
problem. If the southern reserve should be adequate
(a very uncertain point), then on its merits the case
was probably a good one. Moreover the government's
main fault had been to leave the Masai alone. They
must be taught to market their cattle, and some of
their customs were frankly abominable. Sir Charles
Eliot had compared the Masai to panthers—beautiful
but useless. In *Kenya* Leys himself was to liken them
to a herd of elephants in Hyde Park, their way of life
absolutely incompatible with any conceivable program of economic development. [24] Nor was this policy
of removal by any means the worst of the government's iniquities. It was merely the most clear-cut vio-
lation of a formal commitment that lay to hand. He
told Murray:

I hope you don't think it is mainly the moving of the
Masai we object to. We hate the whole policy of government, its attitude to natives, its lack of sympathetic knowledge, its aims to use them for the advantage
of Europeans. The government worships false gods. [25]

The Masai affair was a disturbing precedent. It fore-
told a system of colonial government in which Africans, if they happened to be in the way of white
interests, would simply be removed.

   Leys had expected others to join in a direct approach to the governor, but they shrank away. His own
uncertainty continued. Perhaps he should have gone
straight to the governor instead of writing to friends
in England. Perhaps he had not "played the game."
A meeting with Girouard in June 1910, shortly before
Leys came home on leave, increased his confusion:
"I had answers ready for an attack and another set
for a cross examination but I was not ready for an
extremely able and thorough exposition of native
policy with which I had to agree." [26] Girouard convinced him that the Masai affair was an exception.

His aim was African development and self-sufficiency. Within six months, the governor predicted, the settlers would be enraged. Leys came home perplexed.

When he returned, this time to Mombasa, the situation clarified. What he called "the mechanical part of my conscience" no longer troubled him. Not only was the Masai move on again (Harcourt having temporarily halted it in 1910 largely in response to Leys' own information),[27] but all of Leys' larger fears seemed to be borne out. A European convicted of the killing of an African was merely deported.[28] Above all, Girouard called a demand for self-government inappropriate in the present stage of the protectorate's finances. Apparently the removal of the grant-in-aid from the imperial treasury, which would make the colony self-supporting, was the only necessary condition for the establishment of rule over two million blacks by what were then four thousand whites. He now believed the governor had "diddled" him.[29] In spirit he was now in opposition. On the merits of the case itself he remained ambivalent. The size of the Masai herds must be curbed, else one day the whole protectorate might not hold them. Perhaps in the long run the move was for the best. Best, that is, for the Africans. What he feared most was a rising: "Perhaps it is better for the African to be pushed through fire. But it is bad for us, and our children."[30]

Leys was dismissed from the service of the East Africa Protectorate not for inspiring Ramsay MacDonald's parliamentary questions but for his role in the process by which the northern Masai retained counsel and, in the end in vain, went to law. He himself maintained (privately at the time to Murray as well as later in *Kenya* and in defending himself before the Colonial Office) that others might have persuaded the Masai chiefs to retain counsel. He had helped to find the best lawyer available but only after the Masai had made up their minds. In the "mechan-

ical part of his conscience" he distinguished legitimate from illegitimate opposition. He thought he had
crossed the line by writing to Murray in 1910. He did
not think he had done so now.[31] He must have been
particularly disgruntled by the knowledge that he had
trapped himself.[32]

Facing dismissal from the East Africa Protectorate,
Leys argued that "wherever the boundaries between
legitimate and improper activities be judged to lie, I
have kept far within them." He pleaded to be allowed
to stay. He could easily imagine that he had been
"represented as a visionary, in whom eleven years of
Africa have not destroyed the sentimental dreams
which betoken the mind inaccessible to reality." He
claimed to be

as loyal as any, unless, indeed, it is disloyalty to believe that the Government of this country has still to
undertake its real work—to think its real task is to
gain for the people of the country liberty of mind,
through knowledge, through the cherishing of traditions that still live, and the encouraging of new traditions that create life, and to reach thereby a close
interdependence of interests and a mutual respect and
regard.[33]

Removing him from East Africa would destroy much
of his usefulness, based on his hard-won knowledge of
African languages. But his touching pleas moved
neither the government of the protectorate nor the
Colonial Office, who transferred him to Nyasaland.[34]
Leys left with a sense of personal grievance, and with
what by now was no more than a grudging acceptance
of the ultimate justification of colonial rule.[35]

The heart of the problem, Leys was coming to understand, was not particular abuses but the basic attitude toward Africans that underlay the colonial system. As he wrote in June 1914 from Nyasaland:

Most people don't think liberty good for "natives."
They think all damage to subject races was removed
when individual slavery was abolished. And they think

Government would be impossible in such countries if law were given the place it has in civilized countries. As a fact people believe that Africans are something less than human and so specially suited for arbitrary government. There are no principles to which one can appeal. If I were to write a book and make it clear that the natives of "Protectorates" are debarred from courts of justice, that their land has by a few strokes of the pen been made "Crown" land, that discontent on these and other grounds is widespread and growing, the public of Britain would answer partly by pointing to rapidly increasing trade and revenue and partly by disclaiming the wisdom of admitting rights to these people. So it seems there is nothing to do but wait till Africans prove themselves men, as they certainly will. But what kind of men will a generation of commercialism produce? And what effect on our own countrymen will follow? These are the questions— with the answers growing plainer in daily intercourse with black and white, that pursue me.[36]

Once Leys had longed "for a spark of natural talent, to brand the facts on men's eyes."[37] By 1914, when the war and then his very serious illness all but ended his correspondence with Gilbert Murray, Norman Leys was already contemplating the book that would be *Kenya*. He was looking toward his life's consuming mission, that of awakening the British public to the inhumanity of its attitude toward Africans and to the inherently exploitative colonial system of which that attitude was the root cause. From this point that mission never left his mind. As he lived through the devastation of the war in Africa, where "natives kill their own fellow tribesmen at the order of strangers from Europe,"[38] he continued to contemplate that book. When the rising led by John Chilembwe in Nyasaland in 1915 confirmed his expectations that Africans would "prove themselves men," he interviewed participants in the jail at Zomba. Their testimony would be useful. In 1918, or so he told Murray, he hoped to return to East Africa instead of

retiring on pension. He needed further materials for
his book.[39] At the height of the Masai affair he had
compared the scandal of the East Africa Protectorate
to that of the Congo several years before.[40] Only
gradually did the notion begin to crystallize in the
mind of Norman Leys that he himself might become
the E. D. Morel of East Africa.[41]

In 1918 Leys accepted the fact that his health would
not permit him to return to Africa. He bought a small
country practice at Brailsford, a village near Derby.
Although his varied African activities—his correspondence, publications, speaking engagements, and
committee meetings—would have been a respectable
full-time job, he took his medical profession seriously.
He took over a practice that had deteriorated. After
an early struggle he rebuilt it into a comfortable if not
handsome living. His socialism repelled the gentry
and wealthier farmers. Most of his patients were
therefore village tradesmen and farm laborers who
were covered by insurance or "outdoor relief." Their
families, who were not under insurance, were the
most vexing problem. Like many another country doctor he took care of them by dispensing large portions
of medicine. Transportation was difficult. He made
his rounds by car. Then, his daughter Mrs. Agnes
Avery remembers,

old men and women would come out to receive remedies and painkillers for their chronic complaints. He
knew them all and many of their problems apart from
the medical ones and came to have a very intimate
knowledge of the lives of the rural poor. He said that
they were very like Africans, both being at that time
a deprived and inarticulate people with their potential
abilities stunted and discouraged.[42]

His quiet life had its rewards:

I doubt if there are many jobs in the world with so
varied a human interest as a country doctor's. We

deal neither with things nor with figures but with
men, women and children. And if I am not so well
paid as the top-hatted urban fraternity, I am at least
better paid than the people I am paid to serve.[43]

A larger, more lucrative practice would have left no
time for the avocation, the mission that was to be his
life's work.

To Kenya Norman Leys' commitment was total and
intense. On other issues and in personal relations the
man could be sweetly reasonable. On the subject of
African exploitation he jokingly referred to himself as
a fanatic. To him the problem was a simple one.
There was injustice in Kenya. It must be stopped.
And (perhaps the flaw in his reasoning) all could be
put right by act of parliament. Such he thought had
happened a century before in the abolition of slavery.
Politicians were guided or forced by a public opinion
thoroughly aroused. Therein lay his own role. Expose
the facts, constantly and relentlessly, and the remaining difficulties would take care of themselves. No
compromise could satisfy him. The partial remedy,
cooling indignation but leaving essentially unaltered
the system from which injustice sprang, was worse
than nothing. Any whose zeal flagged must be dis-
carded. Not for him the dictum Oldham lived by that
in the Father's house are many mansions. Not for him
was politics the art of the possible. No issue that involved discrimination against Africans in Kenya was
too trivial to prevent his wanting to go into the last
ditch.

"Balance" is not a word Leys would have used to
describe the "bee in my bonnet."[44] Such a man can
be trying. But without such single-minded individuals
the great reform movements of English history would
have lacked energy, strength, and soul.[45] Others
might be more effective in securing practical reforms.
Leys' gifts and interests lay in creating and influencing public opinion. In that sphere, for any part

of Africa, few could rival him. There is some truth to
Sir William Ormsby-Gore's complaint that Kenya's
ubiquity in discussions of African colonial questions
arose from the fact that it happened to be the particular colony Norman Leys had chosen for his base.[46]

Leys wrote excitingly, vividly, compellingly. Among
contemporary writers of African nonfiction he surely
ranks as one of the best. He knew how to select the
apt concrete illustration. He had a sense of pace and
rhythm. The force and power of his unpublished
paper of 1918, more than its facts or its thesis, attracted Oldham, who told him he had the gift of
awakening the imagination of his readers. Literary
skill and not, as Leys supposed, mere exposure of the
facts made *Kenya* a commercial success in its own day
and a classic worth reprinting in ours. He was not a
professional writer. He lacked confidence in the gifts
others perceived in his work. To find his book admired as "good" instead of merely accepted as "true"
surprised and annoyed him.

Leys was one of the most penetrating analysts of the
nature and impact of imperialism. Until the early
1930s, when Bronislaw Malinowski's students began
to dominate the African journals and to publish their
books, most of the anthropological literature concerning African peoples was descriptive, unsystematic,
untheoretical, and unpurposeful. Leys did not think
himself an anthropologist. Yet, like a few other colonial officials and missionaries, he observed primitive
society keenly. His "fieldwork" lasted for fifteen
years. He had gone to Africa with the idea that his
main task would be to help colonial peoples understand the overpowering forces of Western industrialism. He had worked hard. Although he had no gift for
African languages he had tried to learn them. He had
not made the common mistake of supposing that because they abounded in metaphor they betokened a
people incapable of abstract thought. He found them

poetical, in a way, in their directness, richness of
vocabulary for things seen and heard, and because of
their frequent mimicry of nature. But the most interesting thing to me, and the most difficult, is to work
out the phrases and metaphors that they naturally
employ for the unseen and the unheard. At first one
believes that the so called abstract ideas are incapable
of interpretation in a Bantu tongue. Then one gradually comes to see that it is all a matter of metaphor,
in our own language as much as in theirs.[47]

   As Leys himself realized his anthropological experience was defective. His frequent moves prevented
him from ever acquiring complete knowledge of one
people. For the analysis of imperialism, for his attempt to build public sympathy for "the African,"
his preparation was all the more appropriate. Long
years of interviewing African patients from varied
tribes and backgrounds, reports he had written about
sanitation and labor conditions, his biting frustration
in trying the persuade the ignorant to do what he
knew was good for them: when Leys wrote that *Kenya*
had been "fifteen years in the making" he was describing all that and more.
   Leys did not write anthropology. Yet his work resembles the "functional" analysis of Malinowski and
A. R. Radcliffe-Brown that dominated the craft between the wars.[48] Instead of emphasizing the quaint
or the exotic, he tried to explain how fabrics of social
institutions in communitites so apparently different
as European and African were yet much alike. He
tried to assess the impact of modern industrialism
upon the lives of primitive peoples. He was one of the
first to expose the mythical stereotype that passed for
an explanatory model of "communal land tenure."[49]
He wrote good history too. The very few academic
historians who thought African subjects worth their
attention at all were writing narratives about Europeans, full of cultural bias and empty of serious atten-

tion to Africans. Leys was sketching the grand theme
of cultural interaction that they overlooked. He had
more than detailed knowledge diligently compiled; he
had systematic method. Whether like Malinowski's
it came from his scientific training, his sense of method
gave his writing its coherence and its compelling
power.

For Leys historical forces had to mesh like the pieces
of a puzzle. "I wonder," he asked Murray, "where
you put certain things—where you fit them in. Perhaps you don't fit them. I can't help it. They rattle
about if I don't. But I must be fitting lots of things
wrong."[50] A "structuralist," but not an economic
determinist, he described forces that swept events on
to their logical conclusion unless their causes were
altered. African rebellions, for instance, did not happen in response to the actions of particularly wicked
people. They were as natural a product of the colonial
situation as coffee. Remove the causes of tension and
risings need not occur. Leave the system unchanged
and they *would* happen. When they did, he told his
readers in an ironic aside meant to shock, it was no
use their blaming the governor or the police commissioner. Bloodshed was also inevitable. However unjust
the Pax Britannica must be maintained. The essential
ambiguity that had marked his reaction to the Kisii
expedition of 1908 endured. Even in the colonial situation law was preferable to anarchy. To shoot the participants was "the kindest way of dealing with native
risings. The fact that most of the people who are engaged in them are in no real sense criminally inclined
makes it no less necessary to shoot them. Those who
object to the shooting must go deeper."[51]

Leys took his readers much deeper. George Shepperson has credited Leys' discussion of the Chilembwe
rising with anticipating Frantz Fanon's theory of pur-
gative violence.[52] Leys is due even more than that. He
was one of the first to develop a coherent theory of the

sociology of the "colonial situation"—and now
Georges Balandier comes to mind[53]—one of the first
to see its shape and to measure its impact "from below." The tendency of the Malinowski school to assume the colonial situation as normal horrified him.[54]
"I knew anthropology was all the vogue and believe it
will have a permanent though small place in the field
of knowledge," he told Murray, a man who had himself taken a "functional" approach to the study of
Greek religion. "But I didn't expect that people like
you could be persuaded that it can provide a clue to
right policy." Running after "untrustworthy sensa-
tionalists like Malinowski" was silly and potentially
harmful:

The danger lies in regarding Africans as specimens
for study instead of human beings who react in certain circumstances just as we should if born to their
heritage and placed in their circumstances. Why suppose anthropology to touch the central problems of
the native African any more than it touched those of
the native Irish? It is truly hard to keep people to the
point about Africa.[55]

His reaction to contemporary historiography was
similar if not quite so scornful. In 1936, preparing (as
it turned out in vain) to teach a course on imperialism in an experimental college for adults that was being established in Edinburgh by his close friend A. G.
Fraser, he attended lectures given at Oxford by Professor Vincent Harlow. He thought them excellent
but somehow beside the point. He had learned about
constitution-making. "But when Asiatics and Africans really wake up, how much of the work of all
these solemn Committees and Conferences is likely to
last?" The professor gave him a list of thirty books.
From them he learned a little about the motives and
forces that had shaped Western society and imperialism: "the ethic of the New Testament, modern science, and what Socialists unkindly call capitalist industry." But where might one obtain a clear idea of

the impact of capitalism in Africa and Asia? (Where indeed?) "By Capitalist industry," he continued in a Marxist vein:

I mean industry that is (1) highly mechanised (2) productive of huge numbers of identical articles which by their cheapness kill industry organised otherwise (3) conducted with the incentive of making maximum profit to private owners (4) controlled by a tiny minority with immense power. . . .

In the West capitalism had triumphed (temporarily, he hoped), "having in fact silenced all respectable rivals and reduced the churches to empty shells." In Asia and Africa capitalism was still undeveloped. But it was meeting even less resistance. Uneducated and unorganized, workers bowed their heads before its awesome power:

Hence a unique situation, examples of which are to be seen in Joburg slums, the cotton-mill area of Bombay, the jute-mill area of Calcutta, in Shanghai, in a hundred other places. In each of these places the problem naturally exhibits variations. But its fundamentals are the same, since the forces of private gain operating from Europe are identical, and since those upon whom they operate are all alike politically and industrially helpless.

Was there, he asked, "a single book . . . that gives an account of its [capitalism's] central features?"

Still more important and if possible still more neglected were the attitudes of subject peoples. What were Africans thinking? It was perfectly understandable and even inevitable that Harlow and the other learned authorities did not know. What seemed inexcusable was their insensitivity. Lacking answers they failed to consider the question. "They all just assume it doesn't matter a scrap what all those millions have thought, do think and may think."

To understand the real world even a little—more is possible only to the genius—one must keep one's ears

to the ground, whether in Africa or Scotland. . . .
Whereas all those highbrows who write and lecture on
Imperialism keep their ears in Government Houses
and Downing St. What goes on in such places does
matter. But on the long view how disproportionate is
the place given it.[56]

Nearly all the ideas Norman Leys ever had about the
colonial situation in Kenya are contained in his unpublished letter of 1918 to the secretary of state. The
result of fifteen years' experience, the statement yet
bears the signs of having been written at white heat
within a short period. Its outlines were etched into his
brain. Thereafter he refined, elaborated, and occasionally modified the positions he had staked out.
But they remained essentially unchanged. Moreover
the compressed form of the letter makes this presentation more powerful and more incisive than his longer
published works.[57]

   Leys wrote of colonialism in East Africa as social
cataclysm. Unlike South Africa, the region had suffered no war of conquest or widespread rebellion. But
families and tribes had been uprooted, agriculture
disrupted, herds destroyed, venereal and other diseases introduced and spread. Moral standards had
been strained to the breaking point for peoples formerly among the most moral on earth. The population had declined—perhaps by one-fifth, perhaps by
one-third. For much of this destruction the labor system was responsible. How could a society hold together
when so many of its men were away for long periods?
War had speeded up disintegration, directly or indirectly killing off thousands of porters, increasing the
incidence of malnutrition and disease. It had destroyed
the Western claim to have brought peace by abolishing intertribal warfare. On the coming of colonialism
Leys was passionate. Seldom can its effects have been
portrayed more vividly.

Most anthropologists and some historians would charge Leys with overstatement. Colonialism was more complicated than that. All would admit to the obvious exceptions—the Xhosa or the Zulu of South Africa who fought long series of "Kaffir wars" against Boer and Briton; the Herero of Southwest Africa whom the Germans systematically exterminated—people who never saw a positive side of alien rule. Recent scholarship has usually described a more placid and less traumatic process. Such institutions as the tribe, the family, or customary law have proved resilient and adaptive. Africans normally remained in control of cultural absorption and transformation. There was substantial continuity as well as change.[58]

To Leys "detribalization" was nearly total and inevitable, indeed a fearful thing. The tribal African had been encased in a web of ignorance and superstition. That web had protected him from reality. When the modern world intruded, as it must, he stood naked before fierce winds of uncontrollable change. The institutions that had held together the fabric of society were swept away like fragile orchids in the first gust. Recent scholarship, again, depicts African tradition not merely maintaining patterns of distinctive culture but adapting to new functions demanded by altered conditions.[59] Tribalism was not extinguished. Many of its elements have not proved incompatible with modernization. Leys underestimated its staying power and its dynamism.

If Leys oversimplified the process of social change, so did even the best authorities of his generation. Anthropologists had lovingly described the exotic customs of primitives in the wild, neglecting changes that were going on before their eyes. Malinowski, having himself written a series of monographs on the Trobriand Islands that ignored the traders and missionaries who populated his diary, began in the early thirties to confront this problem.[60] As his student Monica

Wilson argued at the time, his model was insufficient. Fieldwork was supposed to be self-sufficient. But only through history could the investigator distinguish between tradition, modernity, and the "mixed culture" that formed an emulsion of the other two.[61] In Leys' time "detribalization" meant the swift and bewildering devastation of a whole way of life. The old system was supposed to have literally nothing to do with the new. That tribesmen and townsmen might interchange their life-styles easily and painlessly was not perceived.[62] Leys was not alone in exaggerating the brittle fragility of African societies.

Yet the essential facts which Leys depicted were there. Malnutrition and disease, intensified by war, did reduce the population of East Africa sharply. Rinderpest spread south and west from Somalia into eastern and southern Africa, devastating the cattle that were the center of existence of so many African peoples. Human and animal disease wrought deep social malaise. Nativistic and millenarian movements multiplied. Africans rose against whites and were slaughtered. As in Tudor and Stuart England, another era of rapid social disintegration, witchcraft accusations sharply increased.[63] That agriculture, family life, and traditional systems of law were strained sometimes beyond the breaking point cannot be doubted. The recent flood of studies of African resistance has made clear, if it was not made clear before, that colonialism was often if not always a violent process.[64] Of course the curve was jagged. There was more tension at some times and in some areas than in others. The generation of Africans who were adults in the interwar years (the subjects of the first systematic anthropological research) may neither have showed nor fully remembered the experience of the era of "pacification." When historians have adequately studied the impact of the first world war on Africa (there is a serious gap in the literature here),[65] they may well find that for his time Leys was right after all.

Norman Leys had lived through an East African
time of troubles. He wrote sympathetically and power-
fully of what he had known. He did not emphasize
that Africans and other peoples can and do survive
such crises. Anthropologists later found societies that
had managed to maintain some of their integrity.
That is not necessarily a convincing refutation of
Leys' account of the African experience in the coming
of colonialism.

Leys underestimated African resistance. Marx had
likened the French peasantry to sacks of potatoes,
prevented by their lack of economic interdependence
from sustaining either class consciousness or revolutionary action. Leys shared this kind of thinking. For
him tribalism was only a source of weakness, a ready-
made political division which Europeans could ex-
ploit; it was also purely an evolutionary stage, neither
unique nor particularly African. Rooted in ignorant
superstition, it must be overcome before the African
could hope to defend himself. Tribesmen must always
be oppressed and enslaved. As has been said, Leys
had surprisingly little sympathy for primitive Africans
in rebellion. Risings frightened him. But "primary
resistance" was not only dangerous: it was futile and
premature.

It followed that Leys would oppose any system of
colonial administration that attempted to maintain
tribalism. Indirect Rule, which became orthodoxy in
British colonial policy during the interwar years, he
thought reactionary and sentimental. So long as Europeans were installed in Africa—and he never recommended that they simply leave—they should attempt
to develop and modernize. That meant along Western
lines, for the simple reason that no example of a modern African society existed. African traditional institutions should not be artifically preserved. Those that
remained functional would survive; the rest deserved
euthanasia though not murder. Leys, for one, "would
rather see Africa in the hands of the exploiters than in

those of sentimental anachronists." It was not the
business of Europeans to choose what aspects of African civilization ought to be revived. That must be
done by "Africans with new minds."

In practice Leys recognized that there was no alternative. Institutions already obsolete must be used
while new ones took root. He drew a sharp line between the attempt of Sir Donald Cameron to restore
"democratic socialism" in Tanganyika and Lord Lugard's authoritarian system of rule through emirs in
Northern Nigeria.[66] Indirect Rule as administrative
necessity Leys accepted. As ideology he thought it
monstrous. Its premise was that the African was inherently distinctive, that differences ought to be per-
petuated and even emphasized. On the contrary, Leys
asserted, the African had precisely the same needs
and interests as his Western rulers.

The African's politics should also be the same. If
African nationalism were to succeed it must be modern not traditional. Its goals and organization must
rise above tribalism. This attitude persisted. It colored Leys' ambivalent reaction to the tribally based
movements, led by Harry Thuku and later by Jomo
(then Johnstone) Kenyatta, that grew among the
Kikuyu in the interwar years.[67] It prompted him at the
height of the female circumcision controversy to join
in a letter to the Kikuyu Central Association, urging
them to abandon their dispute with the Church of
Scotland Mission.[68] Africans should be fighting not to
preserve medically harmful tribal customs but to gain
a very modern goal, the franchise for the educated.

Yet tribalism over the last half-century has been
one of the most important forces in the fabric of African nationalism. In Leys' own time it was already
serving as a framework for "modern" political agitation of a kind he certainly approved, as with Archdeacon W. E. Owen's Kavirondo Taxpayers' Association or the Kikuyu Independent Schools movement.[69]

As Terence Ranger has insisted Africans did more in
the era of "primary resistance" than to die in long
rows before machine guns, as Leys put it, without
inflicting a single casualty.[70] Leys' own reference
point, the Kisii expedition of 1908 which he had accompanied, was not entirely typical. Moreover nationalism in colonial Africa was a complex and many-
sided phenomenon. It looked both forward and backward. Its strands and phases—tradition and modernity, "primary" and "secondary" resistance—cannot
be disentangled. Leys recognized, insisted upon, the
cultural richness of the African past. But for him,
colonialism and the war had killed this heritage. Cultural relativism, he felt, could be carried to extremes.
No matter how profoundly one might be dissatis-
fied with modern Western culture, he wrote, "with all
its crimes and follies it is better than Masai civilisation."[71] Those who talked of maintaining African differences really meant to keep the people backward. It
seemed to follow that tradition must be impotent as a
base for politics. Leys was intensely committed to the
cause of African freedom. But he opposed or was ambivalent toward many of the motives and means that
were being adopted by African politicians of his own
generation. He thought he knew better. Even Norman
Leys could not escape a tinge of paternalism![72]

Leys had close personal contact with one rebellion,
the celebrated rising led by the American-educated
John Chilembwe in Nyasaland in 1915. The foremost
authority has called Leys' description "the most considered account and analysis of it which was to be published until after the Second World War."[73] Leys as
usual went beneath the surface to an analysis of the
colonial situation that had made violence so likely.
Yet he might have made more of his rare opportunity
of interviewing participants. (Here especially one feels
the loss of his papers.) His brief accounts in *Kenya*
and in the unpublished letter of 1918 are certainly

more thoughtful than the official report of the investigating commission. But they add disappointingly little concrete information. On several points of detail, for instance in his statement that Chilembwe had no knowledge of firearms, he was wrong. George Mwase's account raises the question of whether Leys should not have taken more seriously the hypothesis that Chilembwe was acting symbolically.[74] Finally, although of course Leys could not have known this, he misunderstood the place of this particular rising in the history of African resistance. Like John Buchan, whose novel *Prester John* (the plot of which in some ways resembles Chilembwe's rising) was published *before* 1915, Leys thought this kind of movement would become typical. In the future rebellions would not be organized tribally, and they would be led by religious figures educated in the West. In fact Chilembwe's rising was unique, an aberration not a prototype.

Some of Leys' most original thinking dealt with the struggle between the two established world religions, Christianity and Islam, for the African's soul. Here again he oversimplified when he described these religions as the "heirs of tribalism," as though it were merely a matter of displacement, the ethnicity of tribal Africans being unable to combine, as European nationalism did, with a "higher religion." Although he was not an authority on Islam, he observed its practice closely among the Arabs and Swahili of Mombasa (and presumably among the Yao of Nyasaland), and his treatment seems reasonably competent.[75] His claim that the Germans had discouraged the spread of Islam into the interior of Tanganyika by favoring Christians in subordinate government appointments is clearly inaccurate.[76] But he was surely right in arguing that a developed Islam would be a profoundly anti-European movement, hardly the subservient apolitical faith colonial officials seemed to expect.

On the nature, role, and impact of Christian missions Leys was brilliant. Oldham found his ideas stimulating as well as disturbing. Leys was often critical.
Missionaries were too ready to meet the expectations
of settlers or officials. They were paternalistic. Above
all they did not remain true to the basic principles of
the religion they professed to preach. But Leys resisted the temptation to make simplistic generalizations about them. He did not call them agents or
"running dogs" of imperialism. Some missionaries
were among the most selfless people he had known.
Stations he had visited had seemed like oases if not
utopias. And the missionary movement was more tolerant than it had been a generation before.

Christianity, Leys insisted, was a radical even a
revolutionary doctrine. Jesus had been executed on
suspicion of sedition against an imperial authority. In
law he had probably been guilty, and he had made no
attempt to refute the accusation. St. Paul had failed
to achieve his goal of compromise with the state.
Those who thought Christianity essentially inappropriate in the colonial situation were right. To teach
the equality of black and white in the sight of God was
indeed potentially seditious. How could it be otherwise? A religion could of course be devised that would
not be dangerous. But it would not be Christianity.

Once more Leys identified a basic contradiction. In
Europe the church had largely abandoned its historic
role as the moral arbiter of society. As Tawney was to
argue in his famous essay, life in the West had been
separated into distinct compartments.[77] From these
the church had retreated one by one. Other institutions—the school, the civil courts, the state—had assumed its former functions. In Africa neither the history of retreat nor those institutions existed. Thus the
mission resumed the church's historic role. It tried to
regulate individual and group behavior in ways that
would have shocked the English parishioner. It dis-
pensed knowledge, the keys to the white man's power.

Its prestige was therefore enormous. In Europe, again, the church had compromised after centuries of conflict with secular authority. Religious leaders like Oldham commonly (and Leys thought mistakenly) sought to keep religion and politics separate. In Africa this arrangement too did not exist. There religious and secular authority resumed their historic strife. Mission and colonial government were both authentic projections of British society. But they were extensions of forces which, however much they might have compromised at home, remained in essence contradictory. Leys' ideas on Christian missions could well be made the kernel of an analysis such as has not yet been written.

Christianity had always been a missionary religion. It would be that or nothing. Africans were much like the early Christians. Sophisticated modern Europeans might have become bored to the point of losing sight of what Christianity was really about. The African had no such difficulty. To him it was fresh and exciting. Free from unconscious associations of Western culture with Christianity, he was the more apt to reach its heart. And what he found was the radical, potentially seditious doctrine of racial equality. On racial discrimination, Leys argued, the early Christians had been quite explicit. People might say that St. Paul's view on race had been wrong (Leys thought him mistaken about the role of women) but not that he had been unclear. Here was the bedrock of Norman Leys' message and of what he sometimes called his fanaticism. St. Paul had been right. Racial distinctions were absolutely unimportant and ephemeral. This very simple idea underlay the man's whole approach to Kenya and to Africa. He believed it with all his soul

A committed socialist, Leys thought significant reform in Africa must be preceded by a fundamental revolution in Europe, by a curbing of the economic

and political forces that had created imperialism in
the first place. To be sure he joined campaigns
against specific abuses. But ultimately he had little
faith in the strategy of item-by-item reform. The
Colonial Office might be persuaded to issue instructions. So long as the basic structure of the colonial
system remained unchanged those instructions would
be ignored or watered down in their implementation.
Unless the colonial government were resolutely controlled it would continue to be the tool of the settlers.
Only a committed Labour government, directing an
overhaul that extended throughout the colonial bureaucracy, could achieve meaningful improvement.
British colonial policy in Kenya was no accident. Its
abuses were the logical result of the balance of forces
that had created it.

The short run, usually so crucial to the reformer
or the politician, did not much concern Leys the revolutionary. Ultimately he looked forward to root-and-
branch reform from the Labour movement. A Labour
government properly advised, pushed as well as supported by an educated public opinion thoroughly
aroused, might achieve something. He saw no other
solution. From Labour politicians and the British
public he expected too much, from African nationalism far too little. He was fond of the analogy of the
abolition of slavery by act of parliament. But he might
have realized that a system based in law can be treated
legislatively, whereas colonialism was largely informal. The comparison he used was not irrelevant but
it was by no means exact.

Labour in power certainly depressed him. They
seemed far more anxious to persuade their enemies
and the uncommitted that they could be trusted to
govern responsibly than to remain faithful to the principles they had professed in opposition. After 1924,
when J. H. Thomas had accomplished nothing at the
Colonial Office in a weak Labour ministry, Leys was

always careful to qualify. It must be the right Labour
government and it must be closely watched. But the
victory of 1929, which brought Sidney Webb (Lord
Passfield) and Dr. Drummond Shiels to the Colonial
Office, excited him. A white paper, reaffirming "African paramountcy" and ordering a sweeping reform
of discriminatory legislation in Kenya, seemed to
foretell a new era.[78]

In 1930 Leys applied for reinstatement to the colonial service, this time as district commissioner. For too
long now he had been "telling other people what *they*
ought to do."[79] He wanted "one more whack at the
old Dragon."[80] This was a symbolic gesture. He knew
that he was overage and that his enemies would probably block the appointment. There is no reason to
think that personal disappointment lay behind the
strong attack he launched against Lord Passfield in
his second book, *A Last Chance in Kenya* (1931).
Rather, the reasons he gave in his preface seem convincing. The select committee on closer union had
refused to hear witnesses from the Kikuyu Central
Association. Their testimony had shown that Governor Sir Edward Grigg and the settlers were as intent
as ever upon maintaining white supremacy. Above all,
the white paper of 1929, such a promising first step,
had apparently been stillborn. Nothing seemed to
have been done to carry out its spirit in the colony.

Last Chance—and these remarks also apply to the
final book, *The Colour Bar in East Africa* (1941)—is
a very different kind of work from *Kenya*. It is a clear
restatement of views but not a systematic analysis of
the colonial situation. It is a propaganda tract not an
artistic creation. That he provided no index is symptomatic of his different aim. *Kenya* had been written
to inform. *Last Chance* was meant to indict. *Kenya*
had avoided personalities. Now he attacked the Labour government and Lord Passfield.[81] The bitter
tone reflects his disillusionment and despair. Labour

had betrayed Kenya's Africans. That it was Labour—
he quoted their explicit promises—made it all the
worse. The white paper had seemed to fulfill those
promises. But nothing of substance had been done to
change the way the iniquitous system worked on the
ground. Official pronouncements repeated the old
insidious cant about "associating the settlers in the
performance of the trust." The African delegates who
had not been listened to would return to Kenya and
spread the word. What would happen once Africans
were convinced they could no longer look to Britain?
The prospect frightened him. In 1930 he had told
Harris that they were at the crossroads. Labour must
act now or the opportunity would be lost. The Conservatives were sure to win the next election. That
would mean victory for the settlers, "which means un
til Africans get to the stage of rebellion. And they [the
settlers] think, though I don't, that they are safe from
that for fifty years." Never had he felt so lonely or
so futile: "I suppose the fact is that I ought to have
realised years ago that in the absence of either private
means or of a job like yours it was silly of me to bother
myself with what happens to Africans."[82]
    In fact the tide had turned. The settlers would not
win. Labour in power (aided by the white colony's
financial difficulties during the depression) had made
more of a difference than Leys realized, more than
might have appeared at the time. By 1931 the closer
union movement was dead. So was the settlers' strongest leader, Lord Delamere. As Leys had hinted, the
new governor Sir Joseph Byrne simply did not pay as
much attention to the settlers.[83] The Kenya controversy was weighted down with paper, notably by the
Carter land commission report of 1934 which put definite limits on white settlement.[84] And it became insig-
nificant in comparison with Hitler's rise to power, the
Spanish civil war, and the coming of world war.
    There was nothing like the root-and-branch reform

that Leys had hoped would follow Labour's victory of
1929. The "last chance" for an equitable multiracial
society (supposing such a thing had ever been possible) had indeed been missed. Near the end of his
life, in *The Colour Bar in East Africa* (1941), he described discrimination that still severely restricted
opportunities for Africans. Britain's "traditional policy" of equal rights for all had never been expressly
repudiated. But the African child was being given a
different and an inferior kind of education. Behind it
lay the usually unspoken assumption that this child
had inferior abilities. It was the same problem Leys had
identified so long ago. Mau Mau was to be the violent
if delayed result that for so long had frightened him.
How he might have reacted to that largely tribal revolt, to what in many ways was the kind of movement
he had expected to be absorbed into a larger pan-
African nationalism, is probably fruitless speculation.
So too is to ask what he might have thought if, as he
once wished, he could have seen the Nairobi newspapers in 1960. The ultimate justification of his life,
he thought, took place in 1942. Then the Burmese
and many Malays refused to fight for the British Empire in its hour of defeat. "Facts of that sort," he told
Gilbert Murray,

hit me harder than military defeats or than exposures
of incompetence in Whitehall. I don't claim to have
foreseen them. But I did foresee and tried to explain
how the state of mind out of which they arise is
coming about in the part of the Empire I used to live
in. I know you thought I gave certain discreditable
facts unfair or at least undue prominence. But I think
you will admit that if a dozen other men had written
as frankly, and accepted the consequences of doing
so . . . we might now have less to be ashamed of.[85]

Among those to whom Norman Leys' long letter to the
secretary of state circulated privately in the spring of

1918 few were more strategically placed than a secretary of the Conference of British Missionary Societies, Joseph H. Oldham. Born in India in 1874, the son of a colonel in the Indian army, he became active in the Student Christian Movement while at Trinity College, Oxford. An overseas missionary career began with the YMCA at Lahore, India, but ill health soon forced him to abandon it. He studied theology in Germany, becoming a fluent speaker of German. In 1908 he began his rapid rise to prominence in the world missionary movement. He was appointed secretary of the Edinburgh Conference, held two years later, and then of its continuation committee. This conference is one of the great landmarks in the history of the ecumenical movement. It led directly to the founding in 1921 of the International Missionary Council (of which Oldham was one of the secretaries), to a succession of ecumenical conferences (many of which he helped to organize), and ultimately to the establishment in 1948 of the World Council of Churches with its headquarters in Geneva.[86] Oldham's preparation for that momentous convocation of 1910 and his work in following up its conclusions were thorough and successful. He acquired the reputation of a first-class organizer. Edinburgh had made J. H. Oldham.

Organizationally, it had given him an incomparable background. Strategically, it had placed him at a unique vantage point for surveying the whole missionary movement. Personally, it had made him known, admired, and trusted. . . . Quiet, unassuming, brilliant and energetic, a thinker who focussed his whole attention on one immediate task, Oldham was marked for a unique and indispensable role.[87]

The World Council of Churches remembers Oldham as one of the founding fathers. It was only one of the important institutions the man helped to build. He had many talents. But it was in what he called "spadework"—molding disparate interests and personalities into a coherent group, minimizing differences so that agreement could be reached, then keeping the body together—that he most excelled.

During the first world war Oldham sought to maintain lines of communication among the warring nationalities. His annual surveys in *The International Review of Missions*, of which he was the founding editor, preserved a tone of sane detachment. They dwelt upon the consequences of the disruptive tragedy rather than upon its causes. They described the revolt of Asia and the immensity of its challenge. They assessed the postwar situation and looked forward to the day when a reunited world missionary movement would renew the struggle. In protracted negotiations with the British government and missionary boards he strove to prevent wholesale despoliation and internment of missionaries, attempting for instance to save the work among the Chagga of Bruno Guttmann's famous mission on Mount Kilimanjaro.[88] At Versailles he helped preserve from Allied vengeance the principle of missionary freedom. And he set about the painful task of bringing the Germans once more into the ecumenical movement, of helping them to recapture the cooperative spirit of Edinburgh. It was this effort to preserve the achievements of the ecumenical movement that brought him into contact with Africa and that made him receptive to Leys' long letter. He was then only at the outset of his African involvement. Wide as were his interests and activities that commitment would become nearly full-time until 1934, when he withdrew to carry out the "spadework" for the important Oxford conference of 1937 on Church, Community, and State.

By 1918 J. H. Oldham already possessed a network of influential contacts throughout the world. To these he added substantially, particularly in government circles, after moving headquarters to Edinburgh

House off Sloane Square in London. There he joined one of the most influential clubs, the Athenaeum. As editor of *The International Review of Missions* he controlled a journal of high intellectual content and great prestige.

As Leys himself must have anticipated, the British government in the last year of war did not at once respond to his letter with a revolutionary program of reform for East Africa. His effort, indeed, was not acknowledged at all.[89] Oldham's request for a meeting was therefore all the more welcome. For Oldham had all the resources the poor and unknown country doctor lacked. He had a powerful organization, money, an established and respected organ of propaganda, an office with secretaries, a network of influential contacts, and easy access to the government. No doubt the man could work wonders if he chose. But was he committed? Could any member of the Establishment, anyone not a socialist, really have his heart in a fight to the finish for African freedom and equality? Leys was never sure. He probed and questioned. Throughout the years covered by this correspondence Oldham knew that he was being tested.

No question but that Oldham passed the first test, and with results far exceeding Leys' expectations. In 1919 the government of the East Africa Protectorate in the person of the chief native commissioner John Ainsworth, a veteran known for his sympathetic knowledge of African society,[90] issued a circular requiring African males between seventeen and thirty-seven to work two months in the year either for the government or for settlers. The farmers' ranks had just been swelled by the immigration of some 350 retired soldiers. War and the disastrous influenza epidemic of 1918 had severely depleted the African population. Always a matter of concern, the labor shortage was now a crisis. Rather unpersuasively the government argued that its primary objective was to help the Africans by curbing lawlessness among their troublesome young men. The dissolution of the traditional regimental system under the Pax Britannica had left a void. From beer-drinking and debauchery they would happily be converted to "habits of industry."[91] Swayed by this argument the Kenya Missionary Alliance backed the scheme. Three important church leaders (Bishop John Willis of Uganda, Bishop R. S. Heywood of Mombasa, and the Rev. John W. Arthur of the Church of Scotland's Kikuyu mission) grudgingly agreed, provided the recruitment be carried out openly and officially by the government. Forced labor was always unpalatable. But in a crisis so acute as this, they thought, it might just be tolerable so long as it did not depend upon the informal "encouragement" of the chiefs. That worst of systems, so inviting to corruption and cruelty, they hoped to avoid.[92]

Norman Leys' views on this question—his exposure of the myth of chronic African indolence in the mouths of whites with whom manual labor was not exactly habitual; his argument that there were simply not enough Africans to perform the work expected of them outside the reserves and yet survive on what they could manage to grow for themselves; his anger at the church establishment for taking yet again the "wrong side"—are made clear in the correspondence. From Oldham he expected little. He anticipated objections both to the tone and the thrust of his article on forced labor for *The International Review of Missions.* The editor's willingness to publish radical views surprised him. Leys declined an invitation to join Oldham's meeting to plan the campaign. Bishops and other such Establishment folk discomfited him, his radical opinions would offend them, and nothing would come of it anyway. He was mildly surprised when any document emerged at all. He did not take the trouble to read it carefully—an indication that he supposed generally well-meaning but uncommitted people had been carrying on an ineffective ritual. He cannot have been convinced by Oldham's declaration that "we are out, please God, for a fight!"

But fight Oldham did. Mounting a campaign against forced labor in Kenya, he prepared as though for a missionary conference. He convened pilot sessions. He collected names of churchmen, politicians of all parties, businessmen—the longer and more imposing the list the better. Shrewdly he obtained the signatures of the three prominent East African churchmen who had issued the "bishops' memorandum," thus depriving the government of one of its most potent weapons of counterattack. Humbly he offered a memorandum—merely a little something to get discussion started. He quoted the speeches of the government ministers he was trying to influence, along with the classic pronouncements from proconsular archtypes—the Cromers, the Lugards. He invited criticism, incorporating some points, giving way on others, leaving the basic outline unaltered. Carefully he coached Randall Davidson, the archbishop of Canterbury, on the line he should take in the House of Lords. The more memorials the better. He encouraged individual missionary societies to issue their own protests, and a steady stream of documents poured into Downing Street.[93] He commissioned articles for *The International Review of Missions*, inspired letters to *The Times*, and cultivated journalists. He organized deputations to the Colonial Office. Edinburgh House fairly hummed.

Finally, and this is what set Oldham apart from the usual sort of humanitarian agitator, he set himself up as a medium through which the Colonial Office might secure a compromise. He wrote privately, sympathizing with the administrator's practical problems, but warning that he could not hold off indefinitely the impatience of others in the campaign more radical than he.[94] It would be well to settle the affair quickly. Otherwise, he hinted darkly to secretary of state Lord Milner, such a row as had not been seen since the days

of the Chinese labor agitation in South Africa (of which
Milner as high commissioner had been the principal
target) might be in the offing.

The forced labor campaign was a classic study in
the mobilization of public opinion. And it succeeded.
That the Ainsworth circular was withdrawn, that first
Milner and then Churchill turned against Governor
Sir Edward Northey, were the fruits of Oldham's cultivation. Leys knew all this, recognized a good job of
propaganda when he saw one. His admiration was immense, all the more because he had been surprised.

For the next few years Leys remembered Oldham's
impressive victory. He wrote intimately and unreserv-
edly. He defended Oldham when J. H. Harris attacked him.[95] He trusted and depended on him. Leys
the agitator, Oldham the builder; Leys the expert with
the knowledge born of long African experience, Oldham the novice with organizational genius and influential contacts: although it is hard to imagine two
men more different in temperament, background,
cast of mind, or philosophy of life, they made a perfect team. In a sense however their partnership was
doomed from the beginning. Leys had been right from
the first. The Kenya labor campaign, J. H. Oldham's
first outright confrontation with a British government, was to be his last.

What, Oldham began to ask himself, had all that
work accomplished? His files bulged with correspondence. He had organized petitions and deputations,
had planned parliamentary debates, had kept up a
stream of press releases. He knew that at "spadework" he had few peers. He had done this sort of
thing before. He could do it again, though if the trick
were repeated too often it would rather lose its force.
The question was what it had achieved. A colonial
government had withdrawn a labor circular. A governor had been eased out. These were negative things.
Had those two years of hard work really changed any-

thing? Would anyone suggest that the Africans were
essentially any better off? Did the long-range prospect
for racial harmony in East Africa appear the least
more hopeful?

As Oldham pondered the problem of Kenya in its
broader African context certain fundamental facts
thrust themselves forward. White settlers and business interests were there. Perhaps it might have been
better if they were not, but there they were. They
already held the effective balance of power in the politics of Kenya. Presumably their influence would
increase still further. All the available precedents fore-
told this. Like South Africa and Rhodesia the white
colony of Kenya would one day become self-governing.
Once that happened the kind of campaign he had led
would become impossible. One might not like it. One
might even try to prevent it, but there it was. If that
were true then the foremost task should be to build a
strong foundation of goodwill among the settlers
toward the African majority and the imperial government. Kenya's whites must be persuaded to join in the
mission to which Great Britain had pledged herself
before the world. They must become associates in
trusteeship.

Unfortunately all the indicators seemed to be pointing the other way. Relations between the British government and Kenya's white community were growing
daily more hostile. If winning the settlers to trusteeship were the main goal, then the labor agitation must
be counted as a net loss. How much criticism could
the whites of Kenya stand before they should decide
that their only recourse lay in a complete identifica-
tion with the racist policies of South Africa? General
Smuts' expansionist aims were all too clear.[96] The
unity of the white-settler communities of Africa, turning their backs upon Great Britain and the principle
of trusteeship, bringing into being a far-flung coun-
ter-empire based on racial discrimination from the

Cape to Nairobi: that was the ultimate evil which must
be resisted at all cost. Flagrant abuses in the administration of Kenya must of course be identified and
corrected. But the ultimate aim must be reconciliation
not antagonism between the Kenya settlers and Great
Britain.

It seemed all too easy to carry on negative resistance.
What was far more difficult was to frame a positive
program that would do some good. It must be of genuine benefit to Africans, else his own conscience
would balk and British humanitarianism would not
support it. But it must also win acceptance from powerful commercial interests—the Empire Cotton Growing Association, chambers of commerce, mining
companies, shipping magnates. It must appeal to
officials at home and on the spot. At least a substantial number of settlers must be won over. Righteous phrases would not work. These groups must see
in the plan something for themselves. To reconcile
these diverse interests, satisfying each while moving
the aggregate toward the general goal of the realization of trusteeship: that was a formidable undertaking. It was however what Oldham had been doing ever
since the Edinburgh Conference of 1910. To Norman
Leys the problem of Kenya was a simple one. To J. H.
Oldham it was baffling and incredibly complex. And
it took, he wrote to Donald Fraser of the Church of
Scotland mission in Nyasaland, "a most powerful
hold on my mind" (see below, p. 222). With characteristic thoroughness and cautious thoughtfulness he
began about 1921 to think the problem through.

What the Africans seemed to need most was education. Not even Leys supposed that more than a tiny
handful of them were ready for immediate participa-
tion in politics. By default missions had hitherto exercised a monopoly over what education had been available. Beside the task of educating an illiterate
continent their resources had been pitifully inadequate. Colonial governments would and should do

more. Still the missions would be necessary, and a
working arrangement between secular and religious
educational authorities had to be achieved. Given the
severely limited resources, education would have to
become an integral part of a plan for the economic
development of backward countries. It must be made
to pay a return. Practical education would be wanted.
It should equip and motivate Africans to improve
their living standards and to participate in the material betterment of their own societies. If this should
mean that they would also become more useful employees of European planters and farmers that did not
unduly trouble Oldham.

Africa desperately needed investment in the "human factor." Capital would presumably be induced to
flow into industry and communications—the Conservative government with Leopold Amery and Sir William Ormsby-Gore at the Colonial Office would soon
be urging the guarantee by the imperial treasury of
transport loans. Money must somehow be diverted
into education, public health, and native agriculture.
Such social investment might not pay a quick return.
Without it, as any sophisticated economist knew, the
building of a sound "infrastructure" for a healthy
economy would be impossible. If one took a sufficiently long-range view, Oldham came to think, the
interests of settlers and Africans did not necessarily
conflict. Both groups above all wanted a sharp increase
in the black population—blacks because they were being threatened with extinction, whites because sparse
numbers made labor hard to get and raised its price.
Aid for research into endemic and epidemic disease
was needed desperately. Some might be obtained
from colonial revenues. Perhaps the British government and other colonial powers could be persuaded to
contribute. The interest of Rockefeller, Carnegie, and
other great American foundations might be stimulated. There were several possible sources. But investment in the "human factor" must be had.

Most important, Africans needed a fundamental shift in the basic beliefs and attitudes of their white rulers. Everything else would depend on that. Most Europeans on the spot, government officials as well as settlers, were prejudiced and intolerant. Missionaries, he was prepared to admit, were in their peculiar way as intolerant as any. More than any other group they came into intimate contact with Africans: their attitudes were therefore the most crucial of all. The British public too must be converted, not so much from active prejudice as from apathy.[97] Ignorance was the prime cause of both. And ignorance must be corrected, not by a romantic counterprejudice that could easily be refuted, but by the systematic, overwhelming presentation of the facts. Oldham was a rationalist. Detached, scientific knowledge would be the cure for Africa's ills. This last brought Oldham up short. So pitifully little was known about the peoples, the societies, and the environment of Africa.

So far as can be perceived from his private papers J. H. Oldham gradually thought this problem through and came to roughly these conclusions between 1921 and 1924. Most of the puzzle probably came together while he was writing *Christianity and the Race Problem*, which he sent to the press in 1924.[98] By that time, of course, he had already begun to act, moving forward while what was ultimately to become a coherent plan was still but a hazy outline in his mind. But the fundamental personal decision he made relatively soon. The pattern of the forced labor campaign was one he would not repeat. Agitation of course would continue. A certain amount of it might even be useful in strengthening his hand. He would leave that to others. His would be the long-range, positive goals. For them he would save himself, keeping his own counsel, maintaining a proper distance between himself and the radicals who were likely to antagonize

those he meant to influence, with whom he meant to
work. He must expand still further his range of contacts. Oldham would work inside.

From the inside Oldham exercised a crucial role in
the fierce dispute between Kenya's white and Indian
communities which came to a climax in 1923. Indians
outnumbered whites six to one. They had been a force
in East Africa long before Europeans had arrived.
During the war they had taken the offensive. Both
from the Indian nationalist movement and from Indians on the spot had come talk of East Africa's becoming their own colony. That project had been abandoned, its exponents having been persuaded that such
expansive ambitions ill became a people seeking freedom from imperialism. Instead they concentrated
upon the battle against discrimination which Gandhi
had waged for so many years in South Africa.[99] Specifically they sought the end of segregation in Kenya's
"white highlands," the elimination of restrictions
against immigration, and the winning of the franchise
under a common electoral roll.

The whites were thrown on the defensive. To their
minds the possibility that within half a century Africans would govern the country would have seemed
remote if not ludicrous. The Indian threat was immediate and clear. Many whites were in economic
difficulty. If prosperous Indians were allowed to buy
their land, that would be the end of the "white highlands." Immigration must be controlled, else the
millions from India's teeming villages would presumably swarm across the sea. If Indian ballots were
counted from the same box, Europeans would be
swamped politically. The white community (settlers,
merchants, officials, and missionaries alike) united as
on no other issue. The fight for Kenya's future was
bitter and prolonged.

It would have been bad enough if the dispute could

have been contained within the colony. In fact it was an imperial affair with enormous potentiality for divisiveness. Backing the Kenya settlers was South Africa, its interest being the maintenance of its own system of discriminatory legislation. General Smuts raised the issue at imperial conferences and wrote strong letters to the British cabinet.[100] On the other side the Indian nationalist movement made Kenya one of its most fundamental targets. The Government of India joined the affray. The indignation of the Indian authorities may well have been genuine. But they must have been pleased, in the aftermath of the Amritsar massacre and in the midst of Gandhi's noncooperation campaign, by an overseas diversion from their own internal difficulties.[101] The British humanitarian movement, notably the Anti-Slavery and Aborigines Protection Society, generally supported the Indian side of the controversy, leaving the Kenya missionaries isolated and resentful.

The tale of this bitter dispute has been told often and very thoroughly.[102] The correspondence that is printed here is disappointingly thin. Oldham, having wintered in India, recovered in the spring of 1923 from a long bout with influenza only just in time to play his crucial mediating role. Leys spent most of the period in bed with a broken leg, using his enforced leisure to begin *Kenya*. He did provide an interesting position paper (see below, pp. 216–18). Unlike many of his radical friends Leys foresaw a time when Indians in the ascendancy might threaten African interests. But that was only a theoretical possibility. For the whites, who were carrying on systematic exploitation now, to pose as the protectors of Africans against Asians was the sheerest hypocrisy.

Oldham returned from the land of his birth convinced that the question must somehow be resolved. Nothing less than the imperial tie with India was at stake. It was not merely that Indians were angry. The

point was that the moderates, those who were now
participating in the elected provincial councils under
"dyarchy," needed some sort of victory if they were to
survive.[103] If the Indian negotiators in London were to
throw in the sponge, declaring that further discussions were pointless, then "there would be practically
no one in India of character and independence among
the educated classes who would stand for the maintenance of the connection between Great Britain and
India."[104] Gandhi's program of noncooperation would
have been vindicated, and even more radical tactics
could not be ruled out.

As usual Edinburgh House was in the middle. Oldham hoped to maintain its links with both the Indian
and Kenya missionary factions as well as those with
humanitarians at home. Both sides sought his support. To come down heavily in favor of either, he declared, would merely destroy his effectiveness. The
East African churchmen, isolated and still bruised
from the forced-labor agitation, required sympathetic
handling. When the strongly pro-Indian J. H. Harris
of the Anti-Slavery Society sharply attacked J. W.
Arthur of the Church of Scotland's Kikuyu mission
for taking the line of the Kenya government, Oldham
refused to go along.[105] His role in this dispute anta-
gonized the leadership of the Anti-Slavery Society, of
which he himself was a vice president. The strain was
never healed. Within a few years the break would become permanent.

Throughout the spring and summer and on into the
autumn of 1923 Oldham worked at the Kenya Indian
controversy. He kept his lines open to both sides. He
met with Arthur and Lord Delamere of the Kenya
delegation. He saw the Indian negotiators: Charles F.
Andrews, V. S. Srinivasa Sastri, Dr. Tej Bahadur
Sapru, Henry S. L. Polak. As in the forced-labor campaign he worked thoroughly and intently. But there
was a difference. Before he had tried to stimulate

opinion. Now he stayed behind the scenes and tried to keep the problem from exploding.

The eventual compromise, the Duke of Devonshire's famous declaration in support of "African paramountcy," was largely Oldham's achievement.[106] That solution came to the Colonial Office in late May 1923 from the archbishop of Canterbury, who suggested that they fall back on "elementary principles," the first being "that we are in East Africa for the sake of the Africans and that our position is that of trusteeship rather than primarily of ownership or dominion."[107] Four days earlier Oldham had written to the archbishop in almost identical language. Whether the compromise would work he could not foretell, although he was convinced the Indian negotiators would agree. The settlers might not.

In that case the question arises whether we are prepared to sacrifice this principle [of trusteeship] and India at the same time to the demands of the small European community in Kenya. If that is the real issue it ought to be put squarely before the British people.[108]

Oldham saw that both the Indians and the settlers claimed among other things to be protecting the otherwise helpless Africans: the Indians because their experience of imperial rule would make them sympathetic toward a subject people; the whites because they would represent the higher civilization of a race whose genius was colonization. The role of guardian, however, had been assumed as a sacred trust by His Majesty's government. That obligation could not be delegated while the African admittedly stood in need of protection. This compromise proved to be a masterful stroke. It left the settler leaders in an awkward position. They resented this setback to the steady progress toward responsible government which Churchill in a speech of 1922 had implied would be theirs.[109]

But they had been thoroughly frightened by the Indian campaign. Their segregated "white highlands" had at least been preserved. If those had fallen, and if the Indians had also gained full political power equal to their numerical majority, then the "revolution" the settler leaders had plotted for the summer of 1923 would probably have gained very wide support.[110] Now, when the slogan of "African paramountcy" could be shown to have been drawn from their own rhetoric, the case for the rebellious action against a tyrannical Downing Street was severely weakened.

In the end the crisis passed. In the course of it Oldham had moved into the center, between the radical humanitarians and the settlers. He had retreated from the leadership of agitation that he had occupied so effectively during the forced-labor campaign. He had become one of the few able to negotiate with both sides. Moreover the Colonial Office well knew how pivotal his role had been. The first overt sign of his adjustment was Oldham's selection in 1924 as a member of a parliamentary select committee on East Africa. Its terms of reference were narrow, however, and its investigative powers were limited. It was far from being the exhaustive inquiry he had once hoped for from a royal commission. He was relieved, he told Leys, when it was abandoned with the meeting of the new parliament in 1925.

Oldham had come to believe that neither publicity nor official investigations were likely to accomplish anything. Instead he exploited the space he had made between himself and the radicals. He approached people in power. He formed new systems of alliances. He began to build. He never worked alone. He always put forward his ideas as joint proposals. He often thrust others into positions of real or nominal leadership. He never claimed full credit. His achievements were outstanding. His ubiquity was phenomenal.

Turn over almost any project of the interwar period
that seems to have been a "Good Thing," and Oldham is sure to be just off center stage.

The program of reform upon which J. H. Oldham had
embarked must be set in the context of the larger historical forces that were moving in the same direction.
For he—or for that matter Norman Leys—was not
cutting against the grain. In the period between the
two world wars a subtle but quite perceptible shift
was taking place in British attitudes toward the subject peoples of the empire. They were becoming, in a
word, less racist. A trend toward cultural relativism
was replacing the hardening chauvinistic ethnocen-
trism of the late nineteenth century. Respect and understanding were growing. Where Rider Haggard had
found romanticism in Africa, Joyce Cary dwelt upon
the tragic theme of people caught in uncontrollable
currents of racial turbulence. Where Kipling had ex-
tolled the imperial mission in India, E. M. Forster
and George Orwell subjected it to critical scrutiny and
ridicule.

The implications of this shift were enormous. It
heightened the dynamic tension, often an important
theme in British imperial history, between domestic
conscience and overseas performance. It widened dramatically the gap between public opinion within Great
Britain and the attitudes of white settlers in Africa.
The common recognition a century before that the
fundamental historical process which had caused the
American Revolution must be repeated had enabled
the makers of British colonial policy to find through
the innovation of responsible government a way of absorbing demands for autonomy from Canada, Australia, New Zealand, and South Africa.[111] So in the
period between the wars the growth of the idea of cultural relativism prepared the British government and
people to yield gracefully before demands for freedom

that arose after the second world war, a time when
Britain's drastically reduced power made decoloniza-
tion inevitable.

This change is easily oversimplified and overstated.
Some individuals in the late nineteenth century—for
example, Sir William MacGregor—preserved a sense
of respect for indigenous cultures.[112] And it would not
be difficult to find the attitudes that had made the
"new imperialism" possible persisting during the
second world war and beyond. After all, emigrants
from Britain continued to swell the ranks of settlers,
and it is a cliché of Rhodesian politics that new arri-
vals are the least tolerant of all. The rising racial tension within Britain after the second world war in
response to rapidly increasing immigration from South
Asia and the West Indies showed that the well of prejudice had hardly run dry. The change in attitudes
that had undoubtedly occurred among individuals
whose careers necessitated long-term communication
with Africans and Asians—among colonial administrators, merchants, missionaries, and even soldiers—
had disappointingly little effect once race became a
domestic and an economic issue. Yet the shift did
occur. The intellectual forces that lay behind it and
the process by which it gradually evolved and spread
have never been satisfactorily explained. In general
however the outline is reasonably clear.

Perhaps the most crucial force was the intellectual
and political revolt of Asia. Western and Asian schol-
ars had subjected Asian history and tradition to systematic scrutiny. They had published vast collections
of books. They had founded institutes and journals.
Scholarly interest and improved communications had
helped to create cultural renaissances.[113] As in the rise
of European nationalism these movements had important political repercussions. One of the strongest
currents of Asian political rhetoric was the charge
against Christian missionaries that they had subverted

traditional ways of life by giving a Western education, and that Christianity was therefore incompatible with Asian nationalism. Stridently Asians demanded to be heard. Oldham and other missionaries listened and learned. They predicted rightly that before long this same cultural nationalism must be taken up by Africans.

Other forces lay within British and European intellectual history. Freudian psychology was one of these, social anthropology another. Both exploded in the years after the first world war. It was then, largely through the influence of his disciple and biographer, Ernest Jones, that Freud's influence crested. Psychoanalysis taught students of society to probe beneath the surface. From Freud one learned "that the static antinomies around which we were encouraged to build our philosophical essays . . . —rational and irrational, intellectual and affective, logical and pre-logical— were no more than meaningless games."[114] Either the apparently trivial and accidental or the apparently inevitable had their origins in the processes of the unconscious, which patient and perceptive questioning might reveal. Civilized Western man shared with primitives a common slavery to forces in his psyche, unknown and uncontrolled. Freudian psychology pointed toward universality. In psychoanalysis the human race became one family indeed.

Anthropology drew upon many sources of nineteenth-century intellectual history. One of its elements was the sociology which the classical economists had initiated, carried on by Marx and Spencer. Another was the proliferation of folklore societies and journals. A third was heightened scholarly interest in magic and the occult. Yet another was the "functional" approach to classical studies, as in the books of Jane Harrison and Gilbert Murray, in which the Olympian quality of Greek religion was shown to be an elaborate veneer superimposed upon a vast edifice of primitive custom and belief.[115] Many of these strands James G. Frazer brought together in his immensely popular *Golden Bough*, which had its first edition in 1890 and its second (greatly enlarged) in 1911. Frazer's readers learned that primitive customs are amazingly complex and that varieties of culture are almost infinite.

The anthropology that captured the imagination of the 1930s, and of which Norman Leys complained so vigorously, added two important features. One was painstaking investigation in the field by an observer trained to be alert not only to the complexities of primitive customs but to the intervention of his own bias.[116] Whereas Frazer had sat in Cambridge, gathering his material from the books and correspondence of travellers, colonial officials, and missionaries, postwar anthropologists lived among one people for long periods. The second feature was the theory of functionalism, developed by the quarrelsome giants Malinowski and Radcliffe-Brown. Functional anthropology made cultural relativism an explicit assumption. It taught that cultures are whole systems of integrally related, interacting parts. It argued that morality, sexual customs, and so on, can properly be understood only in the context and by the standards of the particular culture in which they occur. It asserted that the apparently irrational derived from its functionality, although as in British constitutional history the particular need it had once filled might long since have vanished while the forms remained.

Whereas Freudian psychology stressed universality, functional anthropology emphasized particularity—a conflict that was personified in the famous dispute between Freud and Malinowski over the supposed pervasiveness of the Oedipus complex. But anthropology had its universal dimension too in arguing that cultural systems arose in response to similar human needs. The two disciplines had largely separate lines of development, but they were explicitly joined by practitioners of both.[117] They were received simultaneously and in practice they went together. They taught intelligent Englishmen to begin to probe their own culture and to take more seriously the ways of life of others.

These currents were reinforced by the deep psychological shock of the first world war and the depression of the 1930s. We must beware of glib generalizations. That some English and Europeans did seriously question the achievements of Western civilization there is no doubt. Few if any really believed in practice that it was not preferable to African civilization. The trend I have been describing is one that moved *toward* the acceptance of cultural relativism. And, although the change was going on throughout the interwar period, it speeded up dramatically on the eve of the second world war. For of course the single individual who did more than any other to make the British reexamine their racial attitudes was Adolph Hitler.

Within this broad context shaped by larger historical forces J. H. Oldham worked. He strove to bring this changing climate of opinion to bear upon the decision-making organs of government and the missionary movement. He sought to transform ideas into action. He read widely and thought deeply about the problem of racial tension in the world and the challenge it contained for missionaries. He knew personally many of the important figures in the intellectual life of his society. Not a true intellectual genius himself, he recognized that quality in others. He was a superb synthesizer, a generalist in a world increasingly dominated by the specialist. He was a man (as he once described the qualifications for a position, candidly admitting that he himself possessed them) of "very wide sympathies enabling him to appreciate different points of view and the capacity to see quickly the

essential elements in a problem."[118] He was a committed rationalist. He believed—and his experience
during the forced-labor campaign reinforced his opinion—in the sane, pragmatic approach to politics. In
knowledge scientifically acquired and dispassionately
analyzed, not in ever-intensifying rhetoric, lay the
only hope of solution to perplexing human problems.

As Oldham saw it the missionary movement was at
the crossroads. Christianity, he agreed with Norman
Leys, was a world missionary religion or it was nothing. Although he was by no means ready to give up
the fight, he realized that the church had probably
failed in Asia. Moreover he believed that missionaries
on the whole were guilty of the indictment which
Asian leaders had brought against them. Prejudiced,
intolerant, and ignorant, they had taught their converts to despise their own cultural heritage. As must
be the case throughout the world Asian nationalism
had risen. Christianity had needlessly been forced into
a position of fundamental antagonism in an ideological
struggle it could not hope to win. Too late missionary
leaders had begun to realize their tragic mistakes.

In Africa Christianity had come to the last continent. If it should fail there then its momentum as a
world religion would be finished. The path St. Paul
had charted would end. Christianity would be condemned to be the faith of a declining number of practitioners in the West. To succeed in Africa was therefore crucial. Missionaries might make other mistakes
there, but they ought not to repeat the causes of the
Asian failure. They must strive to create a church that
was thoroughly African, one that was compatible with
the "best" of the African tradition of which it would
become an integral part. This for Oldham was the
only hope for Christianity in Africa. And he was looking even beyond Africa to the regeneration of Christianity itself in an age when it was beset by materialism
and ideological conflict.[119]

Unfortunately history seemed to be repeating itself.
Missionaries in Africa seemed to have learned little
from their Asian experience. In Africa too they were
taking up a position of cultural intolerance that must
one day place them athwart the irresistible assertion
of African identity. Somehow this apparently inevitable dialectic must be avoided.

The early nineteenth century had witnessed another
kind of missionary attitude. Then missionaries on the
West African coast, full of their nation's sin at having
enriched itself in the slave trade and daunted by the
immensity of a task that dwarfed their numbers and
resources, had adopted a policy of partnership. Africans, both liberated slaves and coastal converts,
would perforce take the lead in regenerating their
continent. Any other plan, Sir Thomas Fowell Buxton
had believed, must fail.[120] Coastal converts had
caught this spirit of partnership. Throughout the late
nineteenth century, while white missionaries were
increasing and closing ranks against them, Africans
had maintained this optimistic outlook. It had made
them the most fervent of advocates for colonial expansion and consolidation.[121]

David Livingstone had shared Buxton's fundamentally optimistic outlook. Evil had been brought into
Africa by outsiders, the Arabs and the Europeans. It
was not the result of a basically harmful structure of
society or of any unregenerate quality of sin within the
African individual. Like Buxton he had believed that
in education and legitimate commerce lay sufficient
means for progress. But the first generation of missionaries who followed Livingstone into the "heart of
darkness" had labored under few delusions. In African society they had found little to praise and much to
condemn. Paganism, polygamy, customary dances,
rites of initiation, witchcraft: the whole fabric of
society had seemed to them a web of evil to be attacked and if possible destroyed at every point. Only

the individual removed from the influence of his society had a chance of saving his soul. [122] Intentionally
they had developed a "detribalizing" kind of education, and they had not been dismayed when the few
converts they could muster had scorned the authority
of their tribe. Had not Christ said that He had come
to turn brother against brother? Missionaries, indeed,
had overwhelmingly advocated and then applauded
imperial conquest.

Such an attitude had rested on an uncritical self-
confidence in the high moral quality of their own society, on the belief that Western civilization "was so far
permeated by Christian ideas that it was a natural ally
of the Gospel." Such an assumption, Oldham added,
"is no longer possible for us." [123] Not all missionaries
had shared to the full this cultural chauvinism even in
its period of ascendancy. Even before the war it had
begun to wane. Some of the individuals referred to in
this correspndence—A. G. Fraser, Donald Fraser,
W. E. Owen, Edwin Smith, and George Wilson—
men who began their careers around the turn of the
century, were of a new generation. The controlling
authorities of missionary bodies began to recognize
the need to reexamine their positions. Conferences
were held. Both the Edinburgh Conference of 1910
and the Inter-racial Congress held in London in 1911
discussed the church's relation to the questions of
race and culture. [124] How might missionaries better
understand the people they had gone to serve? How
much of what they were preaching as Christianity
was really Western accretion that Africans might legitimately disregard? Which African institutions, however reformed, were basically incompatible with
Christianity? Polygamy, nearly all agreed, was one
such practice that could not conceivably be accepted,
the one position where the line must be drawn. (Since
polygamy is the basis for so many African family
systems, it was a fundamental touchstone for mission-

aries and Africans alike.) Even before the first world
war, however, a substantial faction began to argue
that many African customs and practices—dances,
initiation rites—were not only compatible with Christianity but might even be turned to good advantage.
For the church to set a flinty face against the whole
thrust of African culture and society must doom
Christianity to failure. Such a conflict, this faction
believed, was unnecessary and might be avoided. To
them cultural intolerance was the way of ignorance
and despair.

J. H. Oldham, then, was by no means alone in urging that the missionary movement stood in desperate
need of education and reform. Edinburgh House, the
International Missionary Council, the *International
Review of Missions* were his bases of operations. He
was as close to the center of the world missionary
establishment as a man could possibly be. The real
question was not whether the movement was going in
the right general direction but whether the pace of
change would be fast enough to match the speed of
economic dislocation and the growth of African political awakening. In Oldham's perception knowledge
and sophistication had the chance of closing the gap
that loomed beyond. Missionaries must be exposed to
the best available minds and methods. Their influence must not be left to work haphazardly. Institutions must be created that would bring the academic
and missionary communities into continual and fruitful contact.

The education of the missionary movement was but
one part of the problem which Oldham perceived.
The mission did not relate to Africans in a vacuum. It
was but one among many European institutions that,
for better or worse, were transforming African society. The success of Christianity in Africa would depend largely on the climate which European colonialism created there. Obviously outright exploitation
would produce a sullen, hostile, and rebellious people

who would turn against any importation from Europe.
Moreover missions had properly concluded that it was
not enough to preach the word. Their goal must also
be to improve the whole tone and quality of their people's lives. For this object the resources available to
missions were clearly inadequate. Fortunately through
the doctrine of trusteeship European governments
had pledged that colonial regimes in Africa would
seek the same goal. As Leys had observed, missions
and governments had long been at odds. This fundamental antagonism seemed to him both inevitable and
healthy. To Oldham it appeared wasteful and ineffi-
cient. He favored cooperation between missions
dedicated to a tolerant understanding of African
society and colonial governments pledged to making a
reality of trusteeship. In areas such as education,
where the two were already interacting, he sought to
form close working relations. He strove to create institutions that would bring colonial officials and missionaries into a joint search for knowledge of African
society. As much as servants of God, the servants of
the state stood in need of education and a fundamental broadening of outlook. Out of their joint effort
governments might be encouraged to develop policies
of real benefit to Africans, plans with which missionaries might in good conscience cooperate.

These were the broad dimensions of the problem
which preoccupied Oldham during the period covered
by his correspondence with Norman Leys. Specifically
he helped to found the Colonial Office advisory committee on education (1924) and the Institute of African Languages and Cultures (1926). In 1926, after
three years of preparation, he organized a missionary conference at Le Zoute, Belgium, that was one
of the most influential ever held. Finally he tried un-
successfully to create a research institute in Kenya,
an idea that he was instrumental in pushing to its important conclusion in Lord (Malcolm) Hailey's famous *African Survey*, carried out in the 1930s with

the support of the Carnegie Foundation. These ventures occurred separately and must be related individually. In the mind of J. H. Oldham they were
closely interrelated means toward the grand goal of
making colonial Africa a prosperous, healthy, and
Christian continent.

Oldham's initial approach to government came in the
field of education. It was natural that the first step
should be taken there, where the missionary movement's leverage was greatest and its need for cooperation most severe. Missions had previously exercised a
monopoly by default. "This must change," he told the
receptive parliamentary undersecretary at the Colonial
Office, Sir William Ormsby-Gore, "and ought to
change." Clearly government could no longer leave
education to the missionaries. If trusteeship were
going to be taken at all seriously then education would
become an obvious target. Moreover any attempt at
economic development that passed beyond the barest
rudiments would require investment in education.
Still the missions were already at work. Given the
restriction of resources there should be neither dupli-
cation of effort nor working at cross-purposes. Missions and governments must work together. "On our
side this means a considerable education of the missionary body. On the other hand effective co-operation requires a definite policy on the part of Government with which we can co-operate." [125] He did not
need to add that government planning in this field
had been in ludicrously short supply. By his initiative
Oldham sought a compromise under which missionaries might continue to exercise a share of the decision-making power in a sphere hitherto their own, but
one in which they would be increasingly threatened.
     The advisory committee which the Colonial Office
appointed in 1924 was an organization of the Establishment. Radical enthusiasts were notably absent.
Oldham, indeed, expressly warned Ormsby-Gore

against bringing J. H. Harris into the project, lest the
involvement of the Anti-Slavery Society should alarm
members of "our constituency."[126] He had several
constituents in mind: missionary leaders such as himself and his brother-in-law, Alexander Fraser; noted
educators such as Julian Huxley the biologist and
Reginald Coupland the Oxford colonial historian;
former governors such as Lord Lugard; colonial educational experts such as Hanns Vischer (formerly of
Northern Nigeria), Sir Humphrey Leggett (formerly
of Uganda and the Sudan), and Henry Mayhew (formerly of India). Active governors such as Sir Donald
Cameron, Sir Hugh Clifford, Sir Gordon Guggisberg,
and Sir Graeme Thomson were encouraged to attend
while on leave. In an era when the British government
still believed that colonies should ordinarily support
themselves, the committee was meant to carry weight
with colonial authorities.

The advisory committee on education was one of
the first attempts to make reality of what had previously been rather empty declarations of the intentions of British imperial trusteeship. It is easy to dwell
upon shortcomings. Even now the commitment was
without financial support from the imperial treasury.
Funds continued to be limited to what various colonial
governments might be persuaded to invest from their
own revenues. Comparatively prosperous colonies like
the Gold Coast or Uganda could institute ambitious
projects that were impossible for Kenya or Tanganyika. Not until the development loan act of 1940,
passed in the aftermath of the influential Hailey *Survey* and at a time when the need was felt to demonstrate
the benefits of empire to Africans and Americans,
would the British government decide to invest directly
in the "human factor." Still the advisory committee
laid the groundwork. It sponsored the founding of
universities. It arranged for the publication of textbooks for African students, a difficult and expensive
problem. It published *Overseas Education.* A cynical

postcolonial age should probably not judge too
harshly the long-range contributions of this committee or the spirit in which it went about its work.

Oldham contributed directly to two of the more important of the committee's early innovations. These
were the founding of Achimota College in the Gold
Coast and the transplanting from the southern United
States to Kenya of the "Jeanes system" for the training and supervision of rural teachers. Education is
always among the more politically charged subjects.
Once again Oldham became involved in controversy.

Achimota was the realization of the vision of one of
the most remarkable and progressive governors of the
interwar era, Sir Gordon Guggisberg.[127] Others might
wish to establish African universities so that the home
authorities might be spared the agitation of students
attending British universities and the colonies their
angry radicalism when they returned. Guggisberg's
goal was positive. The Gold Coast's prosperity, based
on its thriving cocoa industry, enabled him to think
expansively. He planned a university where African
students might be given an education in no way inferior to what they would have received in Britain. At
the same time the institution would lead a resurgence
of pride and renewed creativity in traditional African
culture. The man and his ideas, his faith in the black
man's future, and his tolerance were exciting and in-
fectious, not least to African intellectuals. Such old
Ghana hands as W. E. F. Ward, one of the founding
staff of Achimota, confirm the impression left by the
documents. There *was* something vigorously ongoing
about the Gold Coast in the 1920s. Its spirit was present in few other colonies, and it wore away after Guggisberg's departure.

Oldham's direct contribution to Achimota was to
bring together at his Surrey home the two men who

were to make reality of a governor's dreams. One was
the "chief," Oldham's own brother-in-law, Alexander G. Fraser. A charismatic speaker, he was a man of
strong character who created controversy and anecdotes wherever he went.[128] The other was Dr. James
E. K. Aggrey, a Fanti who had gone to America for
education and who had remained to become president
of Livingstone College in North Carolina. Recently
he had become famous throughout Africa as the lone
black member of the Phelps-Stokes commission
tours. Aggrey matched Fraser's charisma and inspired at least as many anecdotes.[129] Like Booker T.
Washington he had the knack of telling white men
what they wished to hear, but in a way that did not
compromise his own dignity. He was his own man.
Some white men pointed to his gold teeth, his top hat,
his tan shoes, and his polished language, and pronounced him an unsuitable model for "our Africans."[130] For others he was the personification of
their dreams for the future of the continent and the
race.

As Oldham told Guggisberg either of these two
gifted men would have been a lucky catch. Fraser was
undoubtedly the best principal available. "He has run
in Ceylon a public school [Trinity College] that, apart
from the limitation of its resources, will compare with
any in England and he has the advantage over anyone
fresh from home that he knows about Africa and the
East."[131] Aggrey, whom the Gold Coast had welcomed as a conquering hero when he had come home
in 1920 on the first Phelps-Stokes tour,[132] would be a
"unique asset." The combination would be irresistible: "If you get these two men and their health lasts
you will soon have an institution which will become
almost as widely known as Hampton and Tuskegee."
Then, showing that he well understood the negative
image which black intellectuals such as those of the

West African Congress often associated with the pillars of the American Negro educational establishment, Oldham added that Achimota

will be, of course, of a different type and it will not do to let any impression get abroad in the Gold Coast that these institutions are to be a model. The less said about Hampton and Tuskegee the better. I quote them here only in respect of their renown.[133]

At Oldham's house Fraser and Aggrey agreed that together they would build Achimota. Until Aggrey's sudden death in New York in 1927 they made a close and effective team. Persuading the authorities to confirm the appointment of an African to a high position in the hierarchy proved to be difficult.[134] As it turned out his collaboration was essential. For Fraser soon came under attack from African intellectuals. They were suspicious of his emphasis upon African languages and culture, which smacked to them of paternalism and inferiority. They complained about the lavish scale. Most of all they were disappointed at Fraser's decision to begin at the primary level, working only gradually toward university status. Guggisberg's promises were being watered down. They had been shown a vision of a university; they were being given a public school.[135] Whatever else Aggrey may have been, the man was a genius at public relations. He soothed African feelings. He sold them the school and its principal. Without his work the experiment might have failed at the outset.

Achimota succeeded. Fraser emphasized discipline, sports, and teamwork: the model of the English public school that had been conceived at Dr. Thomas Arnold's Rugby. Like its other models, Hampton and Tuskegee, Achimota stressed "working with the hands." The students (many of them chiefs' sons) resented this as demeaning. The principal gave them the rare example of a white man doing manual labor.

They did well on competitive examinations. And the
staff did interesting things. The young Frank Ward
collected both African music and a priceless collection
of oral history (destroyed by a student's attempt to
burn the evidence of academic failure). He wrote a
textbook of British history for African students that
was candid enough to make the authorities see fit
to suppress it.[136] The school's emphasis upon African
culture was no mere show. There seems no good reason to doubt the testimony of its most famous alum-
nus that at Achimota an "African renaissance" took
place.[137]

The interesting attempt to export to Kenya an American system of village teacher supervision grew directly out of Oldham's contacts with American missionary leaders and philanthropic organizations.
More specifically it came from his alliance with the
leading expert on Negro education for the Phelps-
Stokes Foundation, Dr. Thomas Jesse Jones. Since
Kenneth King has recently written an excellent book
on this subject, his main conclusions can be briefly
summarized.[138]
   Phelps-Stokes was one of several northern philanthropic foundations which, from the late 1870s when
the "Redeemers" virtually abandoned public support
of education in the American south, began to give
money to "uplift" the blacks. Naturally enough they
concentrated their relatively modest resources. Most
of their investment went to a small clique of Negro
colleges, notably Hampton Institute in Virginia and
Tuskegee Institute in Alabama, whose leaders formed
an establishment with enormous power, and not alone
over education.[139] Jones had taught at Hampton. He
regarded himself as the disciple of General S. C. Armstrong, the founder of Hampton, and of Booker T.
Washington. Like them Jones consistently tried to
mold American Negro education in the image of what

northern philanthropists and even southern whites
might consider desirable and "safe." Like them he
favored taking the "Negro question" out of politics.
Like them he disavowed "literary" education, prefer-
ring agricultural and "industrial" training that would
equip black students for the disadvantaged lives they
might realistically expect to lead in a country where
they had to win acceptance. Like them he firmly advocated social segregation. King argues persuasively
that Jesse Jones preached their philosophy and followed their tactics—only more so. The administrator
of one of the few substantial sources of money in the
field, the compiler of influential government reports
(which philanthropists were likely to consult before
investing their money), Jones occupied a unique and
powerful position.[140]

It was also a controversial one. His educational and
political theories, his persistent undercutting of any
save the "right type" of black leadership naturally
made him a primary target of the "wrong type." The
latter included W. E. B. Du Bois, the historian, editor
of *The Crisis,* and founder of the Pan African Congress and the National Association for the Advancement of Colored People, and Carter Woodson, the
founding editor of the *Negro History Review.* Between
these factions ideological conflict was intense.

Far from being a detached observer, dispassionately gathering data for impartial reports on the educational needs of African colonies, Jesse Jones toured
Africa as a committed ideologue. His reports were
essentially written far in advance. They had one important virtue that is easily overlooked. African colonial
governments at the time were doing practically nothing for education, and he strongly recommended that
they begin.[141] What he recommended was another
question. There is nothing wrong, then or now, with
teaching people practical things. The economic development plans of any African or Asian country will

testify to that. Few would now take the position which
educated Africans so frequently adopted at the time
that to encourage African students to take pride in a
rich and distinctive culture is necessarily the telltale
sign of an inferior education designed by paternalists.
Rather than the substance it was mainly the tone of
the reports, the strong implication which he made no
attempt to remove that he intended the sort of education that would make Africans useful to white settlers, that made them controversial. Radicals like
Norman Leys attacked Jones. Reactionaries welcomed
him just as warmly.

King argues further that Oldham committed himself fully to Jones' ideological position, doing all that
he could to stamp the Phelps-Stokes pattern on education throughout the continent.[142] There is strong evidence for this interpretation. Indeed, Oldham did not
merely defend Jones' theories in a negative way. He
might have asserted that only such "practical" ideas
were likely to win the essential support of colonial
governments and white settlers. Instead he embraced
Jones with both arms. Along with Jones and C. T.
Loram (who as a South African director of education
claimed to have drafted many of General Hertzog's
speeches on the "Native Question" and who was one
of the strongest "liberal" supporters of segregation),[143]
Oldham was a member of what Jones at least called a
triumvirate. It would combine Jones' inspired ideas,
Oldham's contacts and genius for "spadework," and
Loram's administrative experience.[144] For this group
Jones' enthusiasm knew no bounds. Its influence
would be immense. It would extend its tentacles into
three continents and perhaps beyond.

Oldham strenuously defended Jones against attacks by Leys and other radicals. He agreed that practical training in agricultural and "industrial" skills,
not "literary education," best spoke to Africa's immediate problems. He accepted perhaps too easily the

proposition that only Afro-American missionaries of the "right type," that is of the Hampton-Tuskegee mold, should be allowed to go to Africa. (The choice undoubtedly lay between them and none. "Agitators" in the tradition of Marcus Garvey or Bishop Henry M. Turner frightened colonial governments, who saw them as potential John Chilembwes.) He encouraged what became a regular sabbatical tour by missionaries and educational leaders to selected American Negro showplaces where they might be shown the fruits of the Hampton-Tuskegee philosophy. Oldham himself would not have resisted King's contention that in the main his own ideas on education in the 1920s closely resembled those of Jesse Jones.

Identical, however, they were not. It is from Jones' side of the correspondence with Oldham that King has drawn his interesting material about the goals of the "triumvirate." Oldham never took out membership. It was not his way to demur unless challenged directly, and he let Jones prattle on. His ultimate aims and scheme of values were simply not the same. To Jones educational theories were ends in themselves. To Oldham they were merely building blocks. In moderate doses and with pragmatic good sense they might be supported until better ones could be evolved. Oldham's own contribution to the literature of education (which he wrote in collaboration with his colleague Betty Gibson) stressed no particular doctrines but cited a broad spectrum of opinion: Julian Huxley, Victor Murray, Bruno Guttmann, Alexander Fraser. Jones cannot have been pleased to find that his own approach was nowhere developed, or that the one explicit reference to the Phelps-Stokes reports was mildly critical.[145]

Jesse Jones was a committed ideologue. Oldham did not in the least avoid associating with ideologues— Jones, Malinowski, Leys, Lugard—but he was not one himself. This Jones learned to his chagrin in the

1930s. Then he found Oldham sponsoring the research tours of Victory Murray, Jones' most formidable British critic, and favorably reviewing Murray's
books.[146] Oldham was very concerned about African
education. He fought to maintain its Christian character in a rapidly secularizing society and to keep a
role for missionaries in decision making. He favored
cooperation with government and thought it essential
that both parties work out their positions. What pre-
cise directions African education might ultimately
take he did not profess to know. Africans, after all,
would presumably have something to say about that,
and they would rightly resent any restriction of their
access to European education so that they might develop "on their own lines."[147] Experience and resources must be attracted. Jones had both. The reason
for Oldham's interest in the Jeanes experiment in
Kenya was not his belief that anything very significant
would be achieved from what was after all a very small
investment of a few thousand dollars in a huge country. Rather it was the first commitment by an American foundation to the cause of African education, and
he hoped to attract more.

Like Norman Leys, Jones gradually and painfully
discovered that neither Oldham's thinking nor his
actions could be controlled. He had intended to use
Oldham, but the reverse had been true. Once he realized this he began to cool. There was no decisive
break. But in the 1930s what had been a continuous
flow of correspondence diminished to an intermittent
trickle. King's attempt to draw others—Oldham,
Aggrey, Guggisberg, even Fraser—into the "Jones
school" seems strained and unconvincing, one of the
few blemishes in a valuable and original book.

Simultaneously Oldham was working through an entirely different set of people toward a related aim,
the founding of the International Institute of African

Languages and Cultures, now simply the International African Institute, one of the foremost African research organizations in the world. He hoped this medium might help to educate the missionary movement and bring it into fruitful dialogue with academics and administrators. He looked toward the accumulation of knowledge and the greater tolerance it would presumably bring toward African ways of life. Africans themselves might be encouraged to revive the creative energy of cultures that were threatened with disintegration. As in the educational field however Oldham was pragmatic. The idea seemed a good one. He was building and for the moment that was enough. Who knew what it all might lead to?

Missionary interest in vernacular languages was nothing new. Missionaries, indeed, had achieved most of what had been done toward the enormous task of compiling dictionaries and grammars for oral languages whose emphasis upon tonality and wide diacritical differences presented extraordinary complexities. The Gospels, catechisms, and *Pilgrim's Progress* had been translated into numerous vernaculars. As C. E. Wilson of the Baptist Missionary Society told the High Legh conference of 1924, "almost every word printed in African native languages is Christian."[148] Beyond that missionaries could rightly claim that they had long preceded academic anthropologists into serious observation of primitive societies in the field. Their literature still constitutes one of the main bodies of material for the study of African history. They had after all provided much of the primary evidence for Frazer's *Golden Bough.*

The High Legh conference met to stimulate missionary interest and activity still further. Its organizers urged that vernaculars should be used much more in church and school. The program of translation was lagging. Too many missionaries seemed content with only a partial proficiency. Only the missionary fluent in the vernacular, argued Edwin Smith

(himself a pioneering missionary-anthropologist),
could fully comprehend his people's point of view.
Intensive anthropological investigation was also part
of the missionary's task. Those ignorant of the significance of African custom (he was fond of citing
the origins of the Ashanti war of the 1870s in support), inevitably blundered.[149] On the depth of his understanding depended the ability of the missionary to
lead his people to Christian salvation while retaining
"all that was good" in their own culture. Ultimately,
he thought, most of the African social fabric would not
prove to be incompatible with the essence of Christianity. Much of what was "bad" could be, to use
Smith's own Freudian term, "sublimated" rather
than eliminated.[150]

The German missionary Diedrich Westermann
went still further. African languages were drying up,
ceasing to be the dynamic vehicles of vigorous cultural creativity. The educated were using English,
French, Portuguese, or Afrikaans in their everyday
discourse, coming to regard their native tongues only
as means of communicating with the ignorant. To
Westermann this was all very tragic. African languages were in no way inferior. They were beautiful,
powerful, and efficient, fully capable of adaptation.
They had been made by their people over centuries
of painful, creative evolution. They bore their national tradition. Westermann echoed Herder and the
linguistic origins of German nationalism: a people
that had lost its linguistic autonomy had lost its
soul.[151]

Out of the High Legh conference came the impulse
for the founding of the Institute. It was a joint enterprise. Most of the rationale and rhetoric came from
Westermann and Smith. Oldham's role was merely
to make it go. He circulated the missionary lists and
brought in subscriptions. These he took to the American foundations in New York. Rockefeller gave him
a "challenge grant." Thus armed, back he went to

the missionary societies for more. He strove to make
the organization truly international; Frenchmen, Germans, Belgians, and Swedes became directors. He
had invited Lord Lugard to the High Legh conference.
Through Lugard he attracted other colonial officials.
Gradually the Colonial Office and colonial governments became contributors. Also came Professor
Malinowski, who established with Oldham a close
working alliance which (given the anthropologist's
well-known agnosticism and habit of using profanity)
was at least as improbable as Oldham's relationship
with Norman Leys.[152] Malinowski's interest was
plain: he wanted research grants for his students.
Oldham was glad to have the professor's brilliant
mind and academic contacts. Different in so many
ways, the two men were alike in being unusually effective "entrepreneurs." Thus what had begun as a missionary enterprise drew in government administrators
and academic professionals, the latter coming in time
to dominate it.

More than any other organization between the wars
the International Institute publicized and tried to
enrich African culture. Its journal, *Africa,* published
interesting and informative articles. It sponsored con-
tests for the best writing by Africans in the vernacular. Its general line was that in their traditional culture there was much of which Africans ought to be
proud and Europeans respectful, much that was in
danger of becoming extinct, much that ought if possible to be preserved. An early article, for instance,
warned that increasing European demand for mass-
produced artifacts and the saturation of the environment by Western junk were ruining African art.[153]
This enthusiasm for African tradition was sometimes
shallow. It sometimes served, as educated Africans
often charged, as a cloak for poorly disguised attempts to keep the African backward. As Leys
pointed out the main problem of Africa was not an-

thropological but economic and political. From that
standpoint the Institute was diversionary. Yet Oldham's object had not been primarily practical. He had
hoped to educate and to help change attitudes. Toward those ends the Institute and its journal were
important contributions.

In the 1930s Oldham, as the Institute's secretary,
presided over its gradual evolution into an academic
organization. It was in *Africa* that Malinowski
launched his campaign for "practical anthropology," the rationale under which colonial governments
were persuaded despite their initial hostility to employ
anthropologists.[154] The Institute sponsored some two
dozen research students, who are now the grand old
men and women of the discipline throughout the
English-speaking world. *Africa* reflects the organization's revolution and the growth of the discipline. In
the twenties general contributions from amateurs pre-
dominated. A decade later highly specialized articles
by Meyer Fortes, Isaac Schapera, Edward Evans-
Pritchard, and Godfrey and Monica Wilson had
taken over. The journal published special supple-
ments on diet, magic, traditional music, and customary law. Oldham had certainly hoped that the International Institute might be an important innovation.
He cannot have foreseen the kind of organization it
ultimately became.

The approach to the Colonial Office to seek a compromise on education and the founding of the International Institute were important ventures in their
own right. Like all living institutions they evolved in
ways that had been unintended, outgrew the percep-
tions that had brought them into being, and left their
place in the original order of priorities. For Oldham
both innovations had arisen in the course of his intensive preparation for the international conference at
Le Zoute, Belgium, in 1926. His ultimate goal was

neither the promotion of educational doctrines nor the sponsorship of anthropologists but the grand design of renewing the missionary movement, equipping it to fight its decisive battle for the last continent.

Oldham's eyes were fixed on Le Zoute. His "spade-work" was incredibly thorough. He scrutinized guest lists. He organized weekly planning conferences. He tried to control the agenda while leaving room for spontaneity. In preparation he even wrote a book, *Christianity and the Race Problem* (1925).

As Leys predicted the book has the defects of being the result of group discussions lasting well over a year. It would probably have been a more cohesive and more powerful work if Oldham had simply written it himself. It attempts too broad a sweep. It is obviously written to avoid controversy. The facts seem mostly right, except for its interpretation of recent American history in which disfranchisement by the illegal enactments and violence of the whites is employed to argue that the *blacks* must have been unqualified for the vote—common though this peculiar piece of circular logic was at the time. On clearly controversial questions, such as racial inferiority or innate differences, Oldham was cautious. The first he skirted by saying that while there did appear to be substantial "overlap" in the available tests (such as the famous survey of black and white inductees into the American army in world war I), no means had yet been devised of separating innate intelligence from the effects of environment. On racial distinctiveness he was a little more direct. As he told Leys later he did believe in racial differences.

Oldham's primary aim had not been to write a good book. He had hoped to answer the highly racist propaganda that was emanating at the time from the American academy, such as Dr. Lothrop Stoddard's *Rising Tide of Color* (1922). Judged against the available lit-

erature of the 1920s Oldham's effort was reasonably
successful. His main purpose however was to use the
book as a vehicle to stimulate wide discussion before
and during the conference. The causes of its defects
were thus its virtues. The truly significant thing about
it was supposed to be the process of its production.
The archives of the International Missionary Council
at Geneva contain documents from India, South
Africa, and throughout the world: letters, memoranda, reports of interviews, minutes of discussions.
Every point was the result not so much of intensive
research as of a survey of "acceptable" points of view.

By all accounts the Le Zoute conference fulfilled
Oldham's hopes. It fully endorsed his program. He
had already won the acceptance of the Colonial Office
for the Phelps-Stokes recommendations. Now the
delegates duly added their approval. They agreed to
the principles upon which the International African
Institute had been founded. They discussed at length
the question of the acceptability of African custom.
Once more they drew the line at polygamy. But their
resolutions were more tolerant than ever before. A
spirit of unity and exuberance emerges from the pages
of Edwin Smith's report.[155] Presumably the delegates
carried it away. A very perceptive undergraduate once
wrote that Le Zoute for the missionaries must have
been what the Woodstock festival was for the rock
culture of the 1960s: its climax, a "happening" which,
however carefully it might have been arranged, could
never be recaptured. More tangibly a recent statistical
analysis of the African independent church movement
(which argues that the principal causes of schism are
the contradictions members discover between mission
teachings and Scripture, that is, between what is
Western and what is essentially universal in Christianity) finds a distinct decline in the incidence of the
phenomenon in the decade after Le Zoute.[156] The

growth of a sense of cultural relativism that had been
rare among previous generations of missionaries did
help to decrease if not to end African religious tension.

Le Zoute had given the Protestant missionary movement a new sense of ecumenical unity. Its resolutions
provided a focus and a coherent policy. Although the
goal was not of the kind that can ever be finally completed, nor Oldham the sort of man who would rest
upon his laurels, yet in truth he had largely succeeded
in setting the tone for the missionary movement
for its task in a rapidly changing Africa. But he had
long ago realized that, while work within the missionary household must be his main concern, it could
not be sufficient. Governments too must think through
their problems and arrive at coherent plans. The environment in which missionaries must operate was
being shaped by forces beyond their control and,
apparently, beyond the ken of government as well. To
surrender to a fatalistic acceptance of economic deter-
minism was irresponsible. As he and B. D. Gibson
put it in *The Remaking of Man in Africa*:

Even the economic forces which seem all powerful
proceed in their inception from the decisions of human wills. The shape which the new Africa will take
will be the result of human choice—of the courageous
acceptance or supine refusal of responsibility. [157]

To stand aside from the affray was impossible. Merely
to offer criticism from the outside would accomplish
little. The responsible attitude was to assume that
other parties—governments and if possible even settlers—were basically right-minded and capable of
being reasoned with. More it seemed to Oldham could
be achieved by rational discourse and cooperation
than by impassioned debate.

In Oldham's view the only hope for Kenya lay in
raising the discussion to a new plane. So long as

settlers and their critics continued to flail away at
each other the government would remain between,
stymied and helpless. Meanwhile the relentless forces
of economic change that were destroying African society before their eyes would be left unchecked. In fact
the government was not the altogether hopeless case
outsiders were prone to imagine. In his series of negotiations—first the forced-labor dispute, then the Indian controversy that had produced the Devonshire
declaration of "African paramountcy," and finally
the approaches in regard to educational cooperation
and the International Institute of African Languages
and Cultures—Oldham had met reasonable men who
had felt constrained like himself by a sense of powerlessness. Milner, Devonshire, Amery, Ormsby-Gore,
even Churchill: these seemed like men who wanted to
do the "right thing." A less heated atmosphere might
enlarge their range of alternatives. The key once more
lay in an increase of knowledge—knowledge about the
nature of the problem itself, knowledge by each party
of the other's needs and interests.

In 1925, when Oldham began to move, several factors made the situation appear favorable. The government had accepted both the recommendations of the
Phelps-Stokes commission that it increase its stake in
African education and his own plan for compromise
between government and missions. Ormsby-Gore
published a long report, based on his tour of East
Africa, recommending a substantial investment in
transportation facilities by means of imperial guarantee.[158] On this document Oldham wrote a tactful
memorandum (see below, Appendix) in which he
praised Ormsby-Gore's farsightedness and then urged
that the idea be taken in a slightly different direction.
In the long run, he agreed, the interests of Africans
and settlers were complementary. Both required an
increasing, healthy, and prosperous native population. Railways and harbors were essential but insuffi-

cient. Production and therefore the labor supply must be increased as well. All those factors which had kept the African population small, and which had decreased it so disastrously during the colonial period and the war, must be investigated: the limitations upon native agriculture, endemic and epidemic disease, the demographic impact of migratory labor. It was no longer enough to think about these problems vaguely in the hope they would somehow solve themselves. In a letter to Ormsby-Gore, Oldham quoted Dr. Abraham Flexner of the Rockefeller Foundation, whose reports had revolutionized the American medical profession:

Up to this time almost all social development has been haphazard, accidental and, therefore, blundering and wasteful. It would seem to be high time that we endeavoured to learn the facts first and to act afterwards. I sincerely wish you may succeed in persuading the Government to try this form of procedure. You will introduce a new era in colonization. [159]

In the place of impassioned rhetoric leading to reflexive action Oldham called for intensive, planned research.

As it happened the government had already begun to think of research as a way out of its dilemma. In the course of a House of Lords debate on Kenya Lord Balfour announced the founding of a Committee of Civil Research. Its purview was so far domestic, but perhaps East Africa might be the subject of a similar program. The idea which Oldham began to push in the spring of 1925 was that a portion of the transport loan should be earmarked for research into the "human factor." Even from a strictly business standpoint, he told the Colonial Office, such investment made good sense. For, he argued,

If there is to be successful economic development of East Africa there is something more fundamental

even than transport. It is *mind* in the creative sense—
statesmanship, policy, mastery of the facts.[160]

The direct economic effects of such a dispassionate
pursuit of knowledge would be substantial. More important still would be the indirect effects of raising
the plane of discussion, of "the permeation of the
public mind with larger and more rational issues."[161]
    Finally the appointment in May 1925 of the new
governor of Kenya, Sir Edward Grigg, formerly secretary to Lloyd George, seemed like the beginning of a
new era. Oldham had not met the man before, but he
took to him warmly. Here, he thought, was the strong
governor the colony had so desperately needed. Grigg
swiftly interested himself in Oldham's idea, and between them they concocted an outline of a scheme for
a research institute in Kenya. The British Treasury
raised objections about whether money voted for
transportation could legitimately be devoted to another purpose. Grigg proposed to take it up with the
conference of East African governors. Meanwhile
Oldham sought support from American foundations.
Kenya, he argued, was the great testing ground of the
race problem in modern Africa which could hardly
leave unaffected the United States with its large black
population.[162] He was deeply committed to the idea.
He even considered seriously Grigg's offer to take a
leave of absence in order to go to Kenya and establish
the institute as its first director. It was not, he said, a
position he wanted. But if the "call" came it was not
one he would be able to refuse.[163] In Grigg's "Dual
Policy" of encouraging both white settlement and
African production Oldham saw a "really statesman-
like and creative idea capable, if carried out, of providing a solution of the difficult problems of the African Continent."[164] It had the chance, he thought, of
bringing together white and black, the settler community and its critics. If the Dual Policy were to suc-

ceed, greater knowledge and hence the research
institute seemed essential.

In the end the idea came to nothing. The "call"
never came. The British Treasury continued to object.
At the governors' conference Sir Donald Cameron
could see little benefit for Tanganyika in a program
based in Kenya. Support from American foundations
was not yet forthcoming. Grigg became preoccupied
with the conflict over East African closer union, in
the course of which Oldham gradually changed from
being the governor's warm supporter into an opponent of his plans. The deterioration in their relations
between 1927 and 1931 lies outside the period of this
correspondence, and is covered in a part of Oldham's
papers that have been detached from the main body
and are not yet available.[165] But the Kenya research
institute was a casualty.

Oldham's idea slumbered but it did not die. In 1929
General Smuts came to Oxford, where he lectured
grandly on the benefits that must be conferred upon
Africans by the rapid extension of white settlement
and European commerce. He urged Oxford to turn
from Greek to Africa, and then embarked upon a
fund-raising tour of America in support of a research
center to be established at Rhodes House.[166] Those
whom the Colonial Office called the "best people"
in Oxford hurried together a proposal to the Rockefeller Foundation, only to find that London (that is
Oldham and Malinowski) was there before them.[167]
It was not Oldham's way to exclude, and besides it
was clear that their American benefactors would be
impressed with unity. But Oxford came to London.
Gradually what became known as the Chatham House
project, under the chairmanship of Sir Philip Kerr
(later the Marquis of Lothian) took shape. Out of that
enterprise eventually emerged Lord (Malcolm)
Hailey's massive and extremely pivotal *African Survey*. Characteristically, throughout the course of

events that he had done so much to chart, Oldham remained behind the scenes. So far as the world knew the guiding hand in the field of African research had been that of Smuts.

All these things J. H. Oldham built or inspired in an amazingly fruitful period in the mid-1920s. Together they make him arguably the single most influential individual in the shaping of British official thinking and colonial policy toward Africa between the wars. He could have accomplished none of this if he had not "gone inside," if he had not removed himself from too close an association with the radicals. He did not inform them fully of his plans or of the drift of his thinking. With most of those ideas, especially when they were presented piecemeal in response to particular situations, they agreed. Only when the coherent pattern of "inside" building based on the hope of compromise between positions that were apparently irreconcilable became clear might they object. He left them to make the break he came to think inevitable and even desirable. J. H. Harris was the first to do so. His relations with Oldham had never been close, and they never recovered from the tension of the Indian controversy of 1923.[168]

Norman Leys was slower. Oldham understood well before Leys did that their approaches to Kenya and Africa were fundamentally incompatible. In the period of their correspondence, and in part because of it, both men altered those approaches. More accurately, both came to define more precisely their positions and to act on very different lines of action. Each was challenged to think through his attitude and to calculate his strategy. Their confrontation became as fruitful as their earlier partnership. Their correspondence helps to identify the turning points and the processes through which they grappled with the problems and with each other.

For Leys there were several crucial points. First was the time, probably as late as January 1918, when he reflected upon his fifteen years in Africa and crystallized his experience. His letters to Gilbert Murray demonstrate that his views had developed with reasonable consistency, but not until the paper of 1918 had he worked them out systematically. The second was a speaking engagement at Edinburgh House (of which there is no record), when he was led to return to the New Testament, and heard St. Paul speak on the race question as though for the first time. The Kenya labor controversy was not for him, as it was for Oldham, a crisis of conscience: he had no decision to make. Leys' third crossroads came in August 1921 when, symbolically, he met Du Bois and Jesse Jones in the same week. The fourth turning point was not so much the writing of his book (for there are no really substantial changes in it from the paper of 1918) as its reception: far more favorable than he had expected, yet nobody did anything. Last came his gradual discovery during the spring of 1925 that Oldham was attempting to damp down the very indignation he had written his book to provoke.

For Oldham there were apparently two crises. The first was when he looked back upon his successful leadership of the forced-labor campaign: so much work, so little accomplished. Twice he asked Leys the way out of his dilemma. What, in this year of grace and given the political realities, could be achieved? Leys evaded. To him Oldham's was not the real problem. For one who wants to abolish the system the question of how to reform within it is meaningless. They were on different wavelengths. It was not that they approached Kenya differently. It was not the same problem. This Oldham perceived if Leys did not. After 1923 he never asked for advice, but only for Leys' opinions.

The second turning point came for Oldham in

December-January 1924–25. It is marked by the two
letters, the first not sent (see below, pp. 231, 235),
which he wrote in reaction to *Kenya*. The second, more
qualified in its praise, gives no hint of action. His
letters to the bishops, saying that he hoped Leys' book
would not become controversial but that he feared it
would, shows that his thinking was completed before
he went to America. (Thus discussions with Jones and
others were not crucial.) He realized that if he were
to maintain his position in the center and on the inside, on which so much depended, it would be well
if he kept clear of too intimate an involvement with
this explosive book. In America he talked about it—
Jones complained that he was leading people to think
he agreed with it fully—and helped to publicize it.
But when he returned he made clear that his own
views were different. Sooner or later Leys would find
out just how much they differed. Characteristically
Oldham left him to decide that for himself.

The wonder is that Leys had not seen it, as Oldham
had as early as the autumn of 1921, long before. Part
of the explanation is Oldham's personality. Those
who knew him say that the man, deafness and all,
was hypnotically persuasive. People of many points
of view who dealt with him desperately wanted to
think that their cause was also his. He was a very
shrewd practitioner of the diplomat's art. At one time
or another Leys, Jones, and Grigg were all firmly convinced that Oldham was their man. Eventually, in his
own time, he disabused them all. Yet Oldham's position on the race question is stated quite clearly in
Christianity and the Race Problem. And he told Leys
explicitly at the time that on some points they fundamentally disagreed. How Leys could have written
the wholly congratulatory letter that he did (see
below, p. 227) is hard to explain. Not until June 1925,
when he read the paper that Oldham had written for
Ormsby-Gore (see the Appendix), did he explode.

To be sure the radical doctor had never felt quite safe with this man of the "establishment." He thought, rightly, that Oldham liked to be close to power. "I hope you will forgive me," he observed,

for thinking that your occupation and habits dispose you to give too great importance to people in high position. You know them well, constantly meet them in many countries. You see the levers of the machinery of government in their hands. It is tempting to think that a thing is done when the hand of such a man is rightly guided. In the modern world it is not so. We are helpless unless the lever moves a powerful engine. That engine is public opinion [p. 242 below].

He complained that Oldham's emphasis upon research was leading people to conclude that things in Kenya were perhaps not so bad. As for the facts they were already available. Further knowledge would always be welcome. But his book provided enough accurate information to enable any reasonable person to make up his mind. What was wanted was action. The call for research was therefore diversionary. In June 1925 he felt further betrayed by Oldham's support for still more government aid to the settlers. The more they received the harder it would be to dislodge them from power. Finally in the autumn of 1926 came the Le Zoute conference and its endorsement of Jesse Jones' educational program. That scheme was based (Leys charged) upon the supposed mental inequality of white and black.

Leys attacked, this time publicly. In private he complained to Harris about Oldham's fundamentally un-Christian betrayal. Oldham joined the Hilton Young Commission. Rumor had it that he was siding with the settlers on closer union and responsible government.[169] (In fact he opposed both.) Harris and Leys continued to fulminate. To them Oldham had "sold out." As Harris put it succinctly: "It was an astute move of the Colonial Office to win Edinburgh

House over some time ago by giving the kind of sweets
to Oldham that he so much likes."[170]

That Oldham moved part of the way toward the settler point of view and away from the radicals, "from
paramountcy to partnership" as George Bennett once
put it, is true.[171] Moreover Oldham was indulging in
what he must have known was wishful thinking when
he said that in a long enough view the interests of
white and black were identical. He attacked that very
argument in 1931 in *White and Black in Africa*, a
book he wrote in answer to the pernicious argument of
Smuts.[172] Still, accurate though it is, Bennett's phrase
seems incomplete. As he would surely have seen if he
had lived to complete the biography he had planned
of Oldham, to see the man primarily in the context of
Kenya or even of Africa is insufficient. For Oldham's
ultimate concern was not really Africa. It was rather
the vitality and continued momentum of the ecumenical missionary movement. For him Africa was a testing ground where the great universal issues that challenged modern Christianity—race, human toleration,
materialism—had to be fought out. Oldham belonged
to none of the contending parties. That is what set him
apart. He remained his own man.

As J. H. Harris correctly perceived Oldham was
strongly attracted by the "sweets" the British imperial
establishment held out to him. To get them he needed
to adopt positions at least generally acceptable to men
in power. The "sweets" were the advisory committee on education and government support for the
International Institute for African Languages and
Cultures and for African research. These have been
described here as great and far-reaching institutional
achievements. Although Oldham did not (as Harris
feared he would) come down in the end on the settlers'
side,[173] yet this man who "went inside" had to surrender some of his freedom of maneuver. Such men always do.

Norman Leys

The Leys-Oldham Correspondence

The Leys-Oldham Correspondence

Letter of Dr. Norman Leys
Medical Officer, Nyasaland
to the Secretary of State
for the Colonies
Downing Street
7 February 1918

2, Clarence Drive
Hyndland, Glasgow

Sir,

I have the honour to request your acceptance of a statement descriptive of the existing situation in the Crown Colonies of East Africa. I write in the belief that civil disturbances are to be expected, disturbances that will eventually prove to be widespread and will in any case be destructive to the life and property of Europeans. I presume that you will already have received warnings from the proper authorities. My apology for making a statement of my own is a residence of sixteen years in British East Africa, Nyasaland and Portuguese East Africa, during which my position, while it has given me no claim to write with the authority due to your ordinary advisers, has permitted me to keep my ear close to the ground, and to study the facts and opinions of native life. These facts and opinions I shall attempt to describe and interpret. The mere discovery of unrest and of the danger of its expression in sedition reveals nothing that can serve for guidance. The unrest can be removed only by a policy rightly informed of its causes. Its various manifestations arise out of common origins, out of common currents of thought and ideas within a wide area that includes much diversity, and out of common industrial and economic conditions.

Analysis reveals the simplest factor of unrest, although not probably the most important in the end, to be economic. Superficially regarded the unrest appears to be due to economic grievances which, however greatly due to misconceptions, act with the force of reality. In Eastern Africa industrial and economic conditions are indeed the most uniform of all the conditions causing social change. They are also everywhere the most consciously felt of these conditions. The grievances arising out of them are easier of definition and easier of removal than the others. Their prompt treatment would at least postpone for some years seditious attempts.

These economic grievances arise out of the conditions of land tenure and of labour for Europeans. No detailed description of the varying conditions under which land is held and cultivated is necessary. It is sufficient to mention the fact that nowhere except in the ten mile strip on the coast—and there almost all the land has passed out of native ownership—has any native individual, family or tribe legal title to any land, and the equally important fact that besides thousands of natives who are entirely dependent for food on land held under Europeans, land for which they often have to pay rent either in money or in unpaid labour, there is a much larger number of natives who have merely just enough ground on which to grow their necessary food, to whom it is quite impossible to grow crops for sale, wherewith to pay the tax money and to buy trade goods. It is an immediate necessity that Governments in Eastern Africa should ensure for every family rent free land as secure in law as the land that the Crown has granted to Europeans. This rent free land must furthermore be situated in the area of the tribe to which the family belongs, and it must be adequate to the cultivation of crops for sale. These conditions are each strictly necessary if the general suspicion natives have that they are being squeezed out of the free occupation of land in their own country is to be dispelled. And if it is the case, as is to be feared, that the one difficulty in the way of such a policy is the existence of large tracts of land, mainly unimproved, granted by the Crown to Europeans, it is most necessary that no further land should be sold or leased to Europeans until the natives of the country are provided for. Unrest is probably nowhere else so great in Eastern Africa as it is among those who pay Europeans every year in rent several times larger than the purchase price paid to the Government by the Europeans for the land so used, land in many cases which natives regard as the property neither of Government nor of individual Europeans but as their own.[1]

A still more potent cause of unrest can only be removed by making labour entirely and universally free. There is no slavery under our flag. But labour is performed under conditions which produce and even exaggerate some of the evils of slavery. These evils are certain to arise, unless actively prevented, whenever a race without civilization and without political rights comes into economic relation with members of the race that controls it. I say economic relation because the active cause is hope of profit. It is most important to recognize that we are dealing with men as moved by impersonal economic forces and not by either philanthropy or by cruelty. The motive of the West African slave trade was not race hatred but profit. The same motive operates now in Eastern Africa. Three generations ago it was believed that by preventing the ownership of the person slavery would be abolished. Servile conditions of a new type have arisen, in consequence of new and unforeseen factors. These new factors are the ownership of immense areas of land by Europeans in tropical Africa, the adoption by Government of the duty of helping European owners to develop their land, and the system of direct taxation. All these are new in our generation. The tax operates by compelling the earning of money. Money can be earned by the sale of commodities or by labour for others. Lack of sufficient land, absence of markets and ignorance of what to grow are causes generally operating to prevent production for sale. In Nyasaland, however, the system of differential taxation whereby the native who stays at home pays double the tax paid by the employee ensures most effectively the sale by natives of labour rather than of commodities and stimulates the flow of labour to plantations.[2] In British East Africa the tax is uniform, so that other means have been necessary to supply the enormous demand for labour that has so rapidly arisen in the last fifteen years. There the size and situation of the land-grants themselves have been a powerful cause of migration of labour. In the Kavirondo plain and in the Kenia group of tribes the population is so thick that there is no room to do more than grow food, and the areas of natural overflow for the native population are in European occupation. In the Kikuyu Country in fact, where individual tenure of land is the tribal custom, land granted in freeholds to Europeans by the Crown is the ancestral home of thousands of natives.[3]

Some six years ago, however, taxation, land restriction and the normal growth of the demand for trade goods among natives proved insufficient to supply the rapidly growing demand for labour. In a really free country wages would have risen, thus restricting industry to the more profitable channels. Wages did rise slightly from about 6 or 7 to 7 or 8 shillings a month, but little if any effect on supply resulted. The settlers demanded that the influence of the Government with the natives should be used to induce them to leave their homes to work for Europeans. The demand was acceded to. Magistrates were instructed to "encourage" labour migration. "Moral suasion" was to be used. These instructions were variously carried out. Some magistrates ignored them and were vigorously attacked in consequence by the settlers and their representatives on the legislative council. Others took the straightforward course of sending police or tax collectors to get men. Such means were officially disapproved. But I doubt whether labour, if it must be got, can be got with less friction and hardship by any other means. Most magistrates tried honestly to carry out their instructions and get the labour somehow without compulsion. Their usual procedure was to summon the chiefs and tell them to get the labour. That course seriously affected friendly relations between magistrates and chiefs and still further undermined the position of the chiefs themselves in the opinion of their own people. That method was, however, in general effective in producing the labour.

It is of the greatest importance to realise the authority carried by a magistrate's advice in most districts. Chiefs are summoned, roads and bridges kept up, food brought for sale, and a hundred other things are done or got, not by legal process but by administrative order. Government in these countries depends for its very existence on obedience to advice, directions, orders—call it what you will—of particular application, and not of the general application of law. Breaches of the law bring definite measurable penalties. Disobedience to Government orders is essentially sedition. Thus when magistrates tell chiefs they are to advise their men to work for Europeans, the "advice" reaches the individual as something he dare not resist though he may try to avoid it. To call the system forced labour, to say that compulsion is used, is no abuse of language. Whatever may be the intention of those who sign directions to magistrates, compulsion is the form in which they reach the people concerned. The law indeed provides a safeguard. But, apart from the fact that natives, in British East Africa, though not in Nyasaland, are too ignorant to know how to appeal to it, the law only enables the individual to refuse any particular offer of employment. It cannot prevent a chief from worrying him because he prefers not to go to work for Euro-

peans at all. Further, it is a gross breach of etiquette in the minds of
natives in British East Africa, except the minority of the mission
educated—and to natives manners, morals and law are in general
indistinguishable—to take a European to court. A native never expects to get a verdict against a European. To prosecute a European
is an unseemly way of trying to get revenge for some real or fancied
wrong. To rob him, or even to murder him, is to natives not only a
more natural, but a less offensive and less disgraceful way of getting
even with him than a public accusation.

Such is the contrast, accordingly, between the picture given by the
text of the law and the terms of administrative directions, and the
picture given by the facts of native life and opinion. It is, of course,
only the extreme docility of the African that allows the system to
work at all. The harm to Government is the fact that natives consider Government and not the settlers responsible for their having to
leave home to work, and for the specific injuries incidental to existing conditions of labour; for the food they get, inevitably inferior to
what is available in the villages; for the diseases so prevalent in many
plantations; for the punishments they receive from employers. The
Government from time to time appoints an inspector to see that
labourers receive their contract rates of pay. No attempt is made to
fix or enforce a standard of hygienic and other conditions of life
among employees. It is very doubtful if an attempt to do so would
have results of any value. Improvement of these conditions can only
be produced by other means which I shall refer to later. I here
merely mention the important fact that the physical condition of
unskilled labourers when they return home is markedly inferior to
their condition on leaving home. One can always tell in which direction men are going when one meets a gang resting on the road from
the appearance of the men.

The economic results of forced labour are important. Most of it is
extremely bad in quality. The complaints by the settlers of deliberate idling are perfectly true. Many go to work with the intention of
doing as little as possible, and how little that is no one without experience can imagine. Hence frequent fines and floggings and general
bad feelings, felt by no means continuously by natives but always
ready to be excited, an abundant fuel for seditious notions.

I have never met anyone in British East Africa familiar with native opinion there who knew of any tribe that would not prefer to see all Europeans leave the country. Of that fact the labour system provides the principal explanation. By itself it would not explain sedition. But it prepares for it in the general mind.

Compulsion affects the price of labour as well as its quality. Free labour in the conditions I have described is difficult to define. But if one calls labour free, when it seeks work without pressure from magistrates or chiefs then most of it is free. The wages of all are kept at a low level by the compulsion of some. Voluntary labour seeks work to get money for use. Forced labour has little or no use for the money it earns. Hence, in the Kenia province superabundance of cash more than doubled in a few years the price of sheep which are the real currency in that province. Scarcity, due to the withdrawal of labour from cultivation in the villages, also caused a rise in the price of all food.

A third result of compulsion is the practice of desertion, so bitterly complained of by settlers. Many natives in obedience to the orders of chiefs engage to work for Europeans with the deliberate intention of deserting. Natives commonly invent special means for entry on labour sheets so that they may not be traced when they reach home. Desertion is in British East Africa a heavily punished criminal offence.

I have drawn no complete picture. If I have emphasized the worst features it is because they exist and because I believe they will cause insurrection. On the top of these pre-war conditions came the immense demand for porters for the military forces.[4] These porters were compelled to serve, explicitly so. In our opinion the occasion abundantly justified compulsion. In native opinion with few exceptions the war is merely the result of rivalry between two conquering races. Tens of thousands of porters have died of disease and privation. The war has destroyed for ever our claim to be the protector from wars of natives with one another. Even in Nyasaland, where five years ago most tribes would have by no means wished us to leave the country, the feeling is now in many parts very different.

I am convinced that if serious trouble is to be avoided in the next few years it is necessary at once to make labour free in fact and everywhere; to forbid and strictly to enforce the prohibition of every kind of influence by magistrates and other government agents over the free choice of natives. Natives must not only be told but be convinced that whether they do or do not leave home to go to work for Europeans is no concern whatever of Government. Furthermore, public departments must themselves treat labourers as entirely free. They must raise wages when labour is scarce and lower them when it is plentiful. In a really free market price will affect supply as it does everywhere else. The first result of the withdrawal of the influence of Government over labour supply will be to make labour scarce and dear. The next result, developing later and more slowly, will be to increase the output of the average labourer. In a very few years, I believe, increased output will more than compensate for increased wages. Whether, ultimately, free labour will prove actually more abundant than forced labour will depend entirely on the attractions offered by the employers on the one hand, and on the other upon the opportunities provided to natives for earning money at home.

I have described the most obvious, the simplest, the least mistakeable causes of unrest. The remedies I have so far defined are purely negative. Alone they will do nothing to increase the production of wealth. And a maximum wealth production is not only highly desirable in our own interests. It is an unqualified necessity to the prosperity of the African race. The race will only become productive to the fullest degree when stimulated by an active Government Policy to industry in the village homes of the people. Such a policy is the natural and necessary complement to the policy of free land and free labour. And it would stimulate rather than hinder production in the estates of Europeans.

II. A prosperous peasantry is a necessity in Eastern Africa for other and greater than economic reasons. The unique condition of native society in these parts in our time makes the preservation and development of village life necessary as nowhere else. That society has undergone, in one generation, a revolution of unprecedented rapidity. Not merely have the extremes of barbarism and civilization met. They have met and mingled so hastily and so violently as to cause widespread destruction of the fabric of native life. Never before has a primitive society been urged at such a pace to change its whole scheme of life.[5] Broadly speaking, the old order of native society no longer performs its functions. It may seem the case that in a

primitive society no government should concern itself with social
and ethical changes. On the contrary it is only in the presence of
stable institutions of a civilized people that the state can afford to
ignore them. When barbarians are turned by the hundred thousand
into a vagrant proletariat, when not only the deliberate influence of
Europeans, in religion, in government, and in industry, but even
every meeting point between men of different tribes and traditions
destroys superstitions that gave security to property, when the new
conditions of life make thousands every year forget their homes and
families forever, the cement that binds individuals in a common
ethic and belief, the cement that makes government of any kind possible, is being dissolved. There are indeed sheltered corners where
the disintegration has hardly begun. In other parts the old worship,
the old sanctions and reverences are quite gone. The fragility of the
old system can hardly be exaggerated. Isolated beliefs and prejudices generally persist but the restraints upon individual appetites
and lusts snap at the first strain. Conduct in an African tribe depends on an artificial code bound up with an imaginative explanation of both the outer and the inner world. The first few breaths
from the world of European ways and thought blow both code and
the explanation to fragments. Society becomes atomic, a mere
aggregation of individuals enslaved by instincts and appetites, and
the social virtues which alone make men good subjects of the state
disappear. That is why crimes and vagrancy are rapidly increasing
in British East Africa, why perjury is becoming almost the rule with
native witnesses, why chiefs complain they are no longer respected.
The whole mechanism of Government is hindered by this social and
ethical decay. Labour needs more and more expensive European
supervision. Relations between individual Europeans and natives
become harder to keep frank and friendly.

    In no other part of the world is society in a similar situation. In
the East as in Europe the subject is an individual embedded in an
integrated society. It needs an effort of the imagination to realise a
people without even the embryonic forms of institutions so familiar
to us that we never think of the life they convey to us. The church,
the school, the town, the trade or friendly society, the newspaper,
the sports club, the public house, form with us a living framework in
which the individual subject of the state grows through maturity to

decline. They are the only channels of human life, and often its very
sources. Through them the national will reaches the individual. The
state up to recent times has been little more than their co-ordinator
and protector. They seem, to the individual, to give far more than
they demand, while the nation claims, in means and in life, much
more than it gives. They rather than national energies and activities
are civilization, and in their health liberty consists. With us so tough
is the tissue of society that change whether religious or political or
industrial only reaches the individual through adaptations of these
the vital organs of society. In Eastern Africa such a fabric does not
exist. Changes have been so rapid and so violent as to give no time
for protective adaptations. The individual stands naked. His child-
ish guesswork of a working theory of life can no longer guide him.
He is the slave of the appetites, lusts and instincts which even the
most barbarous society when intact controls, and at the mercy of
economic forces as incomprehensible to him as they are irresistible.

   Governments in Eastern Africa recognise the danger of social disintegration. They have hitherto attempted to meet it by attempts to
preserve the tribal system. They give chiefs power that old tribal
custom never gave them, they forbid individual families to live in
villages of less than a certain size, they forbid religious propaganda
unless invited by the chiefs, whose interest it is to prevent it. It is to
be feared that conservatism of that type is both useless and harmful.
Chiefs are already in many tribes an anachronism. The very support
Government gives them, and still more the duties Government lays
on them, add to their unpopularity. The old order is already in many
tribes moribund, and is everywhere doomed. It deserves a euthanasia. That only a slowing of the rate of economic change can achieve.
The system itself, the world of old fears, old obediences, old loyalties cannot be carried over into the future. Any policy built on its
preservation whether from its supposed suitability to native character or from its necessity to European Government is bound to fail.
Apart altogether from the presumption, a very large one, that a
primitive tribalism can so develop as to serve human needs in the
future, it is futile with one hand to give the system artificial support
and with the other to stimulate economic and industrial changes
that destroy it.

   The analogy that inevitably arises in the minds of those of our own generation is with the economic revolution in England a hundred years ago. Its disasters and miseries were due, not to any weakness of the national spirit nor to breakdown of the national government but to the partial collapse of the less obtrusive but vital institutions of society before the stress of rapid economic changes. If we imagine the effect of that industrial revolution aggravated by the removal, under pressure, of most of the factory operatives by journeys of days or weeks from homes and families, by the breakdown of municipal government, by the abandonment of the old worship, and the dissolution of old sanctions for respect to persons and property, and if we suppose both factories and government in the hands of an alien race, we have no unfair analogy to what is happening in Africa.

I do not suggest that Governments should attempt the creation of a new social fabric in Africa. In that sense no race can possibly govern another. The new fabric will most certainly come into being. No human creatures ever rest in anarchy. Already indeed new bonds between individuals are in formation, new restraints are winning recognition, new institutions the corporate expressions of the new order are coming into life. These and their proper relations with Governments I shall describe later. In the economic sphere here discussed production of wealth within the circle of village life alone will permit the new order to grow up in place of the old. All that is possible should be done to preserve the tenuous ties between the social system that is passing away and the one that is struggling to life. The true conservative policy is to cherish the new growth while the old is dying. Economically, opportunity must be given to the individual to produce what our world demands of him without wholly cutting himself off from old habits and traditions. It is only in the villages that family life can be preserved, and tribal life can survive until replaced by institutions suitable to new conditions. Thus alone can the state be given a stable social foundation.

The trouble with village life now is sheer poverty. Nothing occurs in the villages but the growing of food. The householder has to work away from home to earn even enough to pay his tax not to speak of the purchase of the material needs of the first stage of civilized life. When at work on plantations or railway he is worse fed and housed than at home. Unions for a month or a day take the place of family life. The tone of plantation life, especially in East Africa, is lower by

far than in villages. Most of the work is as monotonous as a tread-
mill. A large proportion of the workers work as slowly and as care-
lessly as they dare. Not by such means are the habits of industry
taught, and hand and eye trained for wealth production. Many
natives indeed have both gained for themselves and enriched the
community by work for Europeans. But where many have gained far
more have lost. Not that it would be wise to discourage wage earning, except where enquiry shows special prevalence of disease. Its
main defects and abuses can be cured by making labour everywhere
entirely free, and by giving opportunity for livelihood in the villages.
Family life with better food and housing would then be offered to
natives by employers, and the output of labour for Europeans would
be multiplied severalfold, when willingly undertaken as the alternative, not to stagnation and poverty at home but to the life of a
prosperous peasantry. What would be thought at home of a policy
which compelled, by differential taxation and administrative pressure, the English or Irish peasantry to leave their villages for labour
in mine and factory?

  There need be no fear as to the effect, on either revenue or production, of a policy of economic development in the villages. The
principal reason of its absence in British East Africa and its small
result in Nyasaland is that native industry has been deliberately de-
flected from the villages. For that reason the mere cessation of efforts to make natives leave their homes for work will not suffice.
Definite encouragement of production in the villages is necessary, if
only because it is an imperial interest that total production should
not diminish. The fact must further be faced that such a policy will
arouse opposition. European employers in Africa still believe that it
is the duty of Government to get them labourers and to keep their
wages down. And it is probably the case that the whole population
of these parts that can be spared from food growing is insufficient
for the full development of the millions of acres already granted to
Europeans by the Crown. Actively to discourage natives to leave
home to work would be to break faith with these estate owners and
concessionaires. But their opposition to the positive policy which I
describe as both a necessary justice to natives and as a means by
which maximum wealth production and trade activity can be
reached, must frankly be recognised as interested and fallacious.

An even greater difficulty will lie in the attitude of some of those who have been carrying on the existing policy. It is only natural that even opposition should be met with. Yet unless the policy here advocated is genuinely accepted by the local authorities and encouraged by them, it will have no real success. In many parts the new idea that money can be earned by work in the villages will need implantation. And I need not labour the point that bad methods may ruin the most hopeful of schemes. It would be easy, for instance, by giving a price for cotton lower than European planters can get, or by failing to provide markets and transport, to prove that cotton production is only practicable on large estates. But if a small proportion of the money and energy that have been spent by Government on European settlement, on surveys, police protection, imported stock, experimental farms, entomological experts, veterinary inspectors, were to be wisely spent on the encouragement of production by a native peasantry, the results would be astonishing.

III. Islam and Christianity are the two rival heirs of tribalism. Both offer a complete way of life. Both give precisely what tribal life in decay can no longer give, a bond transcending the tie of blood relationship, a bond, moreover, that, once formed, holds fast and constantly grows closer. Both these systems cover a far larger part of life than the part covered by the administrative system. Their influence is, judged by any measure, far deeper than Government influence. The attitude of Government to them is of far greater importance than their attitude to Government.

Mahomedanism in Eastern Africa is often described as being nominal. A better word for it is undeveloped. It owes its undeveloped character to the prohibition of translations of the Koran, to the absence of other religious writings, and to the absence of authorised teachers. There is in fact, in most places, no deliberate propaganda at all. It spreads by the mere attractiveness of a simple creed and ceremonial. Nothing less simple could spread in the automatic way it does spread. In the simplification both ethic and legal system are lost, because neither seem to be demanded by the needs of the moment. It is not the tribal restraints that the detribalised native misses but the loss of tribal solidarity: not the claim his tribe made on him but the support his tribe gave him. It is just that solidarity which the

embryonic Mahomedanism of Africa offers. Thousands of even
those whose homes are still in their native villages will when asked
their tribe call themselves Mahomedans. Further enquiry elicits that
they know nothing of Islamic law, and ethic. They know merely
some ten words of creed with some half dozen ceremonial practices.
Some call the system a freemasonry, but it is really much more. It
gives without requiring fee or exertion or restraint nothing less than
a fatherland. The ceremonies and the formula of the religion are the
symbols of a common patriotism. The entire absence within its pale
both of actual Europeans and of Western ideas makes the religion
in Africa essentially racial. Its racial character is emphasized by the
treatment the religion receives from our Government and their
agents. Most Government servants believe that Mahomedanism is a
"very good religion for Africans." I have heard two Governors say so
when addressing Africans. The reason of this attitude is perfectly
plain. Mahomedans have no appetites for Western ways of thought
and habits of life. They never want to learn to read English. The
religion teaches, not the brotherhood of man but the brotherhood
of Mahomedans, at first sight a much less inconvenient doctrine
to administrators to whom racial superiority is a fundamental axiom
of Government. If Government servants were free to follow the policy they think the wisest most of them would give active encouragement to Islam. As It Is, Government in British East Africa spends
public money in teaching it. The police and the King's African
Rifles are almost wholly recruited from among Mahomedans, who
form in no Protectorate a majority of the population. In Zomba,
during the war, Christian worship was forbidden and Mahomedan
worship was encouraged among the natives in the military camp. In
Nyasaland the compulsory levy for carriers was not enforced on
many Mahomedan villages, while it often took every available man
from Christian and pagan villages. The great majority of Government officers, civil and military, choose Mahomedans as personal
servants, while most of the domestics of non-official Europeans are
Christian or pagan. The general impression thus prevails all over
British East Africa that the authorities wish natives to become
Mahomedans. (The Germans, on the contrary, avowedly gave the
preference in Government appointments in the interior, though not
on the coast, to Christians.)[6]

In attempting a judgment on the situation I have described it must never be forgotten that Mahomedanism in the interior of Eastern Africa is embryonic. Whatever its future may prove to be it will not have the same character as at present. It will either develop or decline. Introduced as the religion of Arab slave raiders and of the Africans who took their part, Arab influence has since died away with the cessation of the traffic to the coast. But with the disappearance of educated men and of schools the time of rapid spread began. Enough of its early association with a conquering caste, mainly African in race, survives to give the religion something of the prestige of an aristocracy. But the movement as a whole consists of an untaught multitude, conscious only of unity and awaiting some inevitable development. Its almost involuntary spread is a sign of so perfect a satisfaction of temporary needs, that when these needs change—and society in Africa is certainly not static—the type of Mahomedanism will also change. A short ritual and a cryptic creed will not remain its sole expressions.

Not that Mahomedanism is ever or can ever be merely a natural response to human demands. It is the most rigid of all religions. Historically its seeds have always developed true to type. The only unusual thing about it in Eastern Africa is the long delay in full development due to political severance from the Mahomedan world. African Mahomedans know that world exists. In hundreds of mosques they pray weekly for the Sultans of Turkey and Zanzibar. It is certain that in future contact will be re-established with Islam as a world religion. The development of Mahomedan thought and practice is certain to follow historic lines. A new Mahomedan political philosophy is an impossible growth on African soil. In one important direction indeed growth is certain to be stunted. No development of the legal system of Islam is possible. Not only in criminal but also in civil law, it is from Rome and Westminster rather than from Mecca that the African will learn a rule of contractual relationship. Educated Moslems in the interior complain that Africans will not follow the Moslem rule in marriage, divorce, inheritance and so forth. Nothing but confusion, of course, would follow the competition of Moslem law with our system. Unfortunately such a prospect removes the main cultural value of the religion to barbarous people. Its sole historic justification is that it was the law-

giver to lawless tribes and discordant sects. And if the introduction
of the Moslem theory of social rights is impossible, the code of private rights and duties is deprived of validity. The two are indistinguishable in Islam, just as church and state are. (The position of
the religion in India offers no analogy. There we found it established
long since, with both legal and private codes in actual operation,
and persisting, as is natural, in spite of political decay.) It is safe
also to predict that African Islam, divorced from its own scheme of
social and private rights and duties, will develop in a direction that
may be called nationalistic. Historically always more of a political
and social scheme than a religion, it has never developed except as
a political system. And in Africa already this character is plain.
Mahomedans feel themselves one people, a people that of necessity
excludes Europeans. The Moslem world is self-sufficient. It has
never from Mahomed's day to our own shown any wish to come to
terms with the Western plan of life, to share in any but its material
accidentals. I have never once met an intelligent Mahomedan who
did not know that he was right and I wrong. I have never got any
distance into the mind of any Mahomedan—except some Arabs who
are thoroughgoing agnostics—without discovering that he actually
did consider all Europeans his inferiors, usurpers for a time of empire, and destined either to conversion or to conquest here and to
damnation hereafter. The Mahomedan does not believe the religion a
good one for Africans. He believes it to be the only truth for all, and
that it is one of his first duties to ensure its supremacy in every walk of
life.

   The wisdom of the policy of encouraging Islam is thus to be
judged according to whether it is to develop or not. If its spread in
Africa proves to be only a temporary fashion due to its peculiar
affinity with a transient phase of African life, official encouragement will prove to have been a comparatively harmless mistake. If
on the contrary the religion is going to live and grow, it is idle to
expect from it the submissive virtues of a consciously inferior caste.
In that case its encouragement will prove a policy only one degree
more disastrous than its persecution would have proved. [7]

IV. In some tribes Islam, in others Christianity, has already won the
inheritance of tribalism. In a few it is competed for by both reli-

gions. Into the life of still fewer tribes neither religion has as yet
deeply penetrated. Over all, the careful observer can reach no other
conclusion than that all the tribes will adopt one or other religion. In
the simplified intellectual world of African Islam there are no differences of opinion to produce the sects found in the older Mahomedan East. It is far otherwise with Christianity. The whole variety
of religious type found in Western Europe is represented in Eastern
Africa by propagandist missions. For the purpose of the present
enquiry, however, which investigates the results rather than the
various programmes of the missions, no serious error follows from
disregarding distinctions between Christian sects.

As taught by every sect Christianity is as complete a system of
life as Mahomedanism. It professes to tell people what to believe
and what to do in every relationship of life. Further, all interpreta-
tions of the religion teach that the Christian scheme is true and right
for all, European and African alike, and that those who reject it do
so either from ignorance or sin. And all alike teach that Christians,
whatever their colour, race or social condition are the children of
one father and equal in his regard. I do not assert that that doctrine
is deliberately given special prominence. I only state that it is taught
wherever Christian propaganda exists. And it is everywhere the most
attractive of the Christian doctrines to natives.

Converts are always more enthusiastic than those who are born in
a faith, and are especially apt to draw inferences applicable to common life from what they have recently come to believe. One unusual
feature of Christian propaganda in Eastern Africa also gave the doctrine of brotherhood special prominence and reality. In Uganda and
Nyasaland missions antedated Governments. In their beginnings they
largely concerned themselves with social emancipation. Missions
rather than governments are looked upon by natives as their liberators from slavery and the slave trade. In this generation, however, it
is rather the converts than their teachers who draw inferences applicable to society from the scheme of the ideal Christian society.
Missionaries discourage these inferences. But the doctrine of Christian brotherhood is too suitable to the needs and instincts of natives,
and too attractive to their imaginations, to be without effect on various aspects of ordinary life.

It is precisely this particular consequence of Christian teaching

that is the cause of the principal trouble that governments, employers and individual Europeans have with Christian natives. It is precisely these consequences from and applications of Christian teaching by natives which administrators and employers consider harmful
to material prosperity and dangerous to the social order. The generally accepted basis of that prosperity and of that order is that the
native as a worker should serve the European as his master, and
that the instructions of all European officers should be carried out
without question. It must be remembered that actual administration
is largely carried out by obiter dicta, that these dicta have a weight
often superior to the law, and that without instant obedience to
them government of the type that exists to-day would hardly be possible. Missionaries certainly teach obedience. But they also teach
doctrines that in the minds of the more intelligent of the younger
men incite enquiry. And it is natural that these men should not always obey first and enquire afterwards. When, furthermore, Christian natives pursue their enquiries and speculations in the belief that
the same standard of conduct that they are taught to follow is also
the duty of Europeans; and when they know that many Europeans
neglect or repudiate the Christian religion and its ethical code, the
natural results are such that there is no wonder that missions are
unpopular with Government officers and employers of labour.

A still more important charge is made against missions. It is alleged that some of them have so imperfect a control over their
agents in the villages that these village teachers sometimes openly
criticize Government measures and Government agents. The Chilembwe rising in the Shire highlands and the Ethiopian movement in
South Africa are pointed to as proof that Christian propaganda
without special precautions is dangerous to the very existence of
Europeans in the country.[8] I admit the danger is real. I go further
and admit that in some parts of the country Christianised natives are
even now less satisfactory subjects of the Governments that now
exist than their pagan neighbours. European opinion in Africa considers that missions should modify their teaching. It is held that they
should not permit native agents to work in the villages without European supervision; that they should not circulate the scriptures except
where an oral interpretation is also provided; that certain doctrines
unsuitable to a race socially and politically subordinate should not

be taught generally; that emphasis should always be laid on the virtues of obedience, humility, respect for civil authority and industry;
and, above all, that the education provided should be technical
rather than literary.[9] Such an attitude is perfectly comprehensible,
and it would be grossly unfair to consider it a quite unjustified criticism.

Unfortunately all these recommendations are regarded by missions and the churches responsible for them as impossible of acceptance. In all communions except the Roman the putting of the scriptures in the hands of the people is considered a primary duty; education in every Christian Church must of a necessity mainly be directed
to produce such a mental development as will make Christian teaching intelligible; and every mission regards the training not merely of
native agents to work independently of European supervision, but of
the whole body of converts to become an African Church, as one of
its most urgent tasks. The popularity of Roman missions with those
in authority is explained by the fact that the Roman Church teaches
that the faith must be taken on authority, and does not foster the
spirit of enquiry. By contrast, in all the other missions baptism is
refused to those who cannot read, unless they are too old to learn. In
these missions, in fact, books play a larger part than men in the
spread of the religion.

The real crux is the teaching of the doctrine that "there is no difference, Jew nor Gentile, slave nor free." That doctrine is the real
root of the trouble. The fact to face is that it is of the essence of the
religion. It would be perfectly possible indeed to make an amended
version of Christianity, suitable in the opinion of administrators of
Government, to the condition of industry and society in Africa to-
day. It is in an Islam thus purged as they hope, vainly hope I believe,
of certain of the features Islam shows in other countries and in previous times, that so many officers of Government trust. A modified
version could be made perfectly well. But it would have two disad-
vantages. It would not be Christianity, and no one would care
enough about it to teach it.

There is, in fact, nothing to cause surprise in the situation of the
moment in Africa. It is a constantly recurring situation. The founder
of the religion was delivered to death by an officer of an empire as
tolerant as our own, on the allegation that his teaching could be

interpreted in a way subversive of the civil order, an allegation he persisted in refusing to repudiate. And its second founder, although proud of his Roman citizenship and for long confident that church and state might be in close and friendly relation, was himself executed for sedition after appeal to the highest court of the empire. Nor are other examples lacking to prove that in the very heart of the religion there has often proved to be a principle that has brought it into conflict with Governments, and these by no means all bad Governments. It is curious that the book with the largest circulation among natives after Bible and hymn book was written by a man who spent some years in an English jail.[10] A related fact worthy of note is that the native converts among whom the difficulties I have mentioned most often arise are those of the missions which lay the greatest emphasis on the individual and inward nature of Christianity. If their teaching encourages sedition it is in spite of their discouraging natives to concern themselves with politics.

Quite beyond the influence of any special doctrine of brotherhood, a doctrine in some form shared by every world creed, the effect in an animistic society of a scheme that has itself been moulded by its share in the direction and formation of civilization, is to liberate mental forces to activity in every direction. Even such a simple matter as learning to read is an immense stimulus to the mind. Much more does a whole philosophy of life, however imperfectly understood, act as a ferment, producing change out of proportion to its mass.

An outline is sharper than a fully drawn picture. In a picture of this kind no details are irrelevant, and the necessary omission of many of them gives the appearance of exaggeration to statements true in themselves. It is nevertheless broadly true that both in their aims and in their effects, the civil authority and Christian missions, although both are truly national expressions of the intention of our country, are in an important degree out of harmony. I am in the position of agreeing with those in authority who believe that much of the teaching of the Christian religion that goes on to-day in Eastern Africa actually operates upon people in their existing economic and social condition in such a way as to imperil the stability of order and government. I differ in attributing the situation, not to imperfect comprehension of the political facts of the case by missionaries, nor to defects in their methods, but to the operation of two conceptions of society, capable no doubt of reconciliation by some practical compromise for the time, but certain from their own nature to create fresh opposition and conflict. There is no case for blaming the mere advocates of the contrasting schemes of life. It is only their directors who can hope, by a full interpretation of the national will which they all alike serve, to reach unity of expression through unity of aim.

Misconception in this matter is largely due to the position of the Christian Church in our own country. With us the Christian Church is so old, and has so deeply affected law and custom, as to seem to have reached the limit of her influence on life, to have abandoned those struggles from which the defeats of so many centuries have taught her to abstain, and to rest content in a compromise that seems final. True, signs that the struggle may be renewed are never wanting. But Christian organizations themselves feel these very challenges to be unwelcome disturbances of a settled practice and position. And the facts that the Church is so much concerned with the fear of losing the position she has hitherto held, and that she so often looks back to some former generation as her golden age, show how often she forgets the hope of complete conquest that she had in her early youth. It is such an equilibrium, uneasy though it may be, between church and society, that makes possible the common view that the Church is, even with those who look on her as a mere picturesque survival, the natural guardian of an order of society threatened by revolution.

Such acquiescence is impossible to the church when she introduces herself into a society she has done nothing to shape. Unconfined by historic compromises, of her own nature rather than by the voice of her authorised teachers, she claims the supreme authority over life. The outward evidence of that claim is plainly to be seen in her discipline. In an African mission church, church discipline, public penance, excommunication, are practised and feared. Further, a mission church has many of the energies of youth that churches in Europe have lost. Missions offer education and civilization, and these bring a tremendous reinforcement to the church's influence. Mission schools are almost the only avenues of education: not only of the education that can multiply manyfold earnings and wealth, but also of the education that interprets the spectacle of the new ways of life so suddenly revealed to the native. Missionaries offer him what other Europeans do not, a share in that life itself as distinguished from a share in the labour of its production. When other Europeans seek natives it is to get something from them, their money in taxes or their labour: both, natives believe, for the personal advantage of those who receive them. Missionaries, although from natives their demands both in money and in labour are as great, do offer something in return.

Once again I would emphasize the means by which Christian teaching reaches the native. He first learns as a child at school. The first words he learns are the 'Our Father'. The next are rhymed translations of hymns, sung daily, easily memorised, many of them—too many—painting the glories of the world to come. These he learns, and more besides, in his own colloquial mother tongue, not as we learn them in an obsolete literary dialect. The Christian scheme thus comes to have, from many causes, a precision and a vividness, a nearness to life, scarcely possible to Christendom.

Islam is attractive to natives because it is, as it comes to them, distinctively African: to all, contra-European, to the aggrieved, anti-European. It offers, without fee or exertion, an assured place in a society that replaces dissolving tribalism: satisfaction, complete for the time, to a nascent but universally human sense of nationality. In contrast, the Christian scheme offers a place, at the price of effort, and in proportion to the measure of individual effort and capacity, in the world, present and to come, of which his fathers had never heard. It says a great deal for the African that the Christian scheme is far more attractive to him than its rival. It would be irresistible, if it were not for the price. Missions demand a large expenditure of money and effort and insist on a very difficult ethical standard. In most missions even the child may pay a trifle for education. As the child grows older the cost rises until, in the largest secondary schools, one year's education costs the ordinary earnings of a labourer for six months. In most the convert is expected to give a tenth of his earnings to the church, and in one at least those who fail to give liberally are expelled. And the ethical standard demanded—I can here make no attempt to describe or define it—is on the whole a more difficult one than the church in Europe ever enforced. These circumstances explain the fact that thousands who in a sense accept

the church's teaching remain outside her organization. Even so, if
a religious census were taken in Nyasaland to-day, I suppose that a
fifth of the people would describe themselves as Christian. A much
larger number would claim the name if it were not for the cost. It is
no exaggeration to say that whole tribes are Christian in the sense
that they accept the truth of the teaching and consider the standard
of conduct the right one. They reject the standard as applied to
themselves because they cannot bring themselves to give up what it
demands. This is to some extent true even of Mahomedans, though
less true of them than of pagans. If there is a place where Christian
propaganda has entirely failed it is Mombasa. In more than two
generations it has scarce won a convert, and the church's own people
of escaped slaves and their descendants are mentally and morally as
libertine as the freed slaves of whom the word was originally used.
But even there, in a solidly Mahomedan population, polygamy is
becoming obsolete. It is just beginning to have the flavour of a custom not quite reputable. And this is an effect, so far as I can judge,
not of economic but of ethical change.

Present indications, therefore, point to Eastern Africa becoming
in certain areas Christian, in others Mahomedan. It is not too much to
say, indeed, that the ordinary African unconsciously feeling rather
than realising that his own world is falling away from him, must of
necessity passively receive rather than actively take one or other of
the rival schemes of life the two religions offer him. It seems also
probable that in that part of the world the precision of both creeds,
the completeness with which they prescribe for every relation and
occasion in life, and on the other hand the plasticity of the human
material, and the looseness of structure of a tribalism in decay, will
give those religions a commanding position in life and society.

V. I have investigated the operation of economic and industrial
forces, and the prevailing currents of feeling and opinion which
issue in unrest. There remains to view the subject from its opposite
end, to discover the means, whether by the direction of these currents or otherwise, to right relations between governments and their
subjects.

The view is hindered by a presumption in the political thought of
our time which must be deliberately set aside. We are accustomed

to the control of industry by the state. All governments freely man-
ipulate economic forces. In Africa they are even more completely
under control than elsewhere. A whole tribe is transported to a new
home, or the labour of a hundred thousand men at a time is diverted, by the stroke of a Governor's pen. And no state, least of all
in Africa, is likely to lessen its control over the material means of
life. By contrast, modern governments profess to have abandoned
control over opinion and belief. "A free church in a free state" represents a principle commonly believed to be universally valid. I
suggest that it cannot be considered so, and that in tropical Africa
in particular its application is impracticable. I believe it has been
accepted in Europe only in consequence of the transfer from ecclesiastical to civil authority not only of many of the functions of society, such as education and the care of the insane and of the sick,
but of the transfer also to the state of the feeling of religious reverence formerly conceived of as due to the church alone. I suggest that
these changes in Europe are coincident with and mainly dependent
upon the changes which have identified states and governments with
nations. The separation of church from state does not with us, as
might appear, imply the withdrawal of civic and national aims and
activities from the influence of the individual and corporate conscience. The bond between state and subjects has become a religious
as it has become a national bond, so that the life of the modern
state now depends less on obedience than on active loyalty. The religious nature of that loyalty is shown by its dominance. Far more citizens in our time would die for their country than for their faith.
Separation of church and state is accordingly natural only to those
states in which active loyalty is felt by the general body of citizens
to be the supreme religious duty.

In Africa this natural and active loyalty does not exist. Loyalties
there indeed are, but no loyalty is given to the state because none is
felt for the state. Sedition in Africa is thus due, not merely to causes
in economic and religious life, but to the absence of resistance to
their force. At present the African cannot or dare not rebel. Western
education and the contact with world religions will enable him and
make him dare. The future will depend on whether before he ceases
to say "I dare not" he begins to say "I ought not." The heart of the
question has been reached.

Solutions applicable elsewhere are here inadmissible. Over the rest of the empire the question has been or is being settled, for our generation, by the extension of political liberty. In Africa the problem is for us unique. Rome like us governed races with creeds and social systems in decay. To her, as to us, the problem of their loyalty arose. She solved it partly by sharing such political rights as the age conceived with all her subjects who sought them. She shared these so fully as to make the children of barbarians feel themselves to be Romans; so that citizens of the third and even of the second generation from barbarism gave to the empire generals, statesmen and emperors. These ties of equal status and opportunity for the fulfilment of advantage and ambition were, however, regarded as insufficient. Every subject was in addition explicitly bound to the state by a religious tie. From all Rome demanded the worship of the state. She could conceive of no empire without the devotion of religious worship. It is ominous that the religion that refused all terms except her own with the Roman Empire, and that other creed which finally overthrew the empire, are the only militant creeds in Africa to-day. We need that warning that such problems never settle themselves. We ourselves have moved so far from the old ground of conflict that the compromise in which the old quarrel issued is no longer real to us. With us it is not the divine unction upon the head of our king but the identity of the state with national feeling that is the source of loyalty. But wherever that identity has not been reached we are faced, as even the war in Europe reveals, with the same problem of that older empire. How is loyalty to governments in Africa to arise? Can it be taught? Can it be designedly made to grow? We cannot ask Africans to worship King George, as the early Roman Emperors required worship of our ancestors. Nor can we with Constantine and his successors enforce conformity to a church from which the secular ruler derives reverence and authority.

Loyalty is a kind of affection. It is not given, in gratitude for past nor in hope of future benefits, nor is it withdrawn because of misfortune or disaster. It is felt by people whose government is their own, seldom or never by any others. People indeed may feel loyalty to a government not of their own making. In such cases the sense of ownership is derived from peculiar qualities in the Government, from its adaptation to and service of special institutions and feelings, rather than from general qualities of wisdom and disinterestedness. The loyal are those who feel their government, even if they think it a bad government, to be their own, whether made by them or for them; the disloyal those who feel they are governed by strangers, however wisely they may govern.

It is not that loyalties do not already exist in Eastern Africa. They are inspired, notoriously, by many individual Europeans. In addition, loyalty is evoked in perhaps its purest form by two widely differing relationships. There is a great deal of real loyalty in converts to their missions and there is an even greater devotion shown by the rank and file of the King's African Rifles to their regiment. I believe that the nature of these two particularist loyalties provides the key to the problem of general loyalty to Governments. Both regiment and mission offer leadership, and the leaders in both bridge the gulf of racial difference by sharing always their special knowledge and often their fortunes and their lives.

If that is so, the aim of governments in Eastern Africa must be one of acclimatization, of adaptation to feelings and beliefs widely different from those natural to a governing race or caste. Governments must do more than take directly upon themselves the duty of sharing the knowledge and the arts and the instruments of civilised life according to the measure of the capacity of their subjects. All that they must certainly undertake. But in addition the spirit of government must be African, not in the sense that Imperial problems have an African aspect but in the sense that there must be as instant and intimate a response to the states of mind of the governed as in the case of governments by the governed themselves. If governments cannot be by the people they must be with and in the people. We must leave it to them to set the problems, even if it is we who must decide them. An instance of my meaning is found in the prohibition of the export of Indian labour to Natal. In decreeing the prohibition I suppose Lord Hardinge acted in accordance with Indian sentiment rather than with Indian, not to speak of Imperial, interests.[11] The danger here is not so much one of conflict between Imperial and local interests as from the kind of minds that govern as wisely as they know, without being moved by what the governed think or feel.

Government by consent is an ambiguous phrase. It must of necessity be a temporary phrase turning either into government by co-operation or into government in the face of dissent. At the moment passive consent is in Africa turning into dissent, which, however fitful and purposeless, is the sign of an unguided and untaught life. Unrest, however inconvenient to us, is less the sign of a social disease than the disordered appetite of a social pregnancy.

No purely alien bureaucracy has ever inspired gratitude or loyalty. Yet without such a basis of loyalty government is in a condition of permanent estrangement from its subjects. Elsewhere, in the result, the bureaucracy is superseded. In Africa, so far as our vision goes, it must persist. It must find its own escape from the riddles of nationalism, an apparition that always takes a bureaucracy by surprise. It is certain that a common national feeling will pervade all the tribes from Kenia to the Zambesi during the next generation. Presuming that the solution of self-government is impossible, how are we to meet that African nationalism? To the objection that the prophecy is gratuitous, I would answer by asking what other result can be expected to follow the introduction of a uniform administrative system that pays no respect to tribal boundaries: a precocious economic development rearranging individual status everywhere in accordance with the ability to earn money: the rapid spread of two religions, the notorious unifiers of the past: all these acting on a people with a consciousness of race even while in undisturbed tribalism, now strengthened and defined by the unbridged gulf, political, social and economic, between black and white, and by the knowledge that in all the rest of the world national aspirations are either already satisfied or likely soon to be satisfied? To state these facts is to postulate rather than to predict nationalism. If we cannot satisfy it in the natural way, how can we meet it at all? Certainly not at any rate by relying on the existing title of governments in Africa, on bargains with other European powers: or on treaties with chiefs, treaties the terms of which the people know nothing of, and chiefs, many of them, whose authority is derived from their signature on the treaties.

In proof of the version of history I have given I would refer to one instance from Nyasaland and one from British East Africa. The Kikuyu and other tribes of the same ethnic group which form about a third of the population of the East African Protectorate never had any chiefs at all. There is no such institution among the Kikuyu. [12] The natives who, a generation ago, signed treaties on the tribe's behalf, were mostly not even members of the tribe. One of the most important of them is to this day prohibited under tribal law from owning land because of his foreign birth and descent—and that in a tribe in which practically every able-bodied man is a landowner by individual tenure. Not one of the Kikuyu chiefs has any authority except as a government agent.

I would also instance the case of the North Nyasa administrative district. The soil of the whole district is the freehold property of a financial corporation.[13] How the corporation came to own these thousands of square miles on which some sixty thousand natives live I cannot here narrate. The points I would emphasise are that the corporation pays an annual tax on the land of about £3000 a year to the Protectorate Government, a sum which it can only hope to recover in the future either directly from the natives in rent or indirectly by the profits of their labour: and also that all the enquiry I was able to make in the district failed to discover a single native aware of the facts of the legal ownership of the land. Not even the man who is the successor of the chief who made the original treaty knows that it involved the conveyance of a freehold title to the land occupied by his tribe.

A summary description of the history of our relations with the different tribes in Eastern Africa is impossible, and the instances I have given are not typical. No single instances in fact would be typical. The single common political category under which all the tribes in the East African Protectorate fall is that they are "protected." That status in law is one which gives the protecting power complete sovereignty in practice, while it withholds from the inhabitants every one of the rights of subjects. The natives are neither in law nor in fact British subjects. They are foreigners over whom we exercise administrative authority; whom we tax as we think proper; whose land we take when we think it can be spared for giving to our own countrymen. The treaties with native chiefs are not even cognisable in our courts of law. The law presumes that these treaties are in force as between equally sovereign states, that the subject of the protected power may find redress for wrong complained of by appeal, not to our courts but to those of his own government. It is needless to remark that these native governments have no shred of existence. Protectorate governments legislate and administer without pretence of regard to any such imaginary authorities, and, most reasonably, never give treaties a thought. The sole effect of these treaties in Africa to-day is to prevent the natives acquiring the status of British subjects which they would have obtained had these regions become British territory by conquest or cession.

The actual relations of natives to Governments are naturally very different from what they might be imagined to have as the subjects of protected powers. These relations may be stated in a sentence. To the average native, government is the recipient of taxes, the demander of labour, the arbiter in disputes between Europeans and natives, and the court of appeal for natives themselves. That is literally all. The old claim of governments to be the protectors from inter-tribal warfare has been swept away for ever by the miseries and destruction of the present war.

As a governing race we are apt to regard ourselves in the light of our honest intentions. We like to think ourselves as the liberators, forgetful that for every hundred freed under the flag by the cruisers in the Mozambique channel there were thousands who sailed the middle passage in chains under the same flag. Most of us have more of the blood of the slavers who built the prosperity of modern Bristol and Liverpool than of the Clapham philanthropists. We should not forget if only because the African has not forgotten. Not that the African knows anything of the history of the past as we know it. Hardly any African now alive has heard tell of Livingstone, except from missionaries, and certainly none have heard of Hawkins. But the racial memory lives. Children each generation learn our reputation. We have still the name of being exacting. We are still the wonderfully clever people who take men from their homes and villages to work for us.

It is of the utmost importance to recognise that in such political relations loyalty does not grow. In all the tribes taxes are paid and obedience is rendered, not from loyalty nor from a sense of duty, but because of the disasters that would follow refusal. Our government in these parts rests on the obedience the ignorant and barbarous always give to the stronger and cleverer. So long as it has no other foundation education and civilization will weaken its authority. They are weakening it now. One lesson, furthermore, this war has certainly taught many natives. They believe now that they can fight as well as Europeans. They know they have sometimes fought better.

There is no country in the world where grievances are not widely felt. In a free country the subject has the means of expressing them and of himself attempting their removal. In Africa native opinion has neither the means of expression nor the means of action. And when grievances are laid at the door of an alien government, when its demands fall on all and its services are felt by none, education enables growing numbers to reflect upon and nurse their grievances until some way of resistance offers, however foolish or criminal or hopeless it may be.

VI. A recent event in Nyasaland reveals so sharply the facts that I am seeking to interpret that I shall venture to describe its characteristic features. The essential characters of the Chilembwe rising in 1915 were that it was planned by a man who had received a good education from a mission, which he had left to set up a church of his own; that it was carried out by that section of the native population who grow their food on land which is the property of Europeans, and pay rent in the form of unpaid labour; that most of the people actively concerned were tenants on an estate the overseers of which were reputed by natives generally to be hard drivers and to resort to frequent punishment; and that on that particular estate no schools or churches were allowed. Each of these facts is essential to the true comprehension of the rising. They mark it as the first of its kind, in sharp contrast with previous resorts to violence in Eastern Africa. Neither motive nor aim nor leadership was tribal. The affair was more than the brutal murder of five Europeans followed by the shooting of some scores of Africans and the hanging and imprisonment of more than a hundred others. It was symptomatic, the first attack of a new malady, a malady the pathology of which is not that of ordinary crime but of that species of disorder in the state which affects its ordinary subjects, otherwise law abiding. And as mere suppression of symptoms, to follow the metaphor, cures no social disorder, the sole importance of the rising lies in what hidden processes of disease the symptoms reveal.

In the reports that were made on the rising emphasis was no doubt laid, and rightly laid, on the character of its leader. Chilembwe was an old man, nearly blind, with no experience of firearms or of fighting. His knowledge of English was perfect, he had read widely, and had sent his sons to America for education. His congregation is said to have spent £500 on their church, a very large sum where ordinary labour is paid 5/- a month. He preached to it chiefly from those passages in the Bible that have played so large a part in insurrections among people of our own race. He mutilated his chief victim, and although that would suggest criminal lunacy in a civilised community, it is more likely to have been a reminiscence of certain incidents in the Old Testament, or even possibly of such state executions in our own history as the execution of Sir Thomas More or of the Earl of Strafford. These murders apart, Chilembwe seems to have been a man of good character. He certainly did not encourage loose ideas of property or sex among his flock. The families of the murdered Europeans were well treated. Chilembwe's attraction to his followers was, his ability aside, his claim to be a Christian and a patriot. It is highly probable that he believed himself to be both.

Chilembwe's following, apart from a small group of former adherents of neighbouring missions, was mainly composed of people who during the past twenty years emigrated from Portuguese territory because of alleged harshness in administration there. These people being homeless, settled on land, the property of Europeans, to whom they gave free labour, not only for rent but in order to pay their tax. They followed Chilembwe because he promised them free land.

The actual precipitating cause of the outrage was the belief among the natives that the labourers on a certain very large estate were cruelly treated. The European men on that estate were murdered by their own domestic servants and plantation labourers.

That estate is in the area covered by the mission work of the Church of Scotland. The owner of the estate forbade the work of that mission, or of any other mission, to be carried on among the thousands of his tenants. More precisely, he prohibited churches and schools. The tenants accordingly were not only drawn from a tribe less affected than most by civilization, but were themselves individually ignorant to a degree unusual in Nyasaland.

Each of these characters affords a partial explanation of the rising. There is a natural history of insurrections. They all need soil, seed and climate, without which they cannot happen, with which they must happen. It is safe to predict, in the first place, that in most future risings the leaders will be professedly religious and patriotic. They will use some version of the formula, Africa for the Africans, and they will be either Mahomedans or Christians. In the second place, it will always be the case that the rank and file of rebels will have an economic grievance. And of all grievances, the lack of free land is most keenly felt, especially when others are seen to have it. In Africa as in Europe the landless are always the true revolutionaries. Men are always readier to risk their lives than their homes. Further, only economic grievances that affect the mass of the population will prevent that mass, too timid to join in rebellion, from actively supporting the Government. Law and order, as was the case in the Chilembwe rising, will always have friends among natives. But it would be most unwise for Government to count on much active support on future occasions. In the case of a first attempt almost entirely confined to a single estate, there would be many sympathisers far from being so desperate as to join an undertaking so obviously hopeless, and still others to whose immediate advantage it was to come out on the side of the authorities.

In the third place, it is nearly always the case in insurrections that some reputed outrage or cruelty is the precipitating cause. Stories of assaults on women, floggings, withholdings of wages by Europeans, are always passing round among the natives, particularly in East Africa. Many of these stories are quite untrue. When they collect round some particular European his reputation acts like a naked light in a mine liable to gas. Here, incidentally, I would venture the suggestion that no European who has been convicted of an assault on a native should be allowed to join the local defence force. Nine tenths of the assaults on natives are, however, due not to cruelty but to the exasperating effects on perfectly ordinary people of trying to get good work out of unwilling natives. Thus in Nyasaland, where direct pressure to work was rarely applied before the war, assaults on natives are much rarer than in British East Africa. In Nyasaland, also, thanks to the ubiquity of mission schools, assaults are much oftener brought into court and punished.

Before leaving this matter of grievances I would draw notice to one misrepresentation which the facts are sometimes given. Personal grievances do not need to be real, and general economic grievances do not need to be reasonable, in order to be felt. A false story of some brutality may do just as much harm as if it were true. Similarly, that cultivators should have to pay rent and should be liable to eviction on six months' notice seems to us a very ordinary arrangement. To natives it seems quite unjust. So also with the innumerable regulations with which natives in British East Africa who visit townships and areas of European settlement have to comply. So also with forced labour. To some extent the feelings natives have on these subjects are due simply to their living under an administration over which they have no control, and under laws they are not expected to understand. The need is clear of some easy means of expression for their feelings as an alternative to rebellion.

The last characteristic feature of the Chilembwe rising that I mentioned was that it was carried out by men who, although attracted by certain features in the Christian religion, were uninfluenced by the teaching of any authorised Christian mission. It was one that only desperate or very ignorant men would have engaged in. The influence of the mission, if its work had been permitted, would probably have prevented this particular rising, both by revealing the certainty of failure and by teaching the men on the estate involved to take their personal grievances to a magistrate. At the same time the rising had far more sympathy among Christian natives than most Europeans believe. If and when anything of the kind brews among mission natives the chief differences that may be expected are that plans will be laid longer, over a much wider area, and with some consideration of military means.

To make the narrative complete it may be added that since the rising occurred the Government has passed an ordinance ensuring that native tenants of Europeans should have the option of paying rent in money instead of in labour. But as most of them can only earn money by the sale of their labour the effect of the ordinance will be very small. A planter may still forbid schools on his estate. That circumstance is made all the more remarkable by the fact that it was by the action of this very mission of the Church of Scotland that the part of the Protectorate in which these estates are situated was added to the empire.

It is greatly to be hoped that authority may recognise that this rising of Chilembwe's and those similar risings that I fear are certain to follow it are not due to mere ordinary criminal instincts. I hold that it is true beyond all question that the danger of insurrection in Eastern Africa is attributable to economic and social causes. Sedition always attracts criminals. If it attracted no others it would be no danger. In Chilembwe's case it did attract, and in the future it will attract, large numbers of perfectly ordinary people. Hundreds of ignorant members of the most docile race in the world do not throw their lives away for criminal ends. To kill them is no remedy. Military preparations, and I know they are being made, are positively harmful, if nothing else is to be done.

VII. The scrutiny of a mere phase leads to faults in proportion that can be avoided only by taking a wider angle. Thus seen the perplexities of the day are an inheritance from our relations in the past with the African. In Europe the true work of politics is the liberation of classes formerly servile, in Africa it is the liberation of a whole slave race. The abolition of the slave trade and of the status of slavery was only its beginning. The ignorant will always be enslaved, whatever their legal status. Little more than a century separates us from the time when our own nation had a monopoly of the slave trade. The motives that led our countrymen to engage in it have not been removed by a mere change in the law whereby rights of property in persons were abolished. Whenever the members of a civilised race have opportunity of making profit out of the labour of a barbarous one, especially if it be totally devoid of political rights, enslavement is inevitable.

For it is servility as much as slave owning that makes the slave. The African is treated like a slave to-day because he is a slave. But he is less a slave than he was. He has surprised all observers by proving himself capable of insurrection. That is the proof of the appetite for liberty. It is also the proof that he can now no longer be kept from it. It might have been possible to direct human development in Eastern Africa so as to make the whole race produce great wealth as wage earners for Europeans. Taxation suitably adjusted, restriction of land, and administrative suasion can secure a control over the person as complete as was given by property in slaves. That is, without misrepresentation, the real aim of planters and investors of capital in Africa, as a class. To achieve it the prohibition of Mahome-

dan, and especially of Christian, propaganda would have been
necessary. If our country had intended to turn the race into one of
obedient wage earners, we should have made it a crime to teach a
native to read. But if Africans are to have real liberty, if they are to
give the true obedience of freemen, obedience given to law alone,
and given because the law's inward authority is felt, governments
must make their chief care the ensuring of the conditions that promote liberty. Government with the main aim of promoting economic
development and wealth production cannot be wise or just government, necessary though wealth is to wise and just government. Society in Eastern Africa would have presented a very different picture
to-day if governments had treated their task as primarily a human
problem, of which the problem of wealth production was one of the
derivatives.

I shall venture to describe one instance of the treatment of human
interests as subsidiary to material interests. On Mombasa island
during the past fifteen years quarters have been erected for the
thousands of men whose labour is necessary for the development of
the port and railway. Permanent quarters have been built for government employees, giving to each family less than a hundred feet of
floor space. The housing of the labour of the port was left to private
enterprise. The price of land on the island has risen in a generation
from a nominal sum to anything from £800 to £5000 an acre. The
fortunes that have been made by this rise in value have contributed
nothing to the cost of streets or drains, and these have still to be
made. The decent housing of labourers whose wages are from six-
pence to a shilling a day is impossible on land at such a price. In the
result, slum conditions, overcrowding, filth, prostitution, destitu-
tion, are growing up in a community literally of our own creation.
In housing, food and health labourers are actually worse off than
the domestic slaves of a generation ago. Actually fewer now than
then get education. The sole gain is an almost empty freedom in
status. There has been no lack of money. Nowhere in the world has
economic development been so rapid. But the money has been spent
with the aim of producing more money, not with the aim of the service of human interests.

Finally, I shall venture, with even greater hesitation than I have
felt in the descriptive part of my letter and certainly with a far more

insistent sense of inadequacy, to suggest a programme. There are many reasons why I should not venture the attempt. But there is at least one good reason why I must. No policy should be recognised to be wise until it is tested by its expression in a practicable scheme.

Once again I would repeat that the administrative programme must reach all in its operation. The test of its rightness is the fostering of the loyalty of all. Cautious tentative experiments that affect minorities are here beside the question. The need is of a deliberate orientation of a policy, economic, legal, administrative, which will touch the consciousness of educated native, plantation labourer and pagan villager alike, a policy that will leave governments open to any criticism rather than that of their estrangement from the governed. Governments in tropical Africa may in fact commit any number of blunders and little harm be taken so long as they display devotion and attract attention.

In the second chapter of this letter I have defined the economic policy necessary to be followed, and I need, in this chapter, to do no more than refer to it.

The next requisite is the extension of law. Our law in these parts is a true universal, changing, forming and fixing everyone's opinion and conduct. With us law registers rather than forms opinion. In Africa it is a powerful creator of opinion. It was until recently, for instance, an impiety to question the sanctions or to doubt the results of witchcraft. Our law, which makes it a crime, has, together with education and Christian teaching, brought many thousands to feel witchcraft to be the curse it is. (African Mahomedanism unfortunately, leaves the invisible world as full of demons as it found it.) It is far from being true that our courts are always trusted. But I believe that they are more trusted than they used to be. Their actual civilising and liberating influence is immense. It is most remarkable to observe how rapidly the principles of our law are absorbed into the stock of native ideas, even in the case of Mahomedan tribes. Among the many corrosive agencies that Europe has introduced, law is the one agency of government that is creative as well.

It is a complete mistake to imagine that natives prefer the personal prerogative of a benevolent local despot to the law. The more a magistrate knows of native opinion and feeling the less he yields to the temptation of seeking to do substantial justice by overriding the strict terms of the law. Natives understand perfectly well that many circumstances of great importance in ordinary life are irrelevant in courts of justice. Their tribal law leaves almost as little room for personal opinion, and insists as strictly on proper form and procedure as does our own. In this connection it is most desirable that the judges of the High Court should be given greater authority over ordinary magistrates. The judges of the High Court are given by natives a respect that not even Governors receive. The increase of their influence would have the best result on native opinion and would be welcomed by the best of the magistrates.

The criticism of our legal system which one hears most often from natives is that Government and its agents are outside the law. It is even generally believed that the law is not impartial as between European and native. Theoretical equality before the law is, I grant, not a practical aim.[14] Different punishments for assault by a native on a European and for assault by a European on a native are simply the reflection of actual difference in social and economic status. In practice, approximation to equal justice in the courts, so far as it is possible, will result from administrative justice. Complete liberality would prevent nine tenths of the floggings that occur in British East Africa, very few of which are ever brought into court.

Nothing short, however, of the subjection of governments themselves to the law will give natives confidence. The fact must be acknowledged that in early days the subordination of government to its own law was difficult. But there can be no reason why at this time of day the law should give the occupying native no protection against the confiscation of his land, except the fact that the government never knows when it may discover that it wishes to confiscate. It is a great hindrance to confidence in government that the executive is so reluctant to confer on natives rights enforceable in the courts. It is an immense mistake that natives do not feel the need of secure land tenure. There are increasing numbers to whom the grant of titles to land enforceable in the courts would be the only proof government could give of its good faith. The effect on local opinion of a single decision given in favour of a native against government would be immense. The task, now so difficult as to be almost impossible, of persuading natives that the Government is to their advantage would be immensely easier if there were visible proof that executive government is subject to the law it expects all others to obey. The idea that the security and the prestige of the Government depend on belief by natives in the infallibility of its agents is worse than untrue. On the contrary nothing would raise the prestige of the Government so much as indisputable evidence that public officers who break the law are punished as publicly and as severely as private persons are punished.

It is probably inevitable that Government in the African Protectorates should be autocratic as nowhere else. The small relative importance of these countries, their remoteness, the obscurity and uniqueness of their social conditions, shut them off from the influence of public opinion at home, and prevent the healthy ventilation of proposals and policies in Parliament, in books and in the press. Practically the only influence that reaches governments in these parts from the outside is the constant pressure of financial interests. In the absence of all other checks and safeguards, the protection of the law, a law supreme over the Crown and all its authorities, is indispensable to justice.

Consideration must be given to the law in quite another aspect. In British East Africa, by the influence of European members of the Legislative Council, a large mass of legislation has been enacted with the object of regulating the conduct of natives when they live or travel outside the purely native areas. Sanitary byelaws, regulations to prevent movement of stock, regulations forbidding natives being out at night, forbidding them to travel across land in European occupation, unfenced and uncultivated although most of it is, forbidding them to travel outside the reserves except to and from work for Europeans, are examples of a rapidly increasing body of law under which the younger generation of natives finds itself. Most local ordinances in fact prescribe different duties from, and give a different status to, Europeans and natives. The law itself is thus increasingly partial.

There is so very much to be said for most of this disciplinary legislation that I would omit all mention of it were it not for the fact that it creates immense irritation among the natives, and is thus a contributory cause of unrest. The best judge I know considers it perhaps the chief cause. It is certainly a rapidly increasing cause. I cannot here dissect out the subject and arrange its elements in a scale

with at the one end unfortunate necessities like compulsory vaccination, and at the other purely vicious restrictions like pass regulations.
The whole matter needs to be regarded from different standpoints,
together. In Africa people are apt to forget that in such legislation
they are imitating Europe with the great difference that in Europe
nothing can be done without persuading the public. The whole system of our own invaluable byelaws and regulations would have been
impossible of application in the England of the eighteenth century,
not to speak of the first century. I do not mean that in Africa no law
contrary to native opinion should ever be passed. I had some share
myself in making vaccination compulsory in one district. I have shut
up smallpox contacts behind barbed wire—from which they escaped
nightly in spite of a guard armed with rifles—and I have had natives
punished for washing clothes in a water supply. But it is too often
forgotten that every prohibition and compulsion makes a draft on
an already small stock of loyalty and confidence and adds to already
prevalent dislike and mistrust. All legislation that bears specially
or specifically on Africans should be scrutinised with that consideration in mind, and should be disallowed except on proof of most exi-
gent need. Further, no law of the kind should be enforced until
much work and trouble is spent in explanation and persuasion. (The
value of local representative bodies of natives is here apparent.) Unfortunately the usual difficulty to be overcome in such cases is not so
much ignorance as the steady belief that every new demand of Government should be met on principle with passive resistance. When
natives have for so long been told to do as they are bid and ask no
questions they suspect explanations as being merely preparatory to
fresh demands.

The source of this difficulty is undoubtedly the large measure of
control which the representatives of the European community have
over legislation. Most of the restrictive and compulsory laws are not
the work of experts at all, as they are in this country. Educational
and sanitary experts are indeed notably devoid of influence in Eastern tropical Africa. The only kind of expert who does get his way is
the man who deals, not with some aspect of human life, but with
plant or animal life. Here again is evidence of the primacy of things
in the existing scheme. It is not that a good case may not almost always be made out. It is easy to see that it is impossible to control dis-

ease in coffee plants if every native is allowed to grow a little patch of them. And it is plain enough that thefts of woolbearing sheep from Europeans will be less likely to occur if natives are prevented from breeding woolbearing sheep themselves.

We reach in this kind of problem the great watershed of opinion where people on one side can hardly understand the language and ideas of people on the other. Politics with these means the problems of human relations out of which wealth grows, with those it means the problems of production, with men as its instruments. There is no simple formula in these matters whereby wisdom may be found and tested. As things are, and so long as the opinions of the different classes of Europeans in the country do not change, a great deal of the differential legislation is inevitable. But a great deal of it is not. Much of it could be and should be disallowed from home. And, above all, the fullest recognition should be given to the principle that the representatives of those whose livelihood or profit depends on the labour of Africans should have no concern whatever with legislation that discriminates between European and African or is designed to bear specially on the African. Personal, class and racial interest combine in these men to produce a distorting medium from which they cannot escape, through which they regard the African. Their increasing control over events in British East Africa is the control of an alien plutocracy and oligarchy.

I can best define the more strictly administrative changes that are necessary by reference to a recent experience of my own. Shortly before the war I was given the duty of introducing a scheme of village sanitation into a remote district of Nyasaland. So far as I know nowhere else in our East African possessions has any attempt been made to diminish the prevalence of endemic disease in a native community. The scheme had some success. What prevented far greater success was partly the sheer poverty of the people, due to the absence of so many ablebodied men and to the complete absence of economic development in the villages, and partly the lack of any organ of native opinion. The first point has already been dealt with. The difficulty in the second matter was that I could not persuade tens of thousands of people except through their natural leaders, and these I could not use.

The district, though so remote, was specially favourable for the experiment. A mission had been at work in it for some years before the arrival of Government and mission influence was stronger than usual. On the other hand its distance from industries and trade routes had kept the old tribal organisation comparatively intact. Thus both the old and the new order were, as it were, alive. I was supposed to work through the chiefs. They were mostly old men, highly suspicious of everything new. Some of them were obviously hostile. The younger people were on my side. Large numbers of them did as I advised even though their chiefs gave me no help. But when I met with obstruction or, worse still, inertia, I was helpless. Sanitary regulations cannot be imposed by force, except on a trivial minority. You can burn a man's hut for refusal to pay his tax, but you cannot so compel him to use a latrine. I did get one chief punished, but the effect was merely to increase my difficulties. And even the more willing of the chiefs were naturally averse to put pressure on their own people and thus diminish their own popularity.

The people who could have helped me were rather the village teachers, skilled workmen, and petty traders who had had education from the mission. They had a native association, the only one I have met with in rural Africa. I was invited to attend the annual meeting, and addressed a quite enthusiastic audience on the prevention of disease. Some of the chiefs attended the meeting. They seemed to be rather out of things. One of them was asked to second a motion, and took the opportunity to make an eloquent speech which seemed increasingly to scandalise the younger members until they pulled him down into his chair. I learned afterwards that he had so far forgotten himself as to abuse the Government, although he gave great praise to the local magistrate, who was, indeed, greatly liked. The association reads papers, holds debates, and shows a wonderful persistence in submitting motions and resolutions to the Government. It has recently raised several pounds for the Red Cross. The resolutions it submits to the Government are ignored. No doubt they are often absurd. But I have no hesitation in saying that if I could have worked through that association of the younger men, instead of through elderly, uneducated and often drunken chiefs, if I could have organised and got authority given to local sub-committees in the groups of villages, village sanitation would have been made so real a success as to save many lives and to increase greatly the efficiency of labour.

It must not be inferred that the concrete example I have given is altogether typical. Common action in an association depends on the degree to which the stimulus of the new thought and ethic has inter-penetrated the fabric of the old society. There are at least five dis-tricts in Nyasaland where associations of educated and influential natives could be formed. The best of the chiefs would always have great influence in them. Whatever the constitution of these native associations Government would do well to stipulate that no resident in the district should be debarred from membership: that all dis-cussions should be entirely free and all officers and committees freely elected without interference by Government or mission: and that a copy of the minutes of all the general meetings should be sub-mitted to the District Resident. Perhaps the most valuable function of such associations would be their expression of native opinion and feeling. I venture to think that their recommendations and resolu-tions would be of far greater value than the reports of any European.

Government should give these associations not only recognition, status, places to meet in, and with some small help in money, but also duties. To begin with the duties should comprise the registra-tion of births and deaths, of great value to the sanitarian; sanitation, including the protection of water supplies, the provision of latrines, clearing of bush and swamp to prevent malaria and sleeping sick-ness; and the forming of local assessor's rolls from which chiefs could get help in trying their cases. (The reform of these native courts is in some districts a very urgent matter. The very stability that our administration gives to the position of the chiefs makes it easier for some of them to indulge in petty spite and minor tyran-nies.) In time, in addition to other duties which need not be men-tioned, these associations should be given the duty of surveying cul-tivated land, counting stock and assessing income, so that, district by district, the inequitable hut and poll tax may be transformed into a land and income tax.

The objection that such embryonic bodies of local government are superfluous I would meet by pointing out that the inevitable alter-native to them is secret societies. These already exist. They are prob-ably always seditious. They are certain to spread and multiply until an alternative means of expression is provided. It is only through such local bodies that Government will become native to the soil. It is through them alone that the more intelligent, who are also the

most restless, of natives will find their place of natural responsibility
and a bond both to their own people and to the Government. They
will give warning of the storms presaged by the Chilembwe affair.
And if they are set up without delay, they will be channels, dug before the flood comes, through which the Government may lead the
developing sense of race and nationality. (I should perhaps add that
as administrative districts do not conform to tribal boundaries, these
local bodies cannot be tribal in most cases. That circumstance will at
first be a disadvantage. Later it may even prove to be an advantage.)

VIII. At present governments and missions are two contrasting, and
in effect conflicting, expressions of our country's aim. Their co-
ordination is only possible through a wise scheme of education undertaken by governments. Furthermore, it is by education that governments may most closely relate themselves to their subjects. And it
is only in the schools that the future leaders of the African people
can be influenced. When life and movement appear in a state, if the
Government refuses leadership and guidance, it need expect to have
neither loyalty nor respect nor, in the end, authority.

An adequate educational policy in Eastern Africa must fulfil
three conditions. It must cover the whole area, it must fit in with the
existing educational work of missions, and it must be adjusted to
existing economic conditions and to economic policy.

It must cover the whole area because the aim must be to influence
the race, not to choose a few and lift them out of African life. The
education of the sons of chiefs and a few others who are expected to
be of special use to Government is precisely the wrong kind of programme. In Nyasaland Government makes a trivial grant to missions for education. In British East Africa Government itself edu-
cates a minute number of Africans. The cost per head is many times
the cost of education in mission schools. If for no other reason than
their cheapness, the humble village mission schools—there are
nearly a thousand of them in Nyasaland alone—must be the basis
of the general scheme. Many of them are badly in need of the stimulus of an impartial but sympathetic inspectorate. I need hardly mention that co-operation with missions in education must be neither a
help nor a hindrance to propaganda. I believe that these very difficulties of co-operation, in which both resident magistrates and local

representative bodies should share, would go far to unify the different sections of the European community.

A similar attitude of co-operation with the Mahomedan schools on the coast of British East Africa has hitherto been found impracticable. One hopes that even now it may not be too late to save them from complete decay. In the interior of British East Africa and of Nyasaland alike, however, I have never been able to find a mosque school worth saving.

Just as in scholastic education there is the difficulty of working with religious organisations without injury to the true educational aim, so in technical education there is danger from selfish commercialism. The Bible on one hand and on the other the training to trades whereby natives may find work from Europeans are both admirable means of education. But not even together are they the whole. Too much of the existing industrial education in Africa merely makes natives useful to individual Europeans. The main end to keep in view should not be to supply cooks and laundrymaids, cabinetmakers, attendants on expensive machinery, but to supply skilled workers in wood, leather, iron, stone, bricks for the village communities that will grow up round native industries. And these industries themselves must be no mere anachronistic revivals like basket-making or handloom weaving, but real large scale industries, having insatiable demand from wide markets, like cotton or oil seed growing. Cocoa in West Africa and, in some degree, cotton in Uganda, show what can be done and with what little expense to governments. These very instances, however, prove the necessity of ensuring the proper distribution of the rewards of labour among natives themselves. A faulty system of land tenure would have the most undesirable result of encouraging the growth of a class able to live on rent and profit without giving service in return. Every ablebodied native should have as much land as he can make use of, secure in law, and free except for taxation by public authority.

A tribute, in regard to industrial education, is due to the Directors of the Public Works Departments of British East Africa and Nyasaland. Under both, with little encouragement from others, real educational work has been done. Skilled training in the Uganda Railway Workshops, on the other hand, has almost solely been given to Europeans and Indians.

The touchstone of educational policy, and through education of
all policy in Africa, is the relation of governments with the class of
educated natives. In Nyasaland that class has the very greatest influence, in British East Africa it is only now emerging. The importance
of these men lies, not in their being a necessity, as clerks and so
forth, to the machinery of Government, but in their being taken as
models by an increasing number of their countrymen. They, not the
chiefs, are the real leaders of opinion.

The educated minority of the subject race is never popular with
their governors. Nevertheless, to guide the thought and ambition of
these men, and to gain their sympathy and co-operation, should be
part of Government's deliberate policy. A place must be given them
in the state comparable with their influence on society. Otherwise
they inevitably pass into opposition—and all opposition is potentially sedition—which is merely the reflection of the common attitude of Europeans to them. If "the withholding of knowledge is the
greatest of all injustices," then surely the discouragement and re-
pression of those who have received it is the greatest of political
crimes. The guilt of disloyalty and sedition falls at least equally on
the officer who condemns and discourages natives because of faults
inevitable in the first generation of mental emancipation as on the
natives themselves who, with hope of intellectual and social advancement repulsed, become Ishmaels. A certain officer once told
me that he had had a correspondence with John Chilembwe. Misled
by the style of the letters, he at first answered them as he would have
answered the letters of a European. But, as he told me, when he
learned who his correspondent was, he soon put him in his place.
That officer had his share in the rising. There are few of us who
have lived in these parts who have not some share.

It is most necessary that when in future new chiefs and headmen
come to be elected or appointed, Governments should, whenever
possible, recognise the candidature of none but men of good education. In many tribes the chiefs with their special friends and followers form a party opposed to Christianity and education. Unfortunately that party is generally looked upon as a kind of pro-Govern-
ment faction. Governments should be careful to avoid special alliance with what is already in many cases the diminishing minority of
harmfully conservative and illiterate pagans, and the standing order

under which a chief can forbid his people to build a school should be abolished at once. The position of the chiefs, difficult enough in any case, is not improved by Government support of their opposition to inevitable changes.

It is finally of the utmost importance to face with the greatest frankness the fact that opposition to any educational policy of real value will take the form of a professed inability to find the money. The real meaning of those who cite that reason for delay is that in their view there are other more necessary objects of expenditure. There is a mycologist in Nyasaland with the duty of the prevention of diseases that affect the economic products of the soil. There is no officer whose duty it is to teach or to supervise teaching. There is not even an officer employed in the work of preventing disease in man. In German East Africa there are more than twenty doctors employed by Government in the prevention as distinguished from the treatment of disease, in Nyasaland not one. In British East Africa especially every department spends large sums upon the protection and encouragement of wealth production by European capital, in surveys, experimental farms, a veterinary service, police, means of communication, and in many other ways. I can learn of no other country where Europeans are so lightly taxed. There is certainly none where so much public money is spent on them. I submit that in comparison education, education covering the whole area, is a necessity and that expenditure on these objects is, as a whole, less necessary and in some cases at this state of growth in society even harmful because premature. The natural order of growth in society has been reversed. We have cared for production, not for the producer.

My argument is based on no presumption of what the future may bring. The African may or may not prove to be capable, in the phrase of the day, of self-determination. He is certainly capable of protest by insurrection against what he conceives to be wrong determination. Both the religions he is absorbing teach him that he is capable of more than a mere political equality with Europeans. I hold, indeed, that there is one view that is essentially false to the facts, and fundamentally incompatible with the purpose of our country. In a standard book upon Nyasaland the native is described as a person most wisely treated like a dog to which one has the friendliest of feelings, wayward, quarrelsome, but happy when fed, obedient under discipline, submissive to direction because incapable of self-direction. It would be hypocrisy to pretend that such a conception of native mentality has not been influential and even prevalent among those who have hitherto had the direction and shaped the policy of our governments. In permitting it to continue to influence events our country encourages the one means that, unfortunately, man can always use to prove that he is not canine but human, and not slave but free, the murder of his master.[15] To that expiation the war has brought our countrymen in these parts very near. It is in that conviction that I have ventured to address you.

> I have the honour to be,
> Sir,
> Your most obedient servant,
>
> (Sgd.) NORMAN LEYS
> Medical Officer, Nyasaland

Oldham to Leys
18 March 1918
[from Edinburgh]

A friend of Professor Gilbert Murray has allowed me to see in confidence a copy of your letter to the Secretary of State for the Colonies on the situation in East Africa. The paper has left a deep impression on my mind. The subject is one in which I am much interested and some of the matters to which you refer are closely connected with practical questions which are before me at the present time.[16] I should very much appreciate an opportunity of having a talk with you....

Leys to Oldham
23 March 1918

... Subject to the necessities, chiefly arising from the condition of body & mind which is really one of being very tired and very puzzled, I shall do my best to let you have an article on Xtian missions.[17] How long do you want it to be? Do you pay? I ask because I don't want payment.

I shall rely on you in future to inform me of any use I can be, to Africa, to Christian missions. At heart I am a Quaker. They have kept the idea of a corporate conscience. I don't believe in a man's trusting entirely to conscience, or to what he considers the voice of the Spirit in his heart. I want guidance from my fellow Christians. The old idea was that God speaks through them to the individual. And as you have opportunity of seeing needs, and occasions of helping, will you please simply tell me. I want to write a book, for instance. But I should give no merely personal views. I should write as a member of a corporate body. I don't seem to be able to see how I can. Perhaps you can help me best by printing an article in your Review that will bring me criticisms from unknown friends. . . .

Leys to Oldham
1 April 1918

I am sorry to bother you, but I am getting uneasy about the fact that though it is ten weeks since I sent the letter to Gilbert Murray, and five since he told me he had delivered it, I am still without any acknowledgement.[18] . . . I want to avoid such an accident as for the Colonial Office people to hear of outsiders having read the letter long before the person it is addressed to has seen it. . . .

Leys to Oldham
26 September 1918

I shall know soon, perhaps next week, if I am to go back to Africa or to get a pension. If I am invalided I shall seek a small country practice since the pension will be less than £200. If I find the work I want I hope to have time to write a book. One of the many questions I can't answer is what a public servant on pension may say in a book. I expect the book will be more religious than political. But nothing of any account written about East Africa, from whatever standpoint, can omit a description of social and economic conditions. And as these are in part the deliberate creation of Government, and are mainly the results of its policy, I don't see how I can write at all, however carefully, without at least making the reader critical, as indeed I would have him to be. I suppose that by the old standard that would be a breach of good manners, if not of the regulations. But I

imagine that when peace comes there will be many others besides me
who will want to tell the public what has been done in King George's
name although they have taken his money. I feel that there must be
a standard of some kind, whatever happens. I mean that sound
opinion, irrespective of regulations, would debar me from telling
part of the truth. But I can't discover any rule to follow except to
avoid personalities. Read for instance is a stupid fool.[19] Girouard an
unscrupulous adventurer who thinks he can play Clive's part without his brains and do what Rhodes did without Rhodes' money.[20]
Now the characters of these two men are most important to any
truthful estimate of events in East Africa. These characters I must
not mention. To that extent my account of things will be less than
fully truthful. Does decency demand other restraints?[21] . . .

Leys to Lionel Curtis[22]
London
23 November 1918

  I am acutely uncomfortable about our conversation of last night. I
feel as if it may prove to be the case, as Coupland[23] said, that your
group is the only hope of justice in Africa for a number of years.
And I hate to think of effort so precious to millions endangered by
partial failure to gauge the forces against you. You will forgive me I
know if I attempt a warning. Africa may be a problem separable
from imperial and international politics, just as eighteenth century
slavery or spoliation in India were. I hope it may prove to be. But I
think it necessary to think out its very separability. The root of the
trouble is that when modern industrial methods are introduced
among barbarous people without political rights by others who while
they control government, own the soil, and have in machine guns
weapons irresistible as none owned by former oppressors were, also
have the opportunity of making profit at a rate impossible elsewhere—then in these conditions, while men are men, you will have,
as you do have, enslavement. The enslavers are not scoundrels. Take
perhaps the nearest parallel. Take society in the West Indies from
1750–1840. And now think what fate the *staff* of your philanthropic corporation would then have met with if an earlier Curtis and an
earlier Ashcroft had conceived a similar scheme.[24] The old world is
strewn with futile heroisms, Jesuits licking leprous sores of Indians

in Mexican silver mines as well as Puritans today saving life in
America, life useless unless it is more than merely kept alive. The
men you will send to West Africa won't be heroes. You don't want
heroes. Most heroes are bogus anyhow just as most poets are. But
only heroes could keep their footing in the world of industry in Africa and hold fast to their aims. Ordinary men will either fall in with
the minds of their ordinary fellow countrymen there, or will come
home and tell you your scheme won't work.

What so few at home realise is that ignorance, two hundred years
(W. Africa) 50 years (E. Africa) of enslavement and oppression, and
four years of war, famine and misery (E. Africa) have turned all but
a few Africans into people whom nobody who knows them loves,
except a minority of Christian missionaries. The question is can a
scheme be made to work permitting decent and friendly relations in
industry, while all around you have 20% trying to become 50%? Almost as easily I fear keep a single street alone free from the fog I see
around me as I write.

You see I have lived in the fog myself. I have cuffed and kicked
boys, sometimes because for the moment it seemed that nohow else
could things be done, sometimes just because my mind was tired beyond control, sometimes because I hated the people I kicked, though
I never hated them as I hated myself. And from that mephitic air I
sometimes escaped to a mission station where for the time the whole
world looked and felt different. (Not all mission stations by any
means were like that.) It is only in such a walled in garden that one
can ever be a real European. But your men are going to no monastic
life. They will play bridge and tennis with men in trading firms.
They will sit on verandahs on which half shamed women pass when
the darkness begins. They will hear all the obvious facts that are
only untrue when seen in the appalling splendour of the Kingdom of
God.

You see in Africa of the tropics we reach the last problem of the
human race. Probably when brotherhood and freedom are the conscious aims if not the practice of mankind elsewhere, in Africa ignorant armies will still clash by night. And you are going to solve it
on £60,000. You are going to expect second grade public school
boys to keep intact a relationship with a thousandth part of the population.

You will think me a horrible pessimist. I am not. I hope and believe that this scheme of yours & Ashcroft's—it isn't really new, the early Xtian communities in Asia Minor belonged to the same type and so did the Celtic monasteries—will prove to be one of the things the world is waiting for. But I beg you not to pin your faith on a first success. And be ready for your brothers, black and white, to sin against you seventy times seven.

I have only one suggestion in detail. Your staff must be kept alive mentally. Drunkenness and whoremongering are not the worst men's vices in Africa. (Missionaries won't agree.) Their antidote is partly family life—I hope you may achieve it for your men, and partly the full mind. The public school training fails, to my mind, in Africa because it starves the mind, gives no appetite for knowledge.

Do you mind sending this to Ashcroft?

There is one other thing. I have borrowed from friends in order to buy this practice in Brailsford. And I want to stick to it until debt is paid off. But later on I would give all I have and am to shoulder a gun in the Africa you are trying to call to life, just to pull on the rope as one of the team. I could organise education in East Africa, not to say Nyasaland, as well as anybody likely to be given the job—provided of course I had a Governor and a Secretary of State of the right mind. It is a mighty poor alternative in my eyes, to write letters and articles, instead of lending a hand. So I hope I am to be regarded as on call.

Leys to Oldham
London
27 November 1918

(1) My future address is Brailsford, near Derby.

(2) I shall write soon about the article. (3) I wish now only to explain that if you get a letter I wrote to Curtis it is you I mean by Ashcroft. My memory for names is so bad that I mix them up in the case of men I know even better than you.

(4) I am finally invalided on a small pension and have bought a small country practice in Brailsford. I am just at the end of a most exciting week in London before settling down, talking Africa with all kinds of people in influence in various ways, including both arch-Bishops!

Any time you get a chance to hop off at Derby come and have a day's rest with breakfast in bed. I can meet you in the car.

Leys to Oldham
Brailsford
5 January 1919

. . . I find it very difficult to be truthful without telling all the truth. I mean that I can't be truthful about African politics, as in that New Europe article, without bringing in religion, nor can I be truthful in religious articles for you without bringing in politics. So I feel every single article I write to be more false than true. Anyhow this attempt to say the same thing to readers of various types is becoming very difficult: It would be far easier to say it all finally in a book, and tell each class of reader that part of the truth that interests him in a separate chapter.

Leys to Oldham
5 February 1919

Very good. I shall stick to Fulani bin Fulani for all I write that is signed.[25]
Leave out that sentence if you wish. But I confess that it seems to me very dreadful that mission study circles are only given what is supposed to do them good. That isn't study. The only Christian frame of mind in which to approach the study of missions is to seek the whole truth, each in the company of all,—it makes me wonder if I have any business to write for you and if you have any business to print what I write.
The greatest need of missions is not more enthusiasm nor sacrifice or funds, but for the church to learn what giving the gospel to the world means. Such books as Temple's tell them.[26] The mission study books I have seen don't. They tell people what certain other people wish them to believe and do. What the kingdom of God is built on is not such work. Its foundations must be a knowledge of the mind of Jesus and a knowledge, the result of unrestrained and eager search, of the world to be saved. You can't adapt for the purpose, to use your phrase, the facts of the world for mission study,

any more than you can adapt the facts of chemistry for a student of chemistry. My honest belief is that this mental timidity is the moral fault that paralyses the church and is the explanation of the threatened decline in the whole movement of modern Protestant missions.

Leys to Oldham
7 February 1919

My greatest fear not only in my writing but in my thinking is of Unconsciousness. The reformer is open to worse sins than any other kind of man. But I remember that Jesus scandalised the respectable by his refusal to share their judgement of the "Sinners" and on the other hand came down on the good people of the day. It isn't my business to teach other people their sins. But when I think out Africa, as something inside me compels, the facts and not my own desire force me to find the source of so much evil and misery in two classes of men, the rich whose comfort comes from what Africans do, and religious teachers and leaders who refuse to face both the facts and Jesus' programme. These last do not consider the Kingdom on Earth as in heaven a practicable scheme. They try to carry out an easy part of it, the preaching of a message. By itself that is naught. It is a vast deal when a constant feature of the whole programme. It is futile, and worse because a mockery of the truth, when made into a programme of the church's work.

What you tell me of mission study circles precisely illustrates my meaning. You cannot make the church an instrument to the Kingdom on such predigested fragments. Compare the syllabus of a W. E. A. course![27] By all means cater for starved minds, and have your adult schools with missionary primers. But you must have the same level of energy and enthusiasm, the same standard of thoroughness in your textbooks, to raise the true missionary spirit as others use to raise the true historical or the true scientific spirit. If Temple's book is not suitable for mission study circles they can only be religious Kindergartens. The thesis of the book I believe is wrong. It condemns missions, I believe, unjustly. But if supporters of missions are not to be given the kind of facts the book gives, and if their leaders feed them on the baby food the missionary press is full of, Temple's judgement is proved right.

I believe you agree that the church has no real external enemy

worth fighting. Its enemy is Pharaseeism, a common, subtle, all per-
vading sin, in Jesus' eyes the worst, and commonest, scarcely ever
referred to by religious writers & preachers. My trouble is that I find
the ordinary sinner who doesn't give a rap for church or missions
liker Jesus in belief & conduct than the Christian worker kind of
person. Part of the difference is a definite sense of truthfulness
among so called good people [sic]. I return proof herewith.

Oldham to Leys
17 February 1919

... Nine people out of ten in this country need to be taught in the
first place that there is a continent called Africa and to receive some
elementary information regarding the people who inhabit it. Those
who are as yet ignorant of the most elementary facts about Africa
can hardly grapple with Temple's book. I do not mean that the
whole of the mission study constituency is at this stage, but a considerable proportion of it is, and even in the colleges the mission
study text book is in many cases the first book that a man has been
induced to read about Africa. One of the things the mission study
movement has done has been to raise the standard of missionary
knowledge. There is an endless distance to go yet, and not only I,
but I am certain the leaders of the mission study movement, will welcome any pressure in the direction you indicate. But we have got to
take England as we find it, and if things are not as they should be it
is not the mission study movement that is to blame, but the educational system with which the country has been content.

Anybody who chose to form a study circle with Temple's book as
the text book would have my hearty blessing, and I not only agree
with you but long have felt strongly that there is a type of man most
worth winning who is much more likely to be got through a book like
Temple's than through ordinary missionary literature. On this point
there is not the smallest divergence in view. Indeed there is not a line
in your letter which I do not heartily endorse.

Oldham to Leys
3 September 1919

I met some months ago when he was in this country Dr Thomas

Jesse Jones, the author of the exceedingly valuable two-volume Report on Negro Education in America issued by the Bureau of Education in Washington.[28] Dr Jones is a man of wide knowledge and sound judgment and one of the most influential men in America in regard to negro questions. He will shortly visit Africa and at the suggestion of my brother-in-law, A. G. Fraser,[29] who saw him a few weeks ago in America, will include east as well as west Africa in his visit. Fraser spoke to him of your letter to the Colonial Office which he read while staying with me, and asks if I can send a copy to Jones, to whom it will be of great service. . . .

Leys to Oldham
26 May 1920

I wrote to ask Harris[30] what I could do to protest against the statement published by a committee of missionary societies in support of compulsory labour by Africans.[31] He suggests that I should write to you.

I scarcely know what to say. Harris describes the policy of the statement as dangerous. I would call it by much harsher terms. It is an unChristian, evan an antiChristian policy. It accepts race distinction in its worst shape. It encourages oppression in actual operation that is as cruel as slavery and differs from it only in legal form. The arguments used in its support are those used by those leaders of the church a hundred years ago who opposed liberation. If the missionary societies allow the world to believe that the statement represents their politics, it will prove their unfitness to represent the church, their antagonism to the Kingdom of God, and the hopelessness of extending that Kingdom in the World by their agency. I write dogmatically. The justification is that the occasion is critical. If is not the first time that the church has been led into opposition to the Gospel by the Spirit of the Pharisees in ecclesiastical authority, the Spirit that prescribes to others what those in authority would themselves refuse to perform. . . .

Oldham to Leys
31 May 1920

I too am distressed about the statement which was issued by the missionary alliance in East Africa. I cannot think what can have led the missionaries to take this action. I have already written to the headquarters of the missionary societies concerned on the subject and the question will come up at the international missionary meeting which we are holding at Geneva next month. The action may in the end lead to good as it may show the missionary societies the kind of problems they are up against and hasten what I have long desired to see, the throwing of the weight of missionary influence more definitely and explicitly on the side of justice and the treatment of native populations. . . .

Oldham to Leys
9 June 1920

I am going to take up the question of East Africa with the missionary societies and I want your help.

Have you seen the letter of the Bishop of Uganda and the Bishop of Mombasa?[32] The statement issued by the Missionary Alliance is based on the Bishops' letter, but while it incorporates a good deal of the latter it seems to me to do it in a way that gives the statement a different tone. The Bishops' letter seems to me to be prompted by a very genuine anxiety regarding the effects of the recent circular and by a desire to protect native interests. Unfortunately in pleading for the protection of these interests it gives away a vital point and the situation is made a good deal worse in the pronouncement of the Missionary Alliance. . . .

What do you consider to be the right constructive policy, having regard to the two particular grounds which are alleged to make the circular necessary, i.e. the urgent need of labour by the settlers and native idleness.

In existing circumstances and having regard to the personal element both in the Colonial Office and in East Africa what line of action or suggestion to the Colonial Office do you think most likely to have practical effect? We ought of course to declare our adherence to principles and this I hope the missionary societies may be induced to do. But this will not of itself make any practical difference to the natives. What from the practical point of view is the most fruitful line of action?

I have seen the letter of the Anti-Slavery Society to Lord Milner and while it is very good in certain ways I do not see very clearly what it is going to lead to.[33] This may be partly due to my ignorance. I have as you know no personal knowledge of conditions in East Africa and in taking up the matter I want the best advice I can get. . . .

Can you further let me have by the middle of July an article for publication in the Review, taking the recent circular and the statement of the Missionary Alliance as your text and in the light of this discussing the situation.[34] A good deal of the matter in the document you sent to the Colonial Office could be brought in if you think fit. I want the article to do as much good as possible and for this purpose I hope that your aim will be primarily to instruct. So far as the Bishops are concerned I believe that their hearts and intentions are all right, but that they have failed to see all the implications in their statement. This is true, I believe, of the missionary body as a whole. What we need is education on constructive lines and I hope you will be able to give it. So long as the approach to the subject is that of a teacher to willing pupils there is no reason why you should not express in the most unqualified terms you like your regret regarding the statement of the Missionary Alliance and the sense of the harm it may do.

I am trying to have a talk with Bishop Willis of Uganda.[35]

Leys to Oldham
10 June 1920

I shall try to answer you as briefly as you ask me to.

1. You are right in putting your finger on two dogmas, that the natives of East Africa are lazy as other human creatures are not, and that Europeans who own land in Africa have the right to Africans' labour, and Africans the duty to labour for them. These are the two bases of the policy of compulsion. The first is simply untrue. The African acts and reacts like other human creatures. His hatred of the system of industry in East Africa would be shared equally by every other kind of human creature in the same circumstances. Part of the evil of that system is the degree of compulsion already in use.

Secondly I deny absolutely the existence of any obligation on the part of one man, of whatever race, to work for anybody's profit. To demand that an African should work for a European is as contrary to right as to demand that you should come to drive my car here. The reason you don't think it equally absurd is that you do not think of the African as you think of yourself.

What is slavery? It is compulsory labour for another's advantage. Why do leaders of the church support it now? For the same reasons as they did 100 years ago, because religion has nothing to do with politics. An African Xtian is a King's son. Slavery makes the "inasmuch as ye did" into nonsense. That means, treat the African as we would ourselves be treated.

You won't get any change out of Bishop Willis. Four hundred years ago he would have burnt heretics with a good conscience, out of a sense of right. His face shows his character, that of a soldier of the Cross, but a Saul not a Paul.

The issue underlying this incident is whether the Gospel is as true of public as of private life. Bishop Willis and his school would recoil from the idea that industry and marriage are on the same footing, that in both alike the divine life is revealed, that unless in both the law of love is enacted by the church the church is not fully Christian. The church has not *thought out* Xtian politics and economics. Thousands of volumes on private morals, none on the larger half of life. Hence when faced with a practical issue it is not the law of Christ they apply in politics and industry but the maxims of Mammon. In one of your own articles you wrote "the spheres of religion and politics are distinct."[36] The other view, that I hold, is that there is no part of human life in which there is anything religious more than another. I admit, fully, that to claim that, say, socialism is as much a religious question as, say, monogamy is contrary to the ideas of the last few hundred years. But to the great bulk of men religion is either the whole of life or it is a fraud, and God is either in all human life (the incarnation) or he is imaginary.

Forced labour for private profit for Africans *could* not be supported by anyone who accepts the Gospel in politics.

You ask what can be done. In politics nothing till a Labour Govt. reverses existing policy. So long as men are in power who think the African has the duty of serving the European men like you & me can do nothing. Ask yourself why should not the settlers develop their own land, and then, why should the African serve in his own country men who go there to make money out of him?

But I *do* want to do all I can to save the *church* from repeating its crime of 100 years ago. Some day I shall try to write an article for you. But would you print it? Perhaps you wouldn't be wise to print it.

P.S. I have taken the liberty of sending your letter to McGregor Ross,[37] the best judge of the case—a great friend of Dr. Arthur's,[38] Bishop Willis &c.

If you want from me a definite answer to your question what policy ought missions to pursue in the present emergency, I say, oppose in every way the return of slavery in the form of forced labour, also all kinds of legislation that depend on racial distinctions. Equality before God means, in the sphere of politics, for Xtians, equality before the law. Why should the owner from Europe of 10,000 acres of African soil ever imagine it is anybody's duty to work on *his* land rather than on their own? *His* need creates no special problem at all.

Oldham to Leys
14 June 1920

. . . I enclose a draft of a letter I propose to submit to the Standing Committee on Wednesday, and if they approve, to the Conference of Missionary Societies on Friday. If it goes through I hope the individual missionary societies will back it up by letters of endorsement. . . .

I am quite prepared to defend my statement that "the spheres of religion and politics are distinct" as an important truth in the sense and context in which it was uttered. At the same time I hold equally strongly your view and tried to express it in a review I have written of Woolf's book, "Empire and Commerce in Africa."[39] If I can lay my hands on a proof I shall enclose it in this letter. I cannot sign the letter personally as I have to rush out to a meeting.

I do hope you will let me have an article by the middle of July for our October issue. We ought to use the opportunity of educating the people while this East African issue is fresh in their minds.

Leys to Oldham
15 June 1920

I have no criticisms to offer on your draft which I think very good, especially the para at the top of p. 2. But you will never see the promised circular!!

I am taking the liberty of sending your review of Woolf's book to him. His attitude to religion is not what you imagine it to be.

Conference of British Missionary Societies to Milner
18 June 1920
[CO 533 / 248 / 30445]

My Lord,

The Conference of Missionary Societies in Great Britain and Ireland at its annual meeting from June 16th to 18th had under consideration the recent Memorandum on Policy issued by His Excellency the Governor of British East Africa and the accompanying circular by the Chief Native Commissioner.

The proposals in the circular for obtaining the native labour required for non-native farms and private undertakings aroused great disquietude in the minds of members of the Conference. While compulsion is not explicitly mentioned in the circular it appears to the Conference that in practice compulsion could hardly take a stronger or more dangerous form.

The Conference is not prepared to deny that, as Lord Cromer reluctantly admitted, there may be circumstances in which compulsion may be necessary for "indispensable and recognized purposes of public utility,"[40] but it views with concern any extension of the system and holds that it should be introduced only under all possible safeguards against the occurrence of abuses and that every effort should be made to create conditions which will make it no longer necessary.

The members of the Conference desire to express their unqualified opposition to compulsory labour for private profit, which they believe to be morally wrong and fundamentally at variance with Christian conceptions of life and duty. They note with satisfaction that Colonel Amery in reply to a question in the House of Commons on February 25th[41] stated that he deprecated the application of force or illegitimate pressure to make natives work for private employers, but they cannot see how the proposals contained in the circular can fail in practice to have this effect.

They will esteem it a favour if the Conference can be supplied with a copy of the further circular to be issued by the Governor to which Colonel Amery referred in the House of Commons on April 26th,[42] and also with a copy of the Masters and Servants Ordinance mentioned in the same speech.

The members of the Conference are gravely disquieted also by the statement in the circular of the Chief Native Commissioner that "constant endeavours will be made to obtain native labour from the adjacent conquered territory." They would welcome fuller information as to the meaning of this statement, since in their view endeavours by a Mandatory Power to recruit labour for its individual advantage from the mandated territory are difficult to reconcile with the provision in the Covenant of the League of Nations that these territories shall be treated "as a sacred trust of civilization."

It is a vital interest of the work in which all the missionary societies represented in the Conference are engaged throughout the world that British rule over subject races should be exercized in accordance with Christian standards. Even those which have no work of their own in East Africa, therefore, must view with grave anxiety any proposals which appear to involve a departure from the declared policy of his Majesty's Government that it is the trustee of native interests and governs for the benefit of the population as a whole.

The Conference has had no opportunity of consulting formally the committees of the different missionary societies, but representatives of practically all the missionary organizations in Great Britain and Ireland except those of the Roman Catholic Church were present at the conference and have approved of this letter in their individual capacity.

> I am,
> Your Lordship's humble and obedient servant,
>
> J. H. OLDHAM

Oldham to Leys
21 July 1920

Your paper is excellent. I shall gladly publish it but certainly not with the note you suggest. So far from this article not representing the standpoint of the Review, it represents very definitely the ideas of those of us at this office. At the same time, the Review is not intended to have any special standpoint but to open its pages to the discussion of all sides of a question. . . . I have only one or two minor suggestions to make . . .

I wish I could say how much satisfaction I feel in publishing this article and how grateful I am to you for writing it. . . .

Leys to Oldham
23 July 1920 *

Of some phases of African life Ross' experience and knowledge is [sic] unique, in most it is better than mine. But I think I do know more than he does of the effects of mission teaching. I have lived for probably six months in the aggregate on more than a score of mission stations and have spent many hundred days in exchanging opinions on religion with Africans, Xtian, Moslem & Pagan.

I make that claim because Ross, like Willis and Arthur, never imagines a situation in Africa that can be more than a slightly modified existing situation. For instance I say that both justice and wisdom require the deprivation of the "settlers" of their political authority over their employees. Possibly in the end colonies of them may become self-governing. But in that case self support would be the corresponding economic condition of political independence. Theoretically I ought to concede to this thousandth part of the population of tropical Africa its thousandth share of those influences that determine political events. Actually that influence will for long be a mere hindrance to wise policy. These people are in fact closely similar in opinion, political & religious and in situation, in the weight and kind of influence they exert, to the slave owners in Jamaica and Alabama in the times of liberation.

* On 22 July 1920, after lunching with McGregor Ross, Oldham transmitted further suggestions for revision in hope of protecting the article against attack: Leys was at one point too critical of missionaries; the bishops had reluctantly accepted, not *advocated*, compulsion; Leys' implied recommendation that the settlers should be disfranchised was too "sweeping"; and Leys had painted too idyllic a picture of African life before the coming of Europeans.

I think Ross might agree with me if he agreed with my forecast of political events in Europe. I am not surprised that he differs from me in the place to be given to "settlers" in Africa's future.

But I *am* surprised to learn how ignorant he is of Africa's past. Africa before the XVIIIth century slave raids was, roughly, as civilised as Xth century Europe. The evidence is scattered and scanty. Livingstone's journals describe the last stages of the destruction of African civilisation.[43] The British Museum contains examples of an earlier and higher culture. The arts I describe as existing a hundred years ago did exist over almost all if not all of Bantu Africa. W. P. Young who is with me confirms my opinion.[44] From Zambesi to Nyanza and from Tanganyika to the West Coast traditions still persist of these and other arts. Sir Harry Johnston's books, inaccurate as they are, offer abundant proof of that.[45]

Returning to my first point my faith in Africans' capacity is largely founded on a wider experience than Ross' of mission results, and a greater knowledge than his of a not very remote but now dim African past. To him as to almost all Europeans in Africa the degradation of the present makes that past seem incredible. Further my estimate of future possibilities, real practical changes to be planned and worked for, differs from his because I am certain of revolution in Europe, as a consequence of which the exploiters in Africa will have the same fate as the slave owner 100 years ago.[46]

These are my comments on his two chief criticisms. On one of the others, my statement that in the view of Africans, missionaries always demand work from them, Young does not consider my account an overstatement.

It is no doubt true that only 20% of the land on the Uganda Railway is European owned. But Ross himself gave me 70% as the proportion of *first class arable* land with railway frontage owned by Europeans. He got the figure from the E.A. land office.

If my last page isn't clear I can't help it. I can't make it any clearer.

Please send this letter to Ross. He is my best African friend whose criticisms are *invaluable.* But he forgets that I am a convinced revolutionary.

Oldham to Leys
17 September 1920

We want to follow up this East African labour business. I had a long talk a day or two ago with the Bishop of Zanzibar.[47] He is on the war-path. My colleagues and I have had some talk together and the Bishop is coming to confer with us on the 30th instant at 11 o'clock. Can you join us? We want to find out what is the best ground on which to take issue and lay out a plan of campaign. . . .

Leys to Oldham
21 September 1920

I belong to two committees,[48] one mainly and the other very largely concerned with working out and getting public support for and planning to put into execution the policy for Africa that I think wise and just. I find myself in close agreement with others on these committees and I believe that the group you work with would largely agree too. But to make the work of these committees good enough to be successful I have like others to attend regularly. That means a day in London, nine hours in a train, an expenditure of 50/-, no other work done that day—all these on an average once a month, or even oftener. They cost me £40 to £50 a year. I have no income but what I earn or have earned, no shares or investments I mean. And I don't want my lungs to break down again.

These things being so I cannot go to London for any purpose except one hopeful of real results. If I was rich, if I had say £1000 in shares or something to spend £5 at a time on such visits I would gladly accept your invitation. As it is I am afraid I would find myself imperfectly in agreement with others present. With Harris, Woolf, Tawney,[49] Ormsby-Gore,[50] Bentinck,[51] Wedgwood,[52] Ross I differ so little that we can do things *together*, almost like a single mind. But I find it isn't worth while to try to work with people if we only agree on one or two things. I am afraid I would only cause fruitless argument and be thought impracticable. The B. of Zanzibar's articles don't express my mind at all. He attributes to the African a different nature from the European's. I find it hopeless to look for a common policy for Africans with those who think so.

On the other hand, if your committee makes any plans that I can help to carry out, to however small an extent, let me know. You know I will do anything I possibly can. Perhaps if the Committee draws up an outline or skeleton scheme for articles, so that a number of men could make the same points each in his own way, I might be entrusted to do one or two for missionary papers.

Are you having Harris? He and I are in 90% agreement. He knows, I mean, what I think and can represent me. With Woolf I am in 99% agreement, but as he probably doesn't call himself a Christian I suppose you won't invite him. I am afraid you won't agree that in its modern significance the term has no longer any real meaning. It may come to have a meaning again of course.

So I don't want to come. But even so if you write that you really want me and think my notions wouldn't clash, I will come. But do ask Harris to be there in my place.

On reading this over it seems indecently personal. My reason for explaining so fully is that I hate declining what may seem to promise real use, and I want you to know that conventional excuses are not what I am offering. . . .

Oldham to Leys
22 September 1920

. . . I think you would find if you joined us that those of us at this office at any rate were at least as much in harmony with your attitude as J. H. Harris whom I know very well. I have no difficulty on this score. But I realise the difficulty of making the journey and doubt whether at this particular conference, where we want to get at facts and clear our own minds, your attending would justify the cost to yourself. . . .

Oldham to Leys
5 October 1920

We had a meeting yesterday with the Bishops of Zanzibar, Uganda and Mombasa present. I enclose the draft of a document which we propose to send to the missionary societies. If, as we expect, they are willing to get behind it, we shall try to unite the religious forces of the country in an approach to the Government along these lines. I want to get the document into as good shape as possible. We cannot make radical alterations as time is the essence of the problem and the thing must go forward on the general lines on which agreement has been reached. But there is still opportunity for strengthening the argument, if necessary, at certain places and for making amendments if in my ignorance of African conditions I have introduced anything which will not stand examination.

I think you will feel, even if you disagree on certain points, that the thing is sufficiently thorough-going. The Bishops of Uganda and Mombasa have expressed their entire concurrence with our practical proposals, which are the withdrawal of the labour circulars and of the ordinance of 1920. If we make any impression, this will probably involve the resignation of Northey, but that will be all to the good.[53]

The next step will be to work out a plan of campaign. We are out, please God, for a fight. . . .

Leys to Oldham
7 October 1920

I hadn't five minutes yesterday even for beginning an answer to your letter but I thanked God for it and for its news twenty times and more. Look back, even over only the 2½ years since you came to see me in Glasgow! Bishop Gore writes, what can he *do*.[54] More and more I see that the great thing is to explain things to those who really care for God's will. It soon gets plain then what common duty is.

Your memorial seems to me entirely admirable, in every way adequate to its purpose. You see of course how great that purpose is. You have the opportunity, and are taking it to unite *all* the leaders of British churches in a policy of *action*, for the first time. They have often of course been got to repeat the same words, so long as nothing was to be done. But this time you make a quite definite set of proposals.

Allow me for a moment to attempt a kind of horoscope. You will not, I feel certain overthrow Northey or Ainsworth, or change his policy. But if you get this statement of yours published, over the

names of Canterbury[55] and Gore and all the prelates and prominent
free Churchmen, and if they in turn urge it on their people, then
within five years, perhaps much within the system will be changed.
A complete change awaits either the advent to power of the L[abour]
P[arty] *or* on your part (I include your friends of course) a positive
African political and industrial policy. That of course is your next
step! I know you shudder! I hope you will take years to plan it and
get it right, to make it wholly good and wise, which means part of
God's plan revealed in Jesus. That position and definite, albeit provisional, programme for Africa is your future task. Meanwhile you
will not overthrow Satan in his strongest seat. To do that you must
either persuade Lloyd George that a lot of Conservatives will vote
against his party if he doesn't throw over Milner Northey Hollis[56]
Ainsworth & Co.—and so get the Coalition policy changed, *or* put a
party into office with the contrary policy.

I have one suggestion for your statement to be published. Appendix II on p. 29 of the white paper is a local ordinance. To my mind
it is the worst feature of the whole case. It turns all native authorities into instruments of oppression and ensures that in cases where
they have the courage to resist they will be deposed and be replaced
by more obedient tools. It destroys the fast vanishing remnants of
African society. It means that in future there is no possibility of the
Government finding any channel through which to hear the voice of
native opinion since the only spokesmen they *might* have are entirely
transformed into Government agents with unpopular duties. Logically of course such a development was necessary. But it is and will
prove to be the most injurious of *all* recent measures. In fact there
only remains one more step to be taken, the legal imposition on the
individual of the obligation to "work," and that can be carried out
under this ordinance....

I enclose £1 for the expenses of this particular campaign. Don't
trouble to acknowledge it. I wish it was £100 but I am still in debt!

Oldham to Leys
8 October 1920

Your letter has greatly touched me. It means a great deal to know
that you, who have had this burden on you for so long, think that
we are on right lines. Your generous contribution toward expenses

also means much—infinitely more than the actual amount, though
that in itself is welcome.

Time is of the essence of the matter. . . . I am therefore not attempting to introduce into the present draft your . . . new point. All
we are asking at present, however, from the societies is that they
shall authorize an approach to the Government on these general
lines. During the next four or five weeks we shall work up the material afresh with a view to preparing the strongest possible statement
for presentation. We thus have ample time to deal with the point you
propose.

We are clearing our decks here and shall do everything in our
power to get the strongest possible body of support. There is no use
doing anything at all unless we put into it every ounce we have got. . . .

Leys to Oldham
12 October 1920

You said you were writing a fuller statement for Educational purposes. I venture to suggest points for emphasis.

1. Harris is perfectly right in his insistence on the falsity of the pic-
    ture that shows idle people in their own villages turned into vir-
    tuous and industrious people on European plantations. The
    whole allegation of African idleness is a "rump," a "stunt," the
    work of people who would never get the British public to work
    their wicked will to enslave unless they get the B[ritish] p[ublic]
    to believe the African lives in luxurious idleness. Actually the
    villager works harder than the plantation labourer.

2. That is because what is done under compulsion is badly done.
    The African is human. Compulsion in Europeans means shirk-
    ing, cheating, lying, deserting. So among Africans. Even in my
    time I have seen 100 men do one man's work in a day between
    them. The cause is not because these men hate work as work.
    It is because that kind of exertion brings them nothing of value.

3. To build the church in any country a foundation in a stable soci-
    ety is necessary. There must be marriage for lifetime,[57] homes for
    children, time for children to go to school, work for six days in
    the week that brings in not merely money but the enlightenment
    and discipline of true education, work that a man can be proud

of as his own, that he can thank God for help in doing it well and look back upon in old age while his children do even better in it. That is the only kind of society in which a healthy church is possible, the only kind of circumstances in which real human brotherhood can grow. That involves the political and industrial policy of material development in and round the homes of the people. Africans are hungry for that. Missionaries long for it. Missions cannot carry out such a policy. Only governments can. *In the existing balance of political forces they dare not.* Such a policy would diminish the flow of labour to plantations and raise wages.

4. Most important of all is the fatal blow to native institutions given by the "Native Authority Ordinance" and the amending Ordinance (at end of White paper).[58] These simply turn all native functionaries into slave raiders. Sheer anarchy will be their result. They turn a tribe into a band of Ishmaels.

Slavery on railways and plantations is bad enough. But in my time in Africa there was real liberty in the villages. The people were poor because there was nothing for them to do, at home, but grow food. But they had some real home life and didn't *feel* helpless. They went to church and school and listened to a new plan of life, responsively, like the ignorant crowd in Galilee. But these new laws mean nobody will be safe in any village. The village despot can do as he likes so long as he satisfies the Government. Just read the clauses. How can these people believe in any new plan of life revealed in Jesus? They *experience* a quite different one that breaks up families, takes all the young men away from the girls they court to labour camps where prostitutes abound, denies the *possibility* of *home life.*

Don't trouble to answer this. . . .

Leys to Oldham
23 October 1920

The enclosure explains itself.[59] Please read it carefully. You will find in it an almost perfect answer to the three questions you asked me.

You see my evidence on the whole subject is defective because my sixteen years in Eastern Africa included some ten different stations. I never had time to have really intimate knowledge of any one tribe. That intimacy my friend Wilson has in as great perfection as is possible to a European in Africa.

If I had got the article two months ago I would have wanted you to print it instead of my own. As it is I hope that, with one correction of a mistake due I fear to my having misled him, you will put it in your next issue. If you don't I would like it typed in your office—I will pay for that of course—so that a few copies of it can be circulated. My own judgement of the article is that it is by far the best article on the whole subject yet written. In fact its great merits, its vivid picturing of naked facts, its sobriety of tone, its appeal to what is found in the consciences of all, make me fear it is too good for any periodical except your own—or perhaps "East & West." Its value to you and the movement you are leading is unique.... How wonderfully things are working *together*. It is that feature which makes success certain, and only a matter of time....

P.S. One man who ought to read this is Curtis. You spoke of him as a helper in your cause. I feel bound to tell you that I wrote an article for him a year ago.[60] He accepted it and paid for it—handsomely—and then a month or two later rejected it when he realised how it would offend his powerful and wealthy friends in politics and industry. He called the article overstated. That of course is a personal incident. But everyone I know who has had dealings with him gives him the character of a sympathetic man with a keen sense of justice who always draws back when he counts the cost of action—in his case the word meaning of course publishing the facts. He will never help a cause when it is at the stage of being decided by sensible people. There are plenty of nice people in the world who are quite useless for getting things done.

I see an answer by Amery in the Commons makes it clear that compulsory labour for government is designed, *together with the fixing of the wage by Govt*, to make all who do not work for private employers do their two months.[61] In effect that applies compulsion to all. I do hope you will make that clear to your friends who think that in theory compulsion for public services is justifiable.

Oldham to Leys
27 October 1920

Thank you very much for sending me Wilson's paper, which I
have read with the greatest interest. It is a splendid statement, both
in spirit and matter, and it will be of use to me in the present campaign. I do not think, however, that I can find a place for it in the
Review. . . . If we publish anything directly related to the situation
in the Kenia colony it ought to be something written from the point
at which we have arrived in our own thinking here, rather than from
the somewhat different angle from which Mr. Wilson writes at a distance. . . .

Leys to Oldham
31 October 1920

. . . I have a friend of 25 years standing who is now one of the
secretaries to the Imperial Cabinet. If you ever want advice on matters of procedure, how to approach Lloyd George or other poten-
tates, he would help. He knows about the Eastern African situation
and is in sympathy with our views. He and I are intimate enough to
make it certain that if you want a half hour's talk with him he would
give it to you and would give any help in his power—in an entirely
confidential way of course. I would confidently expect him to be as
frank and helpful to you as he would be to me if I asked his advice or
help. If you ever need him, write to Thomas Jones. . . . [62] He is a
man of great experience of men and things, of great acuteness of
mind, and eminently helpful.

Leys to Oldham
12 November 1920

Your detailed argument is most excellent. [63] But while the alternative policies are clearly described you do not clearly demand the
adoption by authority of the right one. I expect you are wise in using
so mild a tone. But I hope that in the result the C.O. won't find it
easy to say soothing things and make no change in policy in Africa.
My whole difficulty is that I cannot imagine real change until men

with different conceptions are in office in Downing St. & in Africa. If that is so, then your policy of explaining alternatives to the Xtian public, and getting facts investigated, is the only right one. I strongly urge that you get your statement published in every missionary & church paper in the country. That would be of the highest value.

Oldham to Leys
17 November 1920

... I am glad you feel satisfied with the memorandum. I tried to make the tone as moderate as possible, with a view to enlisting the maximum amount of support in order to get the thing through. But our actual proposal is the most effective one for getting something really done that we can think of. It may mean a great deal more than could be accomplished by the mere withdrawal of the Circular. That would not necessarily deal with the real causes of the evil and these would only manifest themselves in new ways. An enquiry gives us the chance of getting at fundamental principles. Of course, everything depends on the terms of reference and personnel. Lord Milner will be told quite clearly that we must be satisfied on these points and the Prime Minister will be given a hint that if the very moderate demands made are not satisfied, there is likely to be an agitation which will re call that on Chinese labour fifteen years ago.[64]

We have got the assent of all the heads of churches and there is promise of very influential lay support. I understand from the Bishop of Zanzibar that the letters of the Labour party will back it. We are getting at a group of Conservatives in the House of Commons....

I think the chances of getting the Commission are not unfavourable. If we do get it, we must spare no pains to see that the things we regard as important are kept fully before it and that there is a steady pressure from the Christian conscience of this country.

Leys to Oldham
18 November 1920

The longer I reflect the more certain I feel that your plan is the best, in spite of the long delay it involves. But by relying wholly on a future enquiry you make everything depend on three points.

1. The members of the Commission.

2. Its terms of reference.

3. The evidence.

Are you going to have the evidence got up by counsel? If so you will want money. I would give £10—perhaps much more. Whether you take that means or some other evidence must be collected & sifted. I strongly urge your keeping Ross informed. No other single witness will be so valuable. A letter from him today suggests that as I feared he will soon be forced to resign. So there is no time to be lost. Get him to start interviewing witnesses & collecting evidence. Also, why not ask Hooper (Kenya),[65] Wilson (Nyasaland) & Cripps (Rhodesia) to act as local collecting agents for evidence. Those heartily on our side should be got to write it down for use (confidentially) by the man getting our case up. We must see to it, for instance, that important points are proved over a wide area. The whole of the evidence must fit together.

But my reason for writing now is to urge another point. Native policy is our subject. But actually existing native policy is a mere consequence of the pursuit of another aim. If you want the whole truth the terms of reference must include in addition to those you mention:

1. The treatment by Govt. of European immigrants—the whole policy of Eur. settlement. The subject of land rights is bound up, for instance, with the history of Eur. land settlement. We *must* bring out the fact that Govt. has given 3 or 4 thousand Europeans land worth millions for next to nothing and in many other ways given them privileges denied to natives paid for out of native taxation.

2. Relations between Europeans and natives, e.g. injustices in courts.

So many commisssions have been stultified by narrow terms of reference. Don't trouble to answer.

Oldham to Leys
22 November 1920

Thank you for your letter. If we get the commission we must certainly set on foot every possible agency to secure evidence from all those who have the interests of natives at heart. This can, however, wait I think until the commission is appointed. We must first know the kind of commission, the terms of reference and the personnel before we can set to work to make effective plans for getting evidence before it. At present I am very much concerned about the terms of reference. The main points seem to me the following:

(1) The extent and adequacy of native reserves.

(2) The amount of land alienated to Europeans, the estimated supply of labour necessary to cultivate these lands and the extent to which the demand can be met from the existing native population without interference with the healthy development of native life.

(3) The extent to which the impact of western civilisation is destroying tribal institutions. The effect of this upon (a) administration and (b) native habits and family life, and the measures necessary to tide over the transformation period and ensure the healthy evolution of native life.

(4) The economic and educational advancement of the people through teaching improved methods of agriculture and development of native industries, education, the dissemination of knowledge of health and sanitation.

(5) The means of securing effective expression of native opinion in the government of the country, the adequate representation and protection of native interests and the means of training natives in responsibility and self-government.

Please let me know what you think of this.

Leys to Oldham
19 December 1920

I am troubled about these terms of reference for your hoped for Royal Commission. I am afraid I think for once that you have not expressed the full nature of the problem. The situation to be examined is that in their own country, where such rights as the British Government has were acquired by the gift of native communities, these native communities have, by a process of legislation and administration pursued for thirty years, at length reached the position of a servile caste. The three characteristics of that servile status are (1) that about a third (a half?) of the best arable land has been granted by the Crown to non-Africans while over the remainder Africans have no rights whatever; (2) that the development of that alienated land by the dispossessed for the profit of the dispossessors has gradually come to be regarded as the moral duty of the natives, as their political duty as loyal subjects (though they were not subjects but until 1920 foreign protected persons!), and now at length as their legal duty and (3) that in many less important matters Africans have by that 30 years process acquired a semi servile status, e.g. being forbidden to travel in certain areas, to sleep in certain other areas, to grow certain crops, even to accept employment in certain conditions—all these legal disabilities lying on the natives of the country only.

It is that whole system whereby Africans rest, in their social, political and industrial relations, in an inferior status from which the law forbids escape that I hope is challenged and will be examined by the Commissioners. Of that system the events of 1920 are a natural and even inevitable development. Recent policy is no new departure. It is merely a new step in a direction already plainly fixed.

I do not know how far the Bishops would agree in that view. I hope you do. If it is the true view then the nature of the task of the Commission should be to examine the whole policy of East African Governments for the past generation. (Does it not support my interpretation of events that Milner, Northey, Ainsworth, the settlers are genuinely surprised that so much fuss has been made?)

I know too little about Commissions to draft detailed terms of reference. I suspect it may be wiser to avoid details, to ask Commissioners to examine the political and industrial policy followed by Government as regards both Africans and non Africans. I hope you will get the very best expert advice on such a point. But I would be most grateful if before the terms are fixed you would do your best to ensure that the following details will be included in those to which the Commission gives attention.

1. The treaties with native communities—how far they have been fulfilled, what future obligations, if any, they confer on Govern-

ments, what rights, if any are by them preserved to native communities, *and especially* whether any such rights have or should be given protection of our courts.

2. Land grants to Europeans, the terms on which granted and held, the sums paid in purchase or as rent, as compared with market values at the present time, the existence of native rights in native law over such grants, and the compensation paid for them or due: the degree to which the alienated land has been improved: the advisability of legislation revising rents or imposing new charges.

3. Lands in native occupation: security of their tenure: adequacy for future development (in case of each important tribe separately): the extent of development of industry in such lands, and of Government help in development, especially as compared with help to European owners: how far in future industry in native communities should be encouraged: whether in any case, and if ever when, natives should be advised to leave home to work and when to develop their own land: how far our courts do, how far they should recognise customary native tenures (in fact of course at present they don't recognise them at all!).

4. The powers and duties of native authorities in tribes: what policy should be followed in their development: what kind of constitutions should be encouraged: what duties should in future be given them.

5. Under what legal or other disabilities do natives suffer? Which laws impose obligations or disabilities or penalties that do not fall on non Africans? How far are these wise?

6. Education. The sums spent by missions, by Governments? The numbers educated, by missions, by Governments? In conquered territory, do. do. do. do, by Government? On what plan future education to be followed?

7. Native opinion, existence, extent of discontent; its causes, its remedies. What chiefs, what educated natives, what ordinary natives desire in policy?

8. Health. Changes in population in 30 years? Causes of loss of population? Health of labourers in different areas, death rates?

Food and housing and facilities for family life among labourers? Measures recommended.

9.   Taxation: *how distributed now*? how it should be?

Terms of reference should include *all above*. May I suggest that you should send a copy of your own draft terms and of this letter both to Ross and to Wilson of the U.M.C.A. asking them for their own and for friends' suggestions?

I do hope you won't be in a hurry. If the terms are too narrow, and especially if they only regard recent developments the whole scheme will be useless.

Oldham to Leys
22 December 1920

... The terms of reference in the memorandum which we submitted are simply an expansion (a.nd to that extent an improvement in the direction you want) of the terms in the earlier draft which you passed. It is, I am afraid, too late now to make any change, as the memorandum has gone in. In any case, I fear that the Colonial Office will draw up its own terms of reference. The only thing we can do is to press on them that the section of public opinion in whose name the approach was made will not be satisfied unless the inquiry raises quite sharply the issue of the discharge of the obligations of trusteeship and unless it is wide enough to cover all the points set forth in our memorandum. There are no means known to us of bringing this home to the Colonial Office which we have not employed and we must hope for the best.

As a matter of fact, several of the points in your letter are actually included in the list in the memorandum. As regards the others, while I should gladly have put them in if I had had time, I think if the main purpose is to face the question of trusteeship, there ought to be no difficulty in getting them looked at. It will probably be an advantage if the terms of reference are not too explicit so that the Commission will be left to draw up its own programme. Everything will then turn on the personnel. This we cannot control, but we are doing what lies in our power to press in various ways for the appointment of a Commission that in its personnel will inspire confidence among those who have made the approach.

There, I think, we must leave it for the present. We have done all that we knew. God has helped us so far and we must trust the matter to His hands with the prayer and hope that he will so order it that the way may be opened for us to continue to press for righteous dealing in our relations with the subject races of the empire. . . .

Leys to Oldham
[n.d., c. 24 December 1920]

Thanks. I had no idea you would have to *define* your demands at this stage. If your legal advisers tell you that you cannot later, when the Commission comes to be appointed, provide it with a fuller set of instructions for investigating then there is no use in sending copies of my letter to Africa—and don't bother doing it. But I don't see why, on the publication of the Govt's terms of reference, you should not successfully press for their amendment; if only you are ready beforehand, with members of Parliament with points at fingers' ends. I do hope you have found a legal adviser with enthusiasm as well as knowledge. . . .

Oldham to Leys
28 December 1920

Thank you for your card. We have taken no legal advice and I do not think that any legal question arises at the present stage.

The position is this. We decided to ask for the appointment of a royal commission. In order to make sure that it would be the kind of commission we want we enumerated some of the points which the enquiry must cover. Much the most important issue is that it should deal definitely with the obligations of trusteeship. If we secure this everything else can probably be brought in under that head. But we thought it well to be more specific and went into greater detail. We took the best advice and you, among others, approved of the few simple heads in the earlier draft. As the result of advice which came to me we elaborated these further bringing in some additional points. Having done this we sent in the memorandum. We cannot now send in a supplementary statement. In any case I suppose the Government will settle its own terms of reference. That finishes the first stage.

We have no intention of letting the matter rest. I quite agree with you that there will be further stages. It is conceivable that the Colonial Office may consult us—probably through the Arch-bishop—regarding the proposed terms of reference. It is quite possible that they may not. When the terms of reference are published I hope that they will be sufficiently wide to bring in everything we want. Our chance then will be with the chairman of the commission. We shall have to persuade him that the points which we regard as important ought to receive full attention.

All this is on the assumption that there will be a royal commission: that, of course, is not yet settled. We have done everything in our power and must now pray that our efforts may bear fruit.

You will see I do not regard the question as in any sense closed . . . .

Oldham to Lionel Curtis
[Nashville, Tenn.]
11 February 1921
[International Missionary
Council (Geneva), Box 315]

I have just completed a week's visit to Tuskegee and Calhoun.[66] It has been my first intimate contact with leaders of the Negro race. It has confirmed and deepened the impressions made by previous more casual contacts.

What strikes one most in contrast with national and racial situations elsewhere is the extraordinary sanity of outlook of the Negro leaders and the absence of any kind of sourness of disposition notwithstanding the discrimination and disabilities of which they are daily reminded. They exhibit restraint and balance of judgment, a power of recognizing and reckoning with facts, patience in working towards a far distant goal, a concentration of their energies in constructive efforts and a cheerful optimism to which I know no parallel. This is no doubt partly due to the magnificent tradition established by Booker Washington, but it is so general and widespread although of course by no means universal that one cannot help recognizing in it the expression of very admirable and valuable racial qualities.[67] The Indian situation would be much more hopeful than it is if Indians possessed a larger measure of those gifts.

I have met two or three men from Africa, and in particular have had two or three long talks with a man from Rhodesia who has been for ten years in the United States, and after taking a two years postgraduate course at Chicago University is now on the staff at Tuskegee.[68] He wants to go back to Rhodesia to help in the uplift of his own people. He is thoroughly loyal and has the Tuskegee outlook. But as I talked with him I touched exactly the same things that one knows so well in one's Indian friends. It may be long in coming but sooner or later we shall have the same situation in Africa that we are facing in India. The African students studying in the United States have formed an African Students Association, embracing all African students studying in America. It holds annual conferences and has a definitely Christian character. The striking thing to me is how all these men have an African consciousness; their loyalty and interest is not Liberian or Rhodesian or Gold Coast, but African. The man to whom I have specially referred is a better educated man than the average missionary. The number of educated Africans at present is small, but they hold their own with the European just as the Indian can do.

We ought to look ahead and see whether we cannot so build that when (at however distant a time) we reach the stage which we have now reached in India and Egypt we shall have a situation more easy to deal with. We must have this Royal Commission. If I felt this before I left England I feel it much more intensely after my experiences here.

Francis Peabody[69] says without exaggeration in regard to Hampton that the visitor there "finds himself observing in a corner of the world the way in which the entire world ought to be directed and controlled—a great spiritual tradition penetrating and illuminating daily life, lifting work into worship, and showing its faith in its works." The same thing might be said of Tuskegee. As I reflect that this achievement, to which I know of no exact parallel in respect of the missionary spirit in the broadest sense which inspires not only the workers in the Institutes, but thousands of others who are carrying the tradition into rural communities throughout the southern states, has been in large part the work of a generation of freed slaves and their children, and as I think of the possibilities in the Negro race which it reveals, I desire intensely that we should do something really worth while for the African peoples of our Empire, and build a monument as great and enduring as that which has been built, and is still being built, as a result of the faith, breadth of vision and courage of Armstrong,[70] Frissell[71] and Booker Washington, and the men and women whom they have inspired.

The news of Lord Milner's resignation just before I sailed was a blow.[72] How do things stand in regard to the appeal for a Royal Commission? Even if we have to do the work over again, or have to wait, we must not let the question rest; and we cannot afford to wait too long. . . .

P.S. This letter was begun at Tuskegee. Since coming to Nashville I have heard a great deal more from the other side of the Negro question, which I knew existed. But this enhances, rather than diminishes, the greatness of Booker Washington's achievement.

Leys to Oldham
[postmark 29 April 1921]

Your letter & mine crossed.[73] I examine the situation afresh every few weeks and am always driven for much the same reasons as formerly to conclude that your plan is probably the best. If only I had time to collect outline evidences! We really need a special person for the purpose to do on a smaller scale what the anti Corn Law people in England or the prohibition people in the USA did. It will be difficult to get a man knowing enough of Africa and enough of political methods too.

Leys to Borden Turner [74]
3 May 1921

. . . There is no such [forced labor] problem, I believe, in British West Africa. That in itself is significant. Indeed the dilemma, "what are you to do when necessary work (Scavenging or transport, for instance) would be left undone if compulsion were forbidden," is no real dilemma. The important question to be answered first is, how are those men employed who in other countries do the necessary work?

There are two kinds of ways in which the natives of East Africa employ themselves. Most of them for the whole or part of each year earn wages from Europeans. There are no figures for the whole area. But the differential tax in Nyasaland proves that over nine-tenths in that Protectorate qualify for the lower rate of poll tax by engaging in some occupation specially approved by the Government, most of them in wage earning. If I said that three quarters of the able bodied males in Eastern Africa worked for wages for the whole or part of each year I would more likely be under than over the mark.

Second, of course, natives grow their own food. In every tribe some part of the annual round of duties is done by men, not women. Where, as is usual, 25 per cent to 75 per cent of them at a time are away from home wage earning, the rest have to work harder or food runs short. It runs short even now. Only in rare perfect seasons does the average village in Eastern Africa get enough to eat in spring. Incidentally, nothing is ever done to improve seed or introduce simple machinery in the so called reserves.

Now most natives do some of both kinds of work. Not one in a hundred does neither. There are no unemployed. And there are no idle rich except among the elderly. The statement may excite surprise. That is because Europeans in the tropics use the word work as synonymous with wage earning. The unstated middle term of the syllogism assumed in the dilemma is that food growing is so easy and pleasant as to be amusing or exhilarating rather than exhausting. No body who has tried it thinks so. The planters of course in Africa are not, with very few exceptions, tillers of the soil. I don't mean that they are idle, though many are, just as many large farmers in England are. I mean that their real work is a manager's work, not a cultivator's. Not even the few who do use a plough are independent of hired Africans. The average European "on the land" in Eastern Africa runs an agricultural factory with from one to two thousand or more hands upon it.

It is the policy of the various governments to induce the natives to leave home to work for Europeans. Various means are used. In one protectorate the stay at home pays double tax. Even that device no longer induces natives to offer themselves in numbers sufficient to satisfy the planters. In every protectorate (I exclude Tanganyika territory because of insufficient knowledge though it is at least highly probable the same course is followed) magistrates instruct "chiefs" (whose source of authority is now mainly of European origin) to send men to work. Generally a quotum of men is given. In Kenya Colony, where the procedure is regularised, most of the wage earners are so recruited, so that to some extent all the labour is "forced." There is less compulsion in the dry and more in the rainy season, less in years of bad and more in years of good harvest, less in certain tribes whose members, like American Indians, violently hate any work but the supplying of their own needs. But, taken all over, the factor of compulsion in supplying the labour market has of recent years so increased as to be the chief. If, that is to say, magistrates and chiefs ceased their efforts I doubt if a quarter of the existing wage earners would come out to work.

It is worthy of note that the noise recently made at home about the whole business has merely aggravated the situation. Magistrates are warned in confidential circulars that there must be no scandals. Moral suasion is the approved term. In a Nairobi newspaper a magistrate is reported to have "turned out" 2,000 natives to serve the flax crop of the planters of his district. I have no doubt his suasion was most moral. But I doubt if the headmen were so scrupulous. And I have no doubt whatever that the same urgency that led to the levy was felt in the native villages and that the flax was won at the cost of grain stores. That flax means young children short of food some day to be weakling shiftless pilfering labourers. It also means that many will leave home for wage earning because food is short at home.

The pretence that the system is not compulsory is the most dangerous falsehood. To both European and native, refusal to follow a magistrate's instructions is sedition. That is an inevitable consequence of two factors, the utter powerlessness of the natives to influence law and administration and the adoption by Governments of a policy of economic as well as political control. Natives of course desert by hundreds. But, since the passing of the finger print and pass law ordinances, that merely means exchanging a plantation overseer and a wage of fourpence a day for a prison warder with a rifle and nothing a day.

I am trying to describe the background of the situation that leads to the dilemma I cited, "necessary work will remain undone or compulsion used."

There is one more phase to be considered. During the war there

was industrial conscription all over Eastern Africa (by legal enact-
ment almost everywhere). The 30 per cent to 40 per cent (at a guess)
of able bodied natives always absent at one time from home in the
average village rose to 70 per cent, 80 per cent or 95 per cent. The
whole machinery of industry in the village ran down. Houses, normally rebuilt about every 6 or 8 years, had to last somehow. Food
was so short that seed corn was eaten. Large areas were literally
devastated by war. Loss of life was enormous—there are no figures
but the Kenya Government admitted 23,000 deaths among its un-
armed porters. When peace came every man was needed in the
villages to build and to hoe. Just then however homes for several thousand heroes were offered by Government in Eastern Africa. A grateful country gave them, or sold them at under market price, land that
neither by treaty nor by cession nor by conquest was theirs to give.
There were supposed to be 2,000 soldier settlers (ex officers) in
Kenya Colony; actually many never settled on their 320 or 640 acre
"homesteads." Not a penny do one of these men earn except by help
of Africans' muscles.

Legal forced labour for "essential public works or services" always
exempts those who have already earned wages during the year.
(Proof of two months "work" is necessary for exemption in Kenya
Colony. In an answer to a question in Parliament it was stated that
proof of having worked at home would also be ground for exemption. Nobody of African experience would have given so preposter-
ous an answer. How is such work to be proved? And anyhow, these
idlers in native villages are as fictitious as ostriches with heads in
sand, lions retreating before the human gaze and other fabulous
monsters. We may be quite certain that the promise to exempt the
peasant cultivator will not be kept. He is the very man who is wanted
for plantation and railway.) What kind of men are public servants
likely to get for "essential works and services" by gleaning among
the leavings of voluntary and semi volunteer labour? Obviously either the bone lazy or those specially attached to home, mainly the
former. Most of these forced men will work after a fashion of course,
but average efficiency will be very low. Hence the open uncompromising opposition to compulsion by law of the Director of Public
Works in Kenya Colony, who is alone in that opposition in Council
and among higher officials. The planters are for that reason deter-

mined to be rid of him and he is likely to be served as the late Colonial Secretary was, who was forced to resign in spite of his quieter and more moderate attitude.[75]

When therefore I say that forced labour is always and everywhere unwise and injurious in Africa it is because in reality it is no more than a bye product of a system founded on prostitution of political power to serve the profits of aliens. Regarded in vacuo it is logically justifiable. But in real African life resort to legal compulsion proves the prevalence of unjust and unwise abuse of Government influence over what should be a free labour market.

Someone on our Committee suggested that my remedy of compelling the payment of extra wages to forced labourers would eventually raise the general wage rate. I admit that in existing circumstances it would. The reason of course is that the factor of compulsion operates throughout the whole system. Where land in England is bought under compulsion, the fact that the seller is given a higher than market rate for his land does not raise the value of neighbouring land. It might of course if there was no free market in land. And that is the true situation of labour in Eastern Africa. Rates of wages, for example, scarcely vary with variations either in demand for labour or in prices of commodities. Three quarters of the wage earners in Africa from Zambesi to Nile are paid three to five pence a day—Why? Why not two pence? Why not a shilling? It is some answer to say that the local rate has some relation to the amount of poll tax. Prices of everything from Europe are over twice what they were but wages have only risen about 25 per cent, because the tax has risen by about as much. Wages in fact are fixed by Governments in concert with planters. That is the last rivet in the iron band of compulsion. None can doubt that men at four-pence a day are wastefully used. The rate in fact makes it cheaper than slave labour since costs of replacement are saved.

One great source of loss in efficiency is of course disease. The two chief diseases are malaria, and ankylostomiasis, infection by a blood sucking intestinal worm. The first is air carried and so the means of protection is mosquito netting. The other is picked up by walking with bare feet over infected ground. If everybody slept under nets, malaria in most places would die out, and if everybody was well shod, ankylostomiasis would die out completely everywhere. How

can labourers buy nets and boots for themselves and their families
on four pence a day? These it may be said are sentimental considerations, irrelevant to economic fact. If industry cannot support a
higher standard of health, then no humanitarian effort can ensure
it. Let us then examine the purely economic problem as a whole.
Some thousands of square miles in Eastern Africa have been alienated to Europeans. There was plenty of room for them. But they do
not fill it. All they do is to divert labour from village to plantation.
They add nothing to its sum except by an all too scanty use of machinery. More than that, I assert that if every native man in Eastern
Africa spent nine months in every year in labour for Europeans the
land already alienated would still be insufficiently developed. From
the streets of Nairobi you can see mile upon mile of fertile land with
adequate rainfall without a hut or an upturned sod. "Scandalous,"
say the big game hunter and the globe trotter. "Turn out the idle
scamps from the villages." For ten years at least Governments have
done all they can to turn them out, short of the power given by owning their persons. What has the result been?

The Belgian Commission that reported last year estimates that
since slavery was abolished the population of tropical Africa has
been halved.[76] Where, in the Belgian Congo, exploitation was most
rapid, it has halved in thirty years. In Kenya Colony official estimates show a fall from about four and a half millions to just over
three millions in thirty years. The more exact figures of recent years
prove that the rate is accelerating. True, the fall, as the Belgian
Commission says, has a variety of causes, many of them interrelated.
Polygamy is one. Disease is a greater but never an independent
cause. With rare honesty the Commission laid its finger on what is
everywhere the preeminent cause, exploitation for profit by alien
landowners.

A society has been founded with a bureau in Paris, to win Africa
for the Africans. At its head is M. Burghart du Bois, a man of character, ability and power to lead in quite exceptional degree.[77] So far
it is only educated negroes who are attached to the movement. But
plans are being laid for a new liberation campaign, to be preached
to Africans, not to Europeans, and to every African. The twentieth
century will find the African no longer the patient docile drudge he
has been. As things are, the field is ripe for one of those devastating

uprisings that carry before them those suddenly become conscious of injustice. There is only one safeguard, the simpler kind of liberty. The only sound criticism of the programme "Africa for the Africans" is that there are not enough of them to use all the continent. Suppose that criticism to be just—though why ignore the fact that three centuries of spoliation have half emptied the continent of human creatures?—then it may be right to give such land as is equitable to take to men from overflowing countries like India, but why not leave Africans not only land that is their own but leave them also free to use it, free to refuse to be helots for the profit of the conquerors?

The alleged necessity of forced labour in Eastern Africa springs from the fundamental wrong and folly of imagining that Africans can be turned into passive instruments for the production of wealth for aliens. In no circumstances is forced labour either politically wise or economically valuable.

I have written with no special reference to Tanganyika territory. Eastern Africa is by every test except those of our introducing a single country, inhabited by a single race. And it is governed from a single source in Downing Street. Even in Portuguese territory most of the people who matter both in official and industrial life, are English. All the higher officials in Tanganyika territory were trained in neighbouring protectorates, and took part in the fatal beginnings of the new policy though I am sure they would disapprove of its latest odious developments, as indeed in private do most of the administrative rank and file. But one of the facts that make the situation of East African politics unique is that there is nothing to stop the gathering momentum of a bad policy except disaster. In a free country public opinion would be at the least a brake, at the most a new corrective force. In Africa private wealth is insatiable. As one form of pressure fails another is demanded. And Governments find no ground of principle on which to refuse, while each year the power of wealth is more strongly entrenched in law, and on legislatures.

The only remedy is to deal with forced labour as with slavery, of which indeed it is one of the endless varieties in form it can assume, to sweep it away, to make it plain to every African that whether he lives and works at home or away from home, whether he persuades an employer to pay him five shillings a day or is persuaded to work for a penny a day are matters with which no public servant has any concern. I freely admit that two thirds of the labourers will promptly go home when they hear that news. But it is just as certain that labourers would be forthcoming for "essential works and services." True, they would ask for more than fourpence a day. But then they would earn, when really free, several times as much. P.S. Public announcement was made in the Nairobi papers in February that the Government would do all it could to co-operate with planters in reducing standard wages.

In summary these are the essential facts. Europeans in Eastern Africa consider that Africans are under a moral obligation to work for them. Since opinion in Europe renders former methods of compulsion impracticable, the prestige and authority of Governments are fully expended in inducing the natives to leave home to work for wages. The plan is successful from the planters' standpoint. By its means a far higher proportion of natives do engage to work for Europeans than would be possible by any other means, and all necessity to tempt them by higher wages or better conditions is avoided. But even the high proportion thus attained fails to satisfy. The few who escape the force of the various kinds of pressure and for as long as twelve months have no master are now compelled by law to work for Government. Finally, by concerted action between Governments and other Employers a wage rate already the lowest in the world is to be further reduced—avowedly to raise profits.

This unique economic policy is rendered possible by the complete absence of political rights among the natives. Just as they have no legal rights whatever in land so they have no influence in law and administration. There is no means of redress except rebellion, and no way of expressing native wishes that is not seditious. So the policy proceeds and developes automatically, propelled by the momentum of its original motive, the profit of European landowners. The scheme is now complete. The hand of the all powerful state reaches each single man, appoints to him his task, decides remuneration. It is slavery. It is a system incapable of reform. It is capable only of abolition.

Oldham to Leys
30 May 1921

I enclose a fresh memorandum which we have sent in to Major Wood[78] privately through the Archbishop. . . . But of course the decision will lie with his chief. Little as I like Churchill, he has imagination and if we can only get him to see that things are wrong he has one great advantage that he is not likely to be deterred by opposition from the permanent officials. . . .

Leys to Oldham
31 May 1921

    . . . I don't know how you passed that sentence by.[79] It seems to be doubtful. Think of it this way. Suppose—by no means a baseless supposition—that maximum assistance to the Empire would result from labour of the other type, i.e. by a native peasantry on its own land, would "help" be wise to get Africans to choose village life rather than plantation life? For note that there is no way of helping European landowners to get labour than by persuading men who are potential wage earners to accept employment rather than support themselves at home. It is the preferential treatment of the non African in Africa from which the whole series of evil springs. And in that sentence you grant its claim—not to be helped, that would merely be a truism, but to be "helped to secure the labour they desire." Economically, I believe there *is* a future for production in Africa under European control. But that future awaits the transformation of Trop. agriculture by machinery. In that day the long rows of men with hoes, or picking cotton into baskets, or pushing trucks among sisal plants will disappear. Industries, in native villages, in which hand work is unavoidable, e.g. tea & cocoa & coffee, will absorb these men while maize and sisal & cotton will be grown at half the cost by engineers not by cultivators. To help the European to "secure the labour he desires" merely postpones that day.

(2)   Did you see the leader on E.A. in yesterday's Manch Guardian? In case you didn't please get it. Chelmsford's demand for a Royal Commission to enquire into E.A. policy ought to be combined with yours, and the enquiry should cover policy in the whole E.A. area for which Imp. Parliament is responsible.

(3)   Forgive me for my anxiety lest no preparations are being made

for coordinating evidence. If you can give time to it you are by far the best man to get up our case. But somebody ought to be doing it now. McGregor Ross should be the most valuable witness of all.

(4)   I should prefer delay until we have a Govt. which would appoint more liberal minded men. You may be right in expecting the wrath of man to praise God and turn men like Churchill into Balaams. It seems to me a risky game. . . .

Oldham to Leys
1 June 1921

. . . The sentence on which your keen and critical eye has fastened in the memorandum is not mine but Milner's. It really should have appeared in inverted commas. If I had had your criticism in time, I should have altered it to remove any chance of misconception. The whole of the rest of the memorandum is, of course, an argument against the interpretation that you place on it. I agree with all you say and it is precisely this interpretation of the sentence that moves me to protest. I am not prepared to deny that the welfare and work of settlers is a legitimate concern of the Government and I do not think that the sentence necessarily conceded more than this. Everything turns on what are "lawful and reasonable means" and the whole purport of the memorandum is to deny that "persuading men who are potential wage earners to accept employment rather than support themselves at home" is wrong. What I should not object to would be a really far-seeing policy which, taking the long view, would aim at developing a healthy, prosperous native life in the reserves, believing that as a result of such a policy there would be a supply of surplus labour which, with power to make satisfactory terms for itself, would, to its own advantage as well as that of the European employer, find employment on plantations and farms. I think we have got to believe that there is a solution if we could only find it which, by being true and just, would be in the interests both of the natives and of the white community. . . .

We shall certainly use the lever of the Government of India demand for a royal commission. Have you seen the white papers issued

by the India Office?[80] The attitude of the Government of India on
the question of the status of Indians in the Empire is quite splendid.

I do not think that there is any fear of the royal commission being
rushed upon us. The danger is all the other way. It is very difficult
to make plans for co-ordinating evidence till we know what we are
going to get, what scope will be left to us and to whom our statement has to be addressed. You may rely on it that as soon as these
facts are available every effort will be turned on to secure the best
results. No doubt the Anti Slavery Society will also swing in with all
its resources....

An initial assault has already been made privately on Churchill
who as yet knows nothing on the subject. He undertook to read my
memorandum. I am doing my best to find out how the land lies and
at the propitious moment we shall probably make a new direct approach.

Leys to Oldham
1 June 1921

... The currency changes in Kenya Colony are being found difficult to carry out and are not yet carried out.[81] Everybody there has
been astonished to learn that to alter the value of the monetary unit
from £0.1 to £0.067 will proportionately add to the cost of all imported articles (i.e. by one third) and that compensation to large
holders of existing notes & coins will take over a million sterling.
The whole incident is a vivid illustration of the political ignorance of
those who run the country....

Oldham to Leys
2 June 1921

... I am clear that what we have to do at present is to keep up a
concentrated fire and I am extremely glad that you are going to have
a talk with Major Wood.[82]

By no means take the royal commission for granted. Tell him you
think it is absolutely essential.

We want, however, not merely to tell those in authority that a
commission ought to be appointed but also if we can (as being far

more effective) to awaken their imagination in such a way as they
themselves see the thing to be necessary. This is a thing you have the
gift of doing. Put all your strength in it. Drive home your point that
we have in East Africa to deal with a coherent, unique problem—
one that requires for its solution the highest grade of statesmanship.
Show him that it is essentially an imperial question too big for any
local government to deal with by itself. If it is left to the local governments it will inevitably be decided in the interests of that section of
the community—on a long view by no means the most important—
which at present is alone articulate and has influence with the Government. They are no worse than other people but like every other
autocracy, political or industrial, naturally see things exclusively
from their own standpoint. This means that if questions are left to
be decided locally it is practically inevitable that they will be decided
against the interests of the whole which are the real ultimate interests of the empire. The only way out is to get the best brains we have
to look at the question in a big and comprehensive way and lay down
the lines that will lead to a real solution. We are really up against a
vital issue, whether our empire in East Africa is going to be laid on
sound, true and enduring foundations or is to be built on sand, or
rather on conflict, slaughter and the devastation and ruin which follow in their train. . . .

Leys to Oldham [83]
10 June 1921

. . . Arthur traverses three of my statements.

1. The area now known as Kenya Colony came under British control 40 years ago in consequence of a series of treaties made with
various natives. None of these treaties conveyed to Britain any right
to the land, except mineral rights. We never conquered the country.
We came, avowedly, as friends to protect the rights of the inhabitants. Where then is the inaccuracy in my description of the land in
Kenya Colony as neither by treaty, cession or conquest the property
of the Government? In equity and by treaty it is the property of native tribes and their representatives.

A variety of Acts have, of course, been passed in Nairobi, which
vest the land in the Crown. These are in complete contrast with our

behaviour in West Africa, where all land is inalienably native property. They conflict with natives' treaty rights, but these are not cognisable by our courts, since they are "agreements between Sovereign
States"!! Quite recently, of course, these "Sovereign States" were
dissolved into thin air by an order in Council making a farcical and
hypocritical Protectorate into a British Colony. By what right except
that of the strongest? Where, I ask again, is the inaccuracy in saying
that land in Kenya Colony is not the Government's to give to British
officers, either by conquest, cession or treaty?

Laikipia, as the exact site of "soldier settlement" never entered
my mind. True, it is ours by treaty, the only one of its kind, made in
1912. But Arthur knows perfectly well that the Masai signed that
treaty lest worse should befall them. I have a letter in my possession
from Hollis, who made the treaty, proving that. I never, of course,
said the land was not *by law* the Government's to give. It is easy for a
Govt. to keep within the law if it can make what laws it pleases. (2)
Arthur's second criticism is a related one. He says natives "have legal rights in land." True, of recent years, the courts acting as appel-
late courts from native tribunals have been asked to decide disputes
between natives as to rights of occupancy. But that does not affect
the fact that not a single native or chief or tribe in Kenya Colony has
any redress in the courts from dispossession of any tenancy or any
claim to ownership by the Govt. *No native has any legal title whatever to land*. Europeans have. Many individuals have several square
miles of freehold, each. None of these can be disturbed except by
process of law that would also disturb other freeholders. No native
has any such security, not even for a few months. Nor is it true to say
that Govt. has respected the rights recognised by native law before
the European occupation. On the very estate Arthur occupies there
are native families whom he could (I don't say would) turn out at
will, who in native law own the land they occupy. The word "Reserve" is utterly meaningless. Natives in reserves are, in law, simply
squatters on Crown Lands with no other right in law to it than they
have when they live on land alienated to Europeans. (3) Fall in population. I take it neither Arthur nor Owen dispute the fact. I admit a
fall of 40% (official estimates) is unlikely. I implied it was. I admit
also influenza. But pandemics of influenza have happened every 40
years or so for centuries, also smallpox, still oftener. Formerly what

happened was, rapid increase in healthy years to make up for losses in epidemics. Can there be any doubt that the separation of large numbers of men from their wives diminishes birth rates? or that it leads to prostitution?

That is my answer to Arthur. I doubt if we differ much about the facts.

Owen it is impossible to answer.[84] He assumes throughout that the satisfaction of the settlers' demand for labour is a necessity. These 2000 souls to my mind matter no more than 2000 Kavirondo. I admit that I treated them in Africa as of greater importance. I took more care, for instance, in attending them when sick. But when I come to try to think straight I find that in actual fact (in the language of our faith "in God's Eyes") they are 2000 humans. What is unique about the situation that handful of people is in is not their importance, not their alleged indispensability economically, but the fact that their profits depend on getting cheap African labour. Everywhere else in the world that would be felt to disqualify them from having control of these labourers politically, would be recognised to make it impossible for them to be impartial. If their demands are to be regarded as "requirements" then our solution to the problem is impossible. I have always defended their characters. They are just ordinary men. But to aim at changing their minds so as to get them to regard Africans as of equal value with themselves and so through that change to change Govt. policy in Africa is mere madness. As well expect publicans to reform licencing laws and wait until they are convinced of their necessity.

I don't understand O's figures at all. If the 77,000 is average number "required" (as I prefer to say, demanded) to be at work at one time it really means at least double as many, probably nearly three times, if separate persons are counted. That may explain our different estimates. Mine I admit were only guesses. I said so. I was drawing an inference from the fact that over 80% of poll tax payers in Nyasaland work at least one month each year for wages. And there were (1914) only 310 Europeans not officials and not missionaries to 950,000 natives, a far lower proportion than in Kenya. (The 310 includes about 60 women & children.) Nobody knows typical Bantu life better than Barlow[85] and G. H. Wilson (see 33–37 of his recently pub. book).[86] Of course youth is disinclined to continuous toil, vide Piccadilly in winter & the Thames in summer. But the allegation that the African is specially lazy comes only from those who want to make money out of him, or from those, alas! not unknown among missionaries, who dislike him.

Providence and improvidence. Don't forget two facts. Take any consecutive 5 years in Africa, and call the crop in the best year 100. In the worst it will be 30–40, in the others 50–80. In the best year the absence [at] wage-earning of 50% of ablebodied males may not cause a shortage. In all the others 25% will. Second, from poverty & ignorance, Africans are *unable* to keep grain from a good to a bad season. I made, and reported, both on Coast & in Highlands, careful tests. Without metal tanks & fumigation, weevils, on an average, diminish the food value of grain 60% in 9 months.

And by the way Arthur knows well enough how vast the loss of childlife is from weevily and insufficient grain in Africa today.

Last of all Owen's criticism of my central thesis. I am simply astounded to learn that my letter was followed by any action. But it fills me with despair to see that I have failed to explain my meaning. I cannot think of plainer language than this, shortage of labour for necessary work is wholly due to *the measure of compulsion used by Govt agents and chiefs to induce natives to work for private employers at rates of pay fixed by Govt. and employers in conjunction.* When I was in Africa I never heard that statement denied. What I did hear was that if Govt. agents and chiefs ceased interfering with the labour market the country (i.e. the settler) would be ruined. Why no tears for the Coast Arab? Food, housing, leisure, in Arab slavery were infinitely better on the average than on Europeans' plantations. I don't defend that system. A full stomach is no compensation for the soul hurt of a servile status, even if, as was the case with most slaves on the coast, they could escape with little difficulty before 1885 or so. But I attack any and every status that restricts true liberty, as partaking of slavery.

I don't mind a bit anything O. says about me. I deserve far more severe, if rather different, kinds of blame. But in return let me ask him one question, is he prepared to ask his settler friends to treat an African pilferer and deserter as Paul asked Philemon to treat Onesimus, namely as he would treat O. himself? None of us in Africa act up to that, I least of all. But I see no hope of carrying out the Xtian

programme without stating it. More than that I believe it is impracticable without corporate, cooperative effort by the church, irrespective of the worldly illusions that distinguish and separate its
members. What proportion of the settlers would accept that teaching? Men talk about the certain failure of effort to help mankind
without the Gospel. All right. Here then, is the true basis of right
action, the fount of wisdom. Without it do men judge aright, see
aright into minds of Africans, of Europeans? Why then does O.[wen]
place such value on the opinions of those who reject it?

Leys to Oldham
[10 June 1921]

I don't allow my fanaticism to blind me to the fact that it is liable to
result in cost to others. So I send this 10/- to pay you for the making
of three typed copies of this letter, one for you, one for Arthur & one
for Owen. . . .

Leys to Oldham
18 June 1921

The only important criticism of Owen's I didn't answer was his
statement that in West Africa chiefs had and used the power of
making whoever of their people they wished work against their will.
I passed it over because my experience of W. African affairs is confined to the enquiries I made from the W. African Congress delegation and a week in Sierra Leone, spent in talk with editors, school-
masters, native clergy, &c.[87] But last night I had half an hour with
Wilkie.[88] So far as he knows the market for wage earners for Europeans in W. Africa is absolutely free. I asked what happens when
labourers are scarce. He said wages rose when they were scarce, and
fell when they were plentiful. As I knew already, he told me that
communal services in tribes (in W. Africa self governing of course)
were done by calling out all the able bodied males. Thus not only
roads and bridges but railways, are made, and kept, in repair. I
asked what happened when a railway passed through desert. There
seems to be little really vacant land, and of course there is none not

tribally owned. But so far as Wilkie knows any labourers beyond the number made available by the local corvée are got by free contract. He says he knows of no instance of pressure by Govt. on native authorities to persuade men to work outside their tribal areas and when compulsion is used it is for work of recognised benefit to the tribe, recognised, that is by the natives.

I strongly suspect (from information got from other sources) that labour in the tin mines in Northern Nigeria is not all voluntary.[89] But there of course the matter of profit for aliens that is the root of all the trouble in E. Africa, is actively present.

I know of course that Owen objects to the forced levy for communal services. So long as it is exacted from all, is confined to work of recognised value to those who perform it, and contributes nothing of advantage to any idle class, I see no objection in theory. It is really of course a tax, and, as Wilkie said, it is the only form of taxation in Southern Nigeria.

A criticism from Donald Fraser was valuable. In the Northern third of Nyasaland tribal authority, though weakened, is still alive. In that area there are at the most, less than a dozen European planters. In Fraser's own tribe the Angoni, none need to live on alienated land and the only Europeans in the tribal area are officials, missionaries & traders. You will appreciate how difficult it is to make generalisations wholly true of a large area. It remains true that the chief differences between W. & E. Africa are due to the disintegrating results of inducing the majority of male natives to leave their villages & families to earn wages. . . .

Oldham to Leys
24 June 1921

I have been putting in a lot of work on the East African question. There is to be a debate in the House of Commons on Thursday. What some of those who are interested in the matter rather anticipate is that Churchill may prefer to deal with the matter off his own bat.[90] A royal commission is not congenial to his temperament. What we want is not a Churchill policy but a national policy, but what Churchill decides to do he no doubt will do and he has at least this merit that he will not be deterred from reaching the decisions

which he thinks best by undue consideration for the views of the
settlers. As a matter of fact we have reason to believe that one or two
things in the right direction are likely to be done without waiting for
a royal commission.

I am to see the Archbishop of Canterbury on Monday and one or
others of those most interested will be there. We have a valuable ally
in Steel-Maitland . . . . [91]

Leys to Oldham
25 June 1921

. . . What you say of Churchill is supported by other opinions I
know of. I really believe we have convinced such as he that votes are
behind us—all men like him care about. And while the supporters
have a lot of influence I suspect C. wants to prove himself a Liberal!
by doing something spectacular in some part of the empire where he
won't alienate either voters in the U.K. or captains of industry.
Also, I am told, he enjoys dressing people down and imposing his
will on people like Northey who think themselves important. And I
feel sure that he wants his name to go down to history. He knows
that only the names of liberators do.

So I won't be sorry if C. makes your commission less urgently
necessary. You can get a better one, and get it easier, from another
Govt. in a year or two. For a generation there will never be a time
when African policy will not be in dispute over principles.

Oldham to Leys
28 July 1921

. . . [Dr. Thomas Jesse Jones] is leaving London this week for a
short holiday before he returns to America. I should very much have
liked you to have seen him as I think a talk would have been mu-
tually valuable: but this must wait now for some other opportunity.
Jones has done splendid work. I think the tour of the Commission
may have proved to have been one of the most notable contributions
made to the education of the African peoples . . . . [92]

Leys to Oldham
7 August 1921

I have just had 24 hours of Archdeacon Owen's company. . . .
I found O's hope of converting the settler is a matter of faith—
almost a credo quia impossible. And as for any alleged overstatement by me—why I never told such horrible tales as O. has in
plenty. The only criticism I could get him to make was that I attri-
bute sins to the settlers of which the real guilt rests on officials. He
even admitted that our agitation at home was necessary.

Of course the whole situation is transformed by the Indian & anti-
Indian agitation. I venture to prophesy it brings your Royal Commission into immediate prospect. It will be the only available refuge
for distracted muddlers in Nairobi.

Leys to Oldham
22 August 1921

Of course you know far more than I do about recent events, but I
want to make quite sure you see one or two points I see clearly.

The settlers used the argument that to grant the Indian claims
would endanger native rights and interests. They did not say how. I
wish they had. I agree the danger is real, but to my mind it lies merely
in the prospect of an increase in the number of people now scram-
bling for the loot of African land and labour. Be that as it may, the
Indians were not slow to take advantage of the introduction of native
interests into the controversy by their opponents. On July 7th there
were two mass meetings in Nairobi. The African one hailed the Indians as, next to the missionaries, their best friends and asked them to
help to get political rights for Africans. The Indians are resolved that
the privileges they claimed should be open to all.

I feel certain that hitherto the average Indian has been more dis-
liked and mistrusted than the average European. But I am equally
certain that now that Indians offer, however vaguely, means for
redress of African grievances, articulate native opinion *must* swing
round to the side of the Indians in the political controversy. The
controversy itself has been the means of changing what were only
confused feelings of resentment into definite desires, consciously

held in common. The sudden realisation of common desires is always a very potent fact. Societies of a kind seem to be springing up and growing like mushrooms. One of them sent a memorial of grievances to the Govt., and I believe Harris has a copy.

I am afraid the European Community, missionaries and all, has missed the tide. I fear they can do little to prevent the Indian from appearing in native eyes as a deliverer from the European. It was left to the Indians to protest against the concerted wage reduction, while tax and prices still remain high, and against the registration ordinance that puts natives at the mercy of any unjust employer. But I am quite clear that if those natives who do not wish an Indian-African political alliance are to have any hope of support from the mass of natives, some considerable body of local Europeans must come forward openly with a reform programme. To make votes for educated natives a plank in that programme might alienate some genuine friends to native interests. But all whose support is worth having would unite on these items as immediately practicable.
1. Legislation to vest all unalienated lands in native ownership, as in Nigeria. 2. The complete cessation of all influence by Govt. agents over natives in regard to labour. 3. The formation of tribal councils, as in Uganda. 4. The formation of an advisory Council for native affairs (of Europeans) to whom would be referred all bills, rules, byelaws affecting natives, with suspensory powers until Imperial Parliament (or Colonial Office?) approves. There may only be a handful of Europeans ready to support such a programme, though I hope recent events have instructed them. All I do say is that unless a considerable party arises with such a programme nothing can stop the immense majority of Africans from gravitating to the Indian platform. Nor will it be fair for missionaries to blame them. In their place we should do as they would.

People in Europe can help in different ways. There are two things to be done. An Indian colonial policy will soon be in process of formation.[93] If I foresee rightly nothing can stop an immense Indian immigration into all E. African ports. Why shouldn't the Indian Govt. encourage farmers and artizans and discourage the people in India who want to buy estates from Europeans and, like them, make natives work for them? Is that quite Utopian? More important, perhaps, than the Govt. in Delhi are the leaders of Indian political life.

There is a large element of idealism among them. They will know the danger, in governing others, of inflicting evils they themselves have suffered from. I have already written a letter to India, through a friend, that will reach the right quarters. There are others who could write, with far more hope of influencing events. We don't want exploiter-Jevanjee to step into exploiter-Grogan's shoes. [94]

Second, assuming that the principal claims of the Indians will be granted—a safe assumption—what can we do to ensure that the change will not merely give votes to well to do Indian shopkeepers? The danger is a purely property qualification, which even if open to all races would in practice exclude all natives except a handful of chiefs whose wealth depends largely on Govt. subsidies and unjust exactions. It would be just like the Govt. to enfranchise a couple of hundred of such men and point to their views as representing native opinion.

What we want is an educational qualification, as stiff as anybody wishes, so long as it applies equally to European, Asiatic & African. Nothing less, if Asiatics are to have votes, would convince Africans that we intend justice and give them hope of attaining through their own exertions, some influence over the direction of their own country.

To those who would oppose, in any event, even if Indians were given votes, the extension of political rights to any African, I would say this. The African looks on the present controversy as a struggle for mastery. He is encouraged in that view by the Europeans who say that if Indian demands are granted their own control of the country will pass to Indians. And it should be remembered that natives don't believe affairs in East Africa are in the control of Parliament. They are perfectly right of course in point of fact. Real control over events has for years rested with the local European community. They have every excuse for failing to realise that British public opinion has real power, if and when it cares to act.

Imagine now the danger of accession to Indian demands. There is bound to be a real loss of prestige. How can such a situation be met? Only by explaining and proving that a share in direction of policy, legislation, executive direction, is for all qualified by knowledge to exercise it—that the real alternative in mastery is not between Europeans and Asiatics but between those who are and those who are not fit for political liberty.

If one thinks of might have beens one can agree with those who say Africans are unripe for any share whatever in a semi national franchise. Far better, I agree, to have begun their political education in tribal affairs, by reviving tribal authorities, by broadening their bases, and so let liberty grow in its natural shelters. That was the right policy thirty years ago. But it was incompatible with exploitation so rapid, so ruthless, so intolerant of whatever did not add to the profits of exploitation. I suppose it is unreasonable to hope that alien governors should have faith in liberty for their subjects at the stage of pure tribalism. They never do believe till they are forced to. And by then introductory lessons are impossible. Even now tribal councils would be killed at birth by forced labour. Until it is stone dead no growth of tribal or village life is possible.

People who want to influence events have really a far narrower range of opportunity than we imagine. Real changes happen mainly through semi-conscious desire awakening in the hearts of thousands. Writing articles, interviewing ministers of state—by such means it is possible to touch the helm, occasionally. But the ship itself moves, and is moved, by forces within and, like tides and storms, outside itself. These we call the Spirit of God. The reason Xtian missions matter more than the armies of any Alexander or Napoleon is that they light these fires, release energies that no man or group of men can create or control. At the moment, in East Africa, these fires and energies are breaking out and spreading. It is folly to fancy they can be controlled. It is not for us to fix a course for events to take and shape them to our will. But we can do just a little that is abundantly worth while. Our weight may even move the helm an inch or two.

Would you send this when read, to Arthur, and will he send it to Owen? I am to visit Jesse Jones tomorrow, and to see du Bois at the end of the week.[95] Isn't it strange to watch one's hopes fructify far more rapidly than one dreamed, and to see the fruit take wholly unexpected shapes? My own hope is that things will soon begin to move more slowly in Africa.

Oldham to Leys
5 September 1921
Strictly Private

. . . The situation in regard to labour in East Africa is encouraging. Major Wood sent for me last month and showed me a draft of the proposals which will be embodied in a new despatch on labour. They seemed to me eminently satisfactory but I said that everything depended on the local application and that I could not commit myself to approval without consulting one or two friends who knew East Africa. He gave me permission to consult Owen, Hooper and Arthur. After doing so I wrote a long letter saying that substantially we thought the new proposals met all that we had been contending for. We suggested modifications on certain minor points and the most important have been accepted. I do not say that we have got everything that you or I might wish; but the Government seems to me to have gone very much further to meet us than I ever expected they would. I do not feel at liberty to say more at present but I shall be glad to know what you think of the despatch when it comes out.[96]

I have, of course, come to hold the view that the stopping of abuses and of forced labour is only a small part of the problem. It is merely negative and there is no real solution without a constructive policy of education and of training in political responsibility such as you suggest. I put these two points as strongly as I could in my letter to Major Wood and he says he entirely agrees and that so do the Government.

I am still of opinion that the problems are so complex and so interrelated that a really comprehensive enquiry by a royal commission is the only way of dealing with them effectively. We cannot get this just now, though I have not the least doubt that we should have had it if Milner and not Churchill had been Secretary of State. But we have succeeded in getting the Colonial Office to take the right attitude in regard to native labour (though, of course, the utmost continued vigilance and alertness will be necessary to see that this is carried out in practice). We have also, I think made some impression in regard to the vitally important matters of education and training in political responsibility. We must keep up pressure on this point.

Your letter seems to me so good that I wish you could write to Major Wood very much on the same lines. Keep the letter as short as you can as it increases the chance of his reading it personally. Assume, as I think you are entitled to do, that he is a friend.

I would gladly write myself on the lines of your letter, but I have already emphasized the importance of the subject, though my statement of the case was not as effective as your present letter. I have within the last two or three weeks let the Colonial Office have my views so fully and at such length that I think it would be wise for me to lie low for a little lest I give the impression that I am an interfering person who thinks he can do their job better than they can themselves. You have, I understand, met Major Wood personally and I think there can be no harm in your writing to him direct and that at this particular juncture the ideas contained in your letter will do good. What seems to me likely to do good at the present stage is very much what you have written to me, somewhat shortened and with the omission of one or two sentences that are a little critical and controversial in tone. . . .

Leys to Oldham
6 October 1921

. . . I have no doubt whatever that your verdict on the terms of the despatch is the right one. I can tell you in advance that I shall have no criticism to offer. You have a full and accurate picture of the situation in your mind such as no one who has never lived in E. Africa, and few who have, has reached.

It is true as you say that much will depend on those who carry out their instructions in Africa. But more important still is what publicity the new directions will receive. I am sure your missionary advisers would all agree. If that is to say, the natives are informed that Government and all its agents are indifferent as to whether they work on the alienated or on the unalienated land there can be no more forced labour (except among those natives whose homes are on alienated land and who have nowhere else to live). So long as natives do not know that Govt. does not care whether they work at home or away from home for Europeans, forced labour will continue.

So I expect to get questions asked in Parliament on that point—not now of course, but when I learn how the despatch is received and enforced in Africa. Perhaps the best thing to hope for is a violent storm of opposition among the planters. Nothing else would make natives realise the change in policy as well.

I simply cannot fathom Northey's mind in going back to Kenya. I cannot imagine what price would satisfy him for having to carry out both an African and an Indian policy so repugnant to his friends' interests and to his own ideas.

... I wish you could have been at the Pan African. I was more deeply moved than ever in my life since boyhood. The last few years have been so full of cause for hallelujahs that I feel I ought never to be unhappy for a moment. As you say of course a positive policy in Africa is still to be undertaken. But everybody knows that and we shall soon see its beginnings. I am more than ever in agreement with your plan of a commission, mainly as a means to influencing the public. If only the subscriber to missions could be reached! The best way would be for all societies to scrap their silly papers and get you & Canon Robinson to run a penny weekly and sixpenny monthly devoted to the depicting of the work of the missionary church. . . . [97]

Leys to Oldham
23 October 1921
[IMC (Geneva), Box 162]

I have waited so long before answering Owen's appeal to me in his letter to you, partly to learn Churchill's policy, in regard to labour and the Indian claims, and partly because I was anxious to discover a point of view from which to harmonise Owen's convictions and my own—my own for once being those of the majority of those with faith in Africans.

I suggested a provisional programme covering everything of importance except the franchise. I explained why I hoped to leave aside the question of political rights for Africans for at least long enough to let people who differ about the franchise work together to some purpose. We all ought to believe if we don't that co-operation in matters in which people do agree throws light on those other matters in which we differ. So I set out a 1921 programme, hoping it would lead to something more adequate in 1922 or 1923.

Owen at first says "yes". He offers no amendments to my programme—I wish he had—it needs amending. He accepts it as it stands. And then, later in his letter, he suggests our pushing the programme as an alternative that would exclude the grant of political rights to Africans. I had thought I had made it quite clear that if the franchise question came up as an issue of practical politics I would

feel compelled to support the grant of equal voting rights to educated Africans. And Owen must know that the great majority in Europe who support the Economic programme (free labour, security of
tenure etc.) take my side on the franchise issue, not his. On my side
are all the Labour Party and many outside it, the League of Nations
Union Group, ordinary liberals like Gilbert Murray, J. H. Harris
and T. E. Harvey[98] and at least some of the High Church group. The
Bishop of Zanzibar in his last letter seems undecided.

Arthur's opinion I don't know. But I hope most fervently that he
and Owen won't take any active part in advocating a less liberal policy than the official one. I made my proposals just because I feared
such a division among us, so that we could work in unison for what
we all see to be justice. The price of such co-ordination is to refrain
from open conflict of opinion. The one great necessity is for people
in Africa who intend justice to publish a programme of practical
reform. I would urge Owen to do so as soon as possible, before the
air is cloudy with contention between interested groups of Europeans and Indians. We must all keep these reforms prominent before the public in Africa as the *real* issues of the time in comparison
with which the catchwords of Delamere and Grogan and of Jevanjee
are as much to the point as hanging the Kaiser and making Germany pay. We must hold fast to justice whatever passion and prejudice may invent to confuse people.

I hope you don't think I take too much on myself. Remember that
in the first article I ever wrote ("New Europe" three years ago) I defined a reform programme exactly as I do now.[99] Let me repeat once
more the terms I suggest for early 1922.

1. Complete security before the law of all land in native occupa-
    tion.

2. The encouragement and organisation of production on the land
    thus made secure.

3. Entire liberty for the occupiers of that land to live and work on
    it undisturbed.

4. The reorganisation and strengthening of tribal authorities so as
    rapidly to ensure

    (a) their complete control of tribal affairs and

(b)   the sharing of responsibilities and privileges by all adult
members of the tribe.

5.   A scheme of education that will make it available to every child
in thirty years and train Africans for the work only Europeans
and Asiatics can now do, for skilled trades, school teaching,
medicine.

6.   The establishing of an advisory council, at first mainly or wholly
European, with power to formulate proposals to be submitted to
the Legislative Council and to hold up questionable legal and
administrative changes until submitted to the Secretary of State.

What I suggest is that in substance that is a minimum programme.
Nothing less will win any substantial support at home, in Parliament,
in the press. And I want Owen and Arthur to get together and express it in better language—not too elaborately or people will get
confused and above all we must make absolutely clear what we are
working for—and then publish in the East African press. After the
publication they will be able to judge by the reception the programme gets and by the letters they will have written to them (of
course the signatories will invite letters) what should be done to get
the reforms carried out. You no doubt saw the very similar scheme
published in the Rhodesian press.

Now I admit such a scheme may come to nothing. But I believe
that if it does an increasing number of educated natives (such as
there are) will become pro-Indian and anti-European. I confidently
assume that rivalry between European and Asiatic will persist for
generations, and don't see how Africans can avoid taking sides. And
I wouldn't care what side they took if it were not that Indian nationalism is on the whole anti-Christian—at least anti-missionary. That
of course opens up *the* fundamental problem. Is any organisation
that permits distinctions of race a Christian church at all? In all my
thinking and planning I assume, you must remember, that the sham
Christianity described so often by Jesus (Matt. XXV parables of
tares and wheat, Good Samaritan etc.) is the one great constant
danger to Christians and churches. There is Pharisaism in every
heart and every church. And its chief mark is behaving to other
kinds of people than oneself as if they were inferior, that "inasmuch
as ye did it not to the least ye did it not to me" is a most appalling

thing as a rule of life. In Africa European looks down on Indian, Indian on African. If out of that welter of arrogances, jealousies, oppressions, the Kingdom of Heaven is to grow up, there must be as real a brotherhood as when at other times religion has transcended these barriers to fellowship. I don't mean that they can be transcended by a proclamation. But I do say both that the proclamation is necessary and that the tendency to provide for and excuse any distinctions, to have separate places with various degrees of importance for different groups of Christians, to give or allow differences of status or responsibility, that these are manifestations of anti-Christ, of the leaven of the Pharisees. How hard all that is I know well, know bitterly. But why pretend that the difference Jesus described between true and false religion is anything else? As always the sinners find such things quite easy. They don't look down on other people and are not tempted by the host of hallucinations about superiorities that vex the righteous.

It is because I believed that the real enemy is not "the world," not scepticism or indifference, but Pharisaism that [I] see the test for the church in Africa is whether it preaches a plan of life the same for all, that relations in so called secular affairs should all of them be of the kind Paul described to Philemon.

It is from such a standpoint that, I suggest, the franchise problem should be regarded. In India itself did wrong judgments not arise for no other reason than that people judged Indians to be inferiors, "unfit" in some sense when they themselves were fit? Nobody that I know of wants a replica of existing European politics made in Africa. What we work for is that world-wide revolution longed for by millions that is impossible except by following the plan Jesus revealed.

Oldham Memorandum
"Inter-Racial Relationships"
3 November 1921
[IMC (Geneva), Box 162]
Private

I have been asked, in the first instance by the United Council for Missionary Education in Great Britain, to write a book on inter-racial relationships. The suggestion has found favour in the United States and Canada. Those who will be responsible for the publication of the book anticipate a demand which might necessitate a first edition of 150,000. The character, scope and size of the book and the method of publication are left open. But in any case it would have the backing of organisations which can reach large sections of opinion, missionary and non-missionary, on both sides of the Atlantic. There appears to be in quite different quarters a strong and urgent demand for a book on this subject; and there can be no doubt that the questions with which it would deal are among the most vital and central in the world to-day.

I am very conscious of my limitations in the writing of such a book and the only consideration that could have prevailed with me to accept the invitation is the fact that at Edinburgh House (the office of the International Missionary Council) we have contacts with those who are in living and intimate touch with inter-racial relations in almost every part of the world. The past few years have also brought us contacts (which can be increased if we so desire) with those whose approach to the subject is from the scientific or administrative side and who can thus supplement the missionary point of view. Most important of all, perhaps, is the fact that we have contacts with members of other races than the white and therefore opportunities of learning something of their mind. This ought to make possible a somewhat broader treatment of the subject than is possible when it is viewed, as is usually done, from the standpoint of one race. The book which I should like to write is one to which I should attempt to give a unity but which would be in very small part mine; a book which would be the result not of an individual but of a common effort and which would represent the contributed experience and thought of many minds and especially of those linked together in the worldwide Christian and missionary fellowship of which the International Missionary Council is an expression.

The greater part of the book, as I at present see it, will consist of chapters in which an attempt will be made to understand and describe the particular concrete situations which exist in different parts of the world such as:

(1)   The relations of Black and White in the United States.

(2)   The relations of Black and White in South Africa.

(3)   The rule of the black peoples of tropical Africa by white governments where there is little or no permanent white settlement.

(4)   The relations between India and Great Britain and the West generally.

(5)   The relations of the West generally and of America in particular with Japan and China.

(6)   The relations of Japan with Korea and with China.

(7)   The situation in the Near East with special reference to the influence of Islam both as a unifying force and as a source of conflict.

There are many other situations that might be treated, such as Egypt, the Malay States, the Dutch East Indies, Eastern Europe, South America and the age-long problem of the Jews. But I think that for two reasons it will be necessary or desirable to limit the ground to be covered. The first is that to make a comprehensive survey would involve so much time as to delay the publication of the book indefinitely or to make it impracticable altogether. The second is that an attempt to be comprehensive would not only increase the size of the volume to an undesirable extent but would weary and confuse the mind of the ordinary reader by inviting his attention at one time to an excessive amount of unfamiliar detail. The main purpose of the book will be sufficiently served and the impact made by it will be much more telling if a limited number of concrete situations are selected for study and from them principles deduced which are capable of wider application.

In regard to each concrete situation the two main questions to which we should seek an answer are:

First, What are the real and fundamental causes of the existing misunderstanding, antagonism and strain?

Secondly, What general forces and conscious efforts are at work to remedy matters, and how may these best be furthered?

In regard to the first of these questions, I think the causes are many and not merely (nor in many instances even principally) racial (i.e. physical) but also political (as predominantly in the relations of England and India or of Japan and China), economic (as predominantly in the attitude of the United States, Canada, Australia and South Africa to oriental immigration), religious (as under the influence of Islam and in part elsewhere) and social, if that term may be used to cover the tendency of a group to keep the outsider at arm's length, which seems to be instinctive and finds many forms of expression in the exclusiveness of various classes, sects and cliques. It would be of advantage to ascertain more clearly what part each of these factors (and possibly others) plays in the different relationships that are studied.

In some of the chapters dealing with concrete situations it may be possible to present a unified, balanced statement doing justice to all the different elements, but such a statement would have to be prepared by a group in which the various points of view were represented, and I doubt whether the time has yet come when a comprehensive statement can be drawn up which would harmonize the divergent views and be recognized by those holding them as doing justice to all the factors in the situation. I think, therefore, we must be content to try to state in turn as fairly as possible the opposing standpoints, recognizing, where they exist, different trends and degrees of opinion on each side.

After the study of some of the more important concrete situations there are certain general questions which will have to be faced.

First (merely in this enumeration and not necessarily in order of treatment in the book) we shall have to come to grips with the claim of race superiority and the assertion of race equality. We shall have to consider what is meant by these general and vague phrases, and what measure of truth (if any) is contained in the different meanings which they might bear.

Secondly, there are certain biological aspects of race which will have to be looked at. It is of course out of the question that a book written by laymen should make any contribution to this side of the subject. But it should be possible to indicate where biological science at present stands in regard to certain matters, and so to remove some current misconceptions and to expose the pseudo-science of such a book as Stoddard's *Rising Tide of Colour*.

Thirdly, there is the difficult question of increase of population and its consequences.

Fourthly, we shall need to seek light on the Christian principles which should govern race relationships. This is the primary purpose of the book and the thing that makes it worth attempting. Has the

Christian Church anything worth while to say in regard to these conditions of racial antagonism and strain, and if so what? In dealing with this subject in particular, though also in the book as a whole, I hope to work in the closest possible co-operation with the Conference on Christian Politics, Economics and Citizenship planned for the autumn of 1923, which through preparatory commissions is seeking to gain fresh light on the application of Christian ideals and principles to the life and problems of our time. The principles the meaning of which they are seeking to discover more fully in their bearing on the constitution of society, the conduct of industry and national and international politics are the same principles from which we must seek guidance in regard to racial relations.

In the fifth place, it will be necessary to recognise and understand the difficulties which confront the practical statesman, who in attempting to deal with these situations has to take account of public opinion and cannot act too far in advance of it.

In a final chapter it will be desirable to consider what practical steps to improve matters are possible and in what ways Christians can best bring the force of their convictions to bear on the situation.

To complete the scheme of the book as I at present see it, I should add that there will probably be an introductory chapter outlining the problem as a whole, showing its significance and importance and emphasizing its gravity and urgency. . . .

Memorandum to members
of the enlarged International
Review of Missions Group, n.d.
[IMC (Geneva), Box 162]

Dr Norman Leys has given permission for the circulation of this private letter of his to Mr Oldham to members of the Group. It was written after he had received Mr Oldham's memorandum proposing the book on inter-racial relationships. In a letter to Miss Gollock[100] Dr Norman Leys ranges himself with Dr du Bois in his view on racial relationships as announced at the Pan African Conference in London some three months back. . . .

Leys to Oldham
14 November 1921
[IMC (Geneva), Box 162]

You and I are made so differently that the only basis of useful criticism, a looking through one another's eyes, is very difficult to reach. But there are one or two things I do want to say to you.

Your idea of a book as the outcome of a common effort is obviously exactly right, splendidly right. But it supposes a common mind. Does one exist? Are there even several common minds, each shared by a group of men seeking the spirit's guidance? If the latter, then the book should describe these group-minds in distinction as well as in the relation you can find between them. Any other plan would result not in a unity but, at the best, in an average, in an unhelpful compromise, at the worst in confusion.

That indeed is the impression left on my mind by your abstract. Let me suggest that you should write no sentence without asking yourself how far what you describe is real. As we all know, every controversy is conducted under misconception. That is why each seems unreal to the next generation. So far I need not supply illustrations. It follows that the only useful contribution to a contemporary controversy is to expose the general elements in it. What I fear you may be tempted to do in your book is to describe, with conspicuous fairness, the position of various schools and types, and the direction of various currents, using uncritically the terms and conceptions they use. You show that you recognise the danger by suggesting the invalidity of equality as a category. But some of your own terms, if they are your own, seem to me of far less value. Equality after all is in certain phases of life a real thing. Jesus taught that the more highly gifted should do their share of the menial work of life. Paul taught that all Christians are priests. I once asked Bishop [Charles] Gore if he thought any difference in *status* compatible (among Christians) with the Gospel. He thought awhile and then said, No, that all differences in status are absolutely wrong. If that is so, if none of the differences between man and man should be reflected in the treatment men are given by Christians, *a fortiori* no differences between groups of men should be recognised and provided for. This may seem to you mere logical analysis. It is not so.

Literally everything depends on what one believes about *real* human differences. If they arise from outside the soul, the real personality, they are tractable, and should be dealt with according as they promote or hinder fellowship in which lies the abundant life. If they promote it then they are the necessary source of life's rich variety. If they hinder they are to be dissolved by the growth of the Kingdom. But in either case, and this is the real point, they are in human control. If the whole case is one of feeding starving bodies and minds, of opening minds to light, then the only wise way of acting (whether in politics, industry, social life) is to deal with every human soul one touches as an equal, of equal importance in God's eyes with oneself, equally capable therefore of the good things in life, these all the gifts of grace.

But if there are real differences inside men's souls, if some are incapable of receiving the good things others enjoy, if there are bits missing in mind and heart and conscience not to be supplied by any effort of help and instruction, then these differences are barriers set by God to free human fellowship. This is the real alternative. In the one case differences are, if welcome, to be cherished, if thwarting to growth and restrictive to fellowship, to be removed. In the other the differences are intractable, beyond human reach.

What I say is that men act differently according as they believe one or other of these alternatives. And there is no way of bridging the gulf between except by confusion of thought. I fear that your readers may be so confused. I fear that on one page they will be thinking on the assumption, for instance, that the Chinese are unlike Europeans because of geographical or climatic or historical facts, and on another that these cannot explain the differences but rather that their soul stuff is different. So I want you to make it clear to the reader whether you are dealing with and repeating current and spurious coin of thought, and whether you are giving the truest picture you can of the facts.

I write in ignorance of your own position. I am fairly sure but not quite that you think as I do that the whole human race is a single family that from sin is ignorant of its single ancestry in God. Jesus nowhere contrasts the logical alternatives. But He constantly referred to "the last" "the least" "the poor" "the sinners" i.e. in actual fact the superiors. And in the parable of the Great Surprise the test is each man's treatment of "the least" of human creatures. There is no sense whatever in trying to treat the least of human creatures as a Jesus if in his soul there are innate deficiencies. Let me give you an illustration of how intensely practical a question the alternative raises. I pressed Jesse Jones to tell me whether he thought American negroes as a whole different in nature and capacity from the Europeans they live among and whether he expected from them a different kind of future. He admitted that he did. I told him that explained everything, to me, of his differences with du Bois and others. If a stable boy is going to be a king some day he has no less need to learn how to sweep the stable well. But stable sweeping should be taught as training for kingly duties. Jones in effect says it isn't wise, it isn't sensible, to teach a negro child what European children are taught because as men they will have a different status. That is not relatively but absolutely contrary to Matt. XXV 40 & 45, and St. Paul's directions to Philemon. That is not to say that Jones' work isn't useful.

The fact is that Jones has a morbid dread of not being thought sensible. On the contrary what is called common sense is the worst of guides in such matters. To shut one's eyes to any relevant fact is a crime. But the sensible people only open them to what facts support their prejudices. Jesus had no common sense. He never thought it wise to avoid extremes. Heaven knows immoderation is no sign of wisdom. But no treatment of any social problem is quite so unwise as that of forcing contradictories into a compromise. Think of all the political and economic crimes and follies that have their root in the assumption by those in authority that those under authority are their inferiors, of the English attitude to the Irish, of the Germans to the Poles, of the Anglo-Indian to the Indian. What is at the bottom of the whole industrial problem in Europe but this that men do not regard those with fewer advantages as their equals? In any dispute the test question is "How would you like it yourself?" Men answer it, not by saying honestly, "I would hate to be in the position of the unemployed or of the workman with 50/-a week" but by saying "These people are not like me, they don't need what I have now, don't deserve what their betters have, must be treated differently because they are different." That is the sensible view. It is the un-Christian view. It is the view that however slowly is bringing Europe to a revolution of violence. The only thing to prevent that revolution of violence is, as people often correctly say, the Christian spirit. But not one in a hundred of those who say so mean treating, thinking of, planning for the bulk of the people as they expect to be treated and regarded themselves, far less as they would want Jesus treated.

Nor is the solution of the race problem any different. All the facts you refer to are important, facts of history, of standard of living, of political liberty. I don't want you to ignore them. I even say you cannot exaggerate their importance. *But* do you look on them as facts to be transformed by the growth of the Kingdom or as facts which the Kingdom in its growth must bow to? As Rome faced the fact of idolatry or as Paul did? I don't say you ought in the book to prescribe to the Church in different countries what policy in detail they should follow. But I do say you should never write a sentence that can bear the meaning that any man-made distinction between men that hinders brotherly love has any other destiny than transformation. Write of these things as you would write of war or of prostitution. You are always scrupulously fair. But you don't always write as if the world could be transformed.

The last Nairobi papers have leaders referring to the news sent from England by cable of prohibiting help by public servants to private employers by getting them labour. Both draw the same inference, that if magistrates are not to be allowed to persuade natives, special powers must be given to "labour recruiters." A new organization must be set up whereby each district is worked over by its own recruiters duly licenced and empowered to deal with chiefs. Rather interesting! The idea of course is for the licence &c in conjunction with directions from magistrates as to which chiefs to apply to will amount in the eyes of chiefs to orders from Govt. And you can imagine how inevitable the bribery of chiefs will be. Still of course such a scheme will be better than the one you got Winston to stop.

Leys to Miss Georgiana Gollock
18 December 1921
[IMC (Geneva), Box 162]

The terms of every real human problem are set by the state of mind of various groups of men. The data are not objective facts but opinions or convictions or feelings. Thus not only is the so called problem of race a different one in different ages. It exists at all as a problem only in certain ages. There was no race problem in either the first or the twelfth centuries. We meet no one in the New Testament who imagined that Phrygian or Libyan ancestry implied any inferiority, or affected a man's capacity or social position. And not even the Crusaders themselves imagined the Saracens to be their inferiors. Far later, the problem had scarcely arisen. Shakespeare's audience saw nothing strange in the marriage of the black Othello to a noble European lady.[101]

The "problem" in fact is wholly composed of the belief in certain minds that certain groups of men, to which they themselves belong, are in some sense superior to certain other groups. So that when Mr Oldham wrote that the question of equality is a false or irrelevant or mistaken way of regarding the problem, he showed that he assumed inequality as between various human groups. There would be no problem at all if it were not that most well to do people who speak English (for the poor as a rule are not race conscious)[102] regard themselves as the superiors of Asiatics and Africans.

But the states of mind of those who regard themselves as superior are not the only data of the problem. Of even greater importance are the feelings and convictions of those who live under the control of those who regard them as inferiors. Of all these alleged inferiors Africans are the perfect example, the test case. The first four pages of the Crisis for November state the mind of the leaders of the African race.[103] And the first four pages of the December issue argue their case in the aspect of the problem felt in our time to be of most importance. These eight pages are more important than everything else together that has been written on the subject. They describe how every non-European with knowledge and active mind inevitably feels and thinks in face of the allegations of racial inferiority by those who control him politically and economically. I fear you will find it impossible to summarise them. They are already summaries of the thought of many thousands.

There is one point I would like to urge on the investigating committee [of the International Missionary Council]. Jesus taught that wealth was so great a temptation as to make it almost impossible for rich men to be good men. And he also taught that his followers must not bear rule and authority. If we remember that those nations that

in greatest degree profess to be Christian exercise authority, fre
quently as in Africa, absolute authority, over the rest of the world,
and that these same nations are out of all comparison the richest in
the world, the dangers of distortion of mind and corruption of soul
are obvious. Britain and America are in authority, which Jesus forbade, and are pre-eminently rich, which Jesus said renders entrance
into the Kingdom supremely difficult—more difficult than prostitution or other flagrant vice. Can we who belong to these nations hope
to judge rightly unless we resolutely reject the prevailing ideas of our
time—unless we attempt to pass the needle's eye? If that is so, no
"sensible" solution of the problem can be Christian. Surely we may
be certain that of necessity the right relation with African and Asiatic will offend and alienate those who exercise authority and those
who have wealth. . . .

Leys, "Memorandum on the
Land Question in Tropical Africa,"
for the Mandates committee
of the League of Nations Union.
15 February 1922
[Edinburgh House, Box 200]

I am so constantly coming across proof that the facts of land ownership and tenure among Africans and their governments are mis-
conceived that I propose to attempt to describe them. I would
suggest that this statement should be typed and sent to Sir Harry
Johnston and to Mr. J[ohn] H. Harris to be criticised and supple-
mented, and that what all three write should then be circulated.

In all tropical Africa outside most of British West Africa the ownership of the land has been assumed by the various governments set
up by European States. The exceptions to that statement are of
importance historically, and as proof that there are other ways of
dealing with the land than appropriating it, but they to-day cover so
small an area, whether in Zanzibar, Uganda or Tanganyika, as
scarcely to affect the general situation. The point to note is that all
titles to land giving either ownership or use with or without rent or
other payments, issue from European Governments. Such rights as
exist in native law may or may not be valid (actual practice varies

very much) as between native claimants, but have no other kind of legal existence in European Courts. The judgment of the High Court of East Africa in the Masai Case in 1912 when certain chiefs sought the enforcement of a written treaty made only six years previously and failed, proved that for British Africa.[104] And the facts of the situation thus illustrated are the same all over the Continent (always excepting British West Africa).

In British Africa no distinction is drawn between the public and private domains of the Crown. In law and practice every acre of Crown land, in Nyasaland for instance, may be granted to anyone the Government chooses. Titles, of course, granted by governments, have transferred the ownership of large areas from the Crown to Europeans. But no such titles have been granted to native tribes or chiefs or individuals (the chief exception is in Uganda where several hundred chiefs were given title by Sir H. J[ohnston] to lands which, though of considerable value, comprise a small proportion of the area of the Protectorate). Over most of Tropical Africa, in fact, British and other, the existing law renders it impossible for any African or African tribe to acquire either the ownership of any land or any security of tenure. The various governments naturally make regulations for the guidance of their land officers and boards. Thus, in 1920 compensation of from one to four pounds was begun to be paid by the government of Kenya to each native family in occupation of land granted to Europeans. But all such rules and restrictions and compensations are in the discretion of the governments. They are related to no legal rights, whether derived from native law or from treaty terms. No European Court takes cognisance, except to settle quarrels between natives themselves, either of treaties or of native land law.

So when France assumed the ownership of all land in the ex-German Cameroons she followed a nearly universal practice. I have done my best to discover what our government has done in Tanganyika. I know that German titles to certain Arabs were confirmed. The area thus involved is trifling. I expect the rest of the territory is just "Crown" land, except of course for the areas, much smaller in proportion than in the neighbouring British Protectorates, granted before the war to Europeans. Most of the alienated land in towns and much of it in the country has since been sold to Indians.

The distinction in non-British Africa between private and public State land is, I believe, of little importance. The former is for exploitation by official or semi-official departments or corporations, the latter being intended for sale. The distinction, so far as I can gather, has nothing to do with the presence or absence of native rights whether customary or of treaty origin.

Plainly if in the rest of Africa, European courts had, as in Nigeria, held that every acre had some native owner, alienation by governments would have been impossible, especially if native ownership had been held to be tribal. Plainly also, governments seeking to be just would, on finding themselves possessed of an absolute power to alienate land to non-Africans, have first ascertained and set aside as much land as Africans could use and so vested it as to make it secure from the cupidity of exploiters. This was exactly what Viscount Grey demanded of the Government of the Congo Free State.[105] Presumably the Belgians informed him that his own government refused to practise what he preached. Yet attempts were made. In 1905 the British public learned of the scandal of the Colonial Office and Governor making contradictory promises of land grants, each ignorant of what the other was doing. Sir Charles Eliot, the Governor of British East Africa, resigned. A treaty was made with the tribe that had suffered the loss of most land laying down its tribal boundary for eternity. Downing Street in 1907 proposed to pass an Act through Parliament which would have had the effect of alienating to trustees for the general African population all the land not yet alienated to Europeans. The local governments in Africa opposed the suggestion. They said they could control their own land policy and feared no pressure from unjust men. Mark what happened. Within six years the treaty, uniquely deliberate, solemn and final was torn up in spite of the scandal of appeal to the Courts to enforce it. Year by year land has been alienated and thousands of Africans driven out or forced to work for its new owners. And now a Colonial Secretary proclaims as official policy that the African is never for all time to have any land rights in the healthier parts of Kenya. These are to be reserved for European ownership for the dispossessed to cultivate for the profit of their protectors.

All this is strictly relevant to the question of policy in territories under mandatories. Until in these areas we know how governments are going to act in regard to land, we know nothing. Until we realize exactly what the real difficulties and dangers are we can do nothing to avoid them. How can we expect from mandatories a record better than that of the country hitherto the wisest and most honourable? British public opinion, Parliament, Colonial Secretaries, Clerks in Downing Street, have all intended justice. How is it that to a record that includes more to be proud of than that of any other country, we have added and are still adding pages filled with shame? The facts in briefest summary of land alienation in Kenya are these. In a country two-thirds desert, with 16 persons to the square mile as compared with 2 in Australia and 3 in Quebec, between 30% and 40% of the arable land (which comprises about 15% of the total area) has been granted to Europeans. Average size of farm is 6,000 acres, average purchase price about a fortieth of market values. The alienated land includes 70% of the land with railway frontage. Since 1914 over two million acres have been alienated, the home of thousands of Africans now homeless. These two million acres consist of land described in official maps up to 1912 as not available for alienation, i.e. in official terminology as "reserves" or "closed areas." These terms, as explained above, have no real meaning. All land not alienated to Europeans is crown land, and, as the facts cited show, can be and annually is alienated irrespective of native law, treaty rights or any other restriction.

The results of this policy for half a generation are these. The country, once grain exporting is now a grain importer. Exports per head are half what they are in Uganda and a fraction of what they are in West Africa. Population has fallen, according to official estimates, by a third, really about a fifth. Standard wages are a third of a penny an hour. Disease and crime are rapidly increasing and baffle all remedies that do not reach their real causes. We cannot hope for better things from mandatories until we are honest enough, first to see clearly what is wise and just to be done in British Africa; second, to recognise frankly and fully the causes of the contrast between our country's intentions and her performances.

What then exactly are the measures in regard to land that Sovereign and mandatory States in Africa should be urged to carry out? I decline to regard the two types of government separately. To ask the French to acknowledge native rights in the Cameroons that we ourselves deny in a British Protectorate is both futile and hypocritical.

I venture to define the needs of Africans by three general statements:

1. That every family should have security in the possession of as much arable land as it is likely to be able to use for fifty years, free of all but public charges imposed alike on all occupiers of land.

2. That the Africans occupying the land thus secured to them should be encouraged (as in Nigeria until very lately) to develop it free from disturbance. In other words that no pressure, direct or indirect, economic, administrative or legal should be used to induce Africans to develop lands alienated to non-Africans in preference to the lands in their own occupation.

3. That Governments should foster in those areas in which Africans may live and work securely the growth, in active response to the changing beliefs and material conditions of the times, of their own social and political institutions.

These three desiderata will, I expect, be regarded as adequate and necessary by all except the less intelligent exploiters and their friends, the latter a surprisingly numerous body. But how to carry them out? Has anything been done, hitherto, to carry them out, in Tanganyika, for instance? I doubt it. I am afraid I regard the section in the Mandates Commission Questionnaire that deals with land, as useless for the purpose. What is needed now is a brief descriptive statement of the facts of land ownership and tenure in every African territory governed by mandatories and from Downing Street. Only when the facts be wisely contrived, can an estimate be made of the steps to be successively followed, of their cost, of the time wise to allow for each.

The kind of information to be elicited can be stated in the form of answers to the following questionnaire, here submitted, of course, merely as a draft.

1. What is the total estimated area of arable land in the territory?

2. What is the area of such land already alienated to non-Africans?

3. What is the area of such land regarded as available for future alienation to non-Africans?

4. What is the annual revenue from such alienated land?

5. What are the approximate numbers of Africans (a) residing on such alienated land in return for rent in money or labour, (b) residing as "squatters" i.e. with no obligation to pay rent in money or labour, (c) non-resident but temporarily employed by non-Africans?

6. State for each important tribe in the territory—

   (a) Population

   (b) Area of arable land in tribal occupation

   (c) The ownership of such land as defined by the law of the mandatory.

   (d) What security against alienation of such land to non-Africans is provided by the law of the mandatory.

   (e) An outline of the law and practice of the tribe regarding land ownership, allocation of tenancies, security of tenure, fees or other charges payable by tenants to chiefs or other tribal authorities.

   (f) Whether a tribal law exists forbidding the alienation of land to anyone not a member of the tribe.

   (g) Whether the law of mandatory regards such a tribal law as valid in restricting alienation.

   (h) Whether assuming normal increase of population for fifty years, and the agricultural development in tribal areas, that events elsewhere in Africa show to be possible, the area in the occupation of the tribe is regarded as adequate.

7. What measures, if any are proposed to render the land still in purely native occupation but not in native ownership secure against alienation?

8. Of the total exports of the territory what proportion is estimated to be the produce of alienated land and what of land occupied solely by Africans?

9. What measures have been taken, and what are to be initiated

for stimulating and organising production on lands in native occupation?

Some of these enquiries could be answered at once, some only after investigation. Until the facts they refer to are known with rough accuracy reformers in Europe can have no idea what to work for. British Governments volunteer none of that sort of information in official reports. Its extraction from unwilling governors is the prerequisite of all reform in Africa.

In conclusion I venture to allude to two common misconceptions among reformers, of importance because they seriously hinder real advance. One is that native law and custom should be decisive. That would only be reasonable if tribal law and institutions had been allowed natural growth and change as in a free country. But in part these have been destroyed and for the rest been stereotyped, an even more disastrous fate. And in any case, no Government could at once conduct a policy of the exploitation of alienated land, and legalise tribal law. I am heartily in favour of the revival of all that is distinctively indigenous in African life. But that revival will be the work of Africans with new minds. Even now much of tribal law is obsolete in general opinion. To support its indefinite perpetuation is sheer cruelty. I for one would rather see Africa in the hands of exploiters than in those of sentimental anachronists. I cannot explain better than by describing what in Bantu Africa the law in regard to land is, or rather was.

Before people learned to fly, the air above the continent of Europe had no owner. The reason of course was that except in slums, everyone had all the air he wanted, and even in slums the shortage of air was dependent on shortage of ground. Also of course no one used air except to breathe and see through. But the discovery of the art of flying created rights, and these had to be provided for in law.

Similarly in Africa with land, in tribes long established the conception of ownership of land is absent. Only while the memory of conquest lasts is the land thought of as belonging to the conqueror. Not even then perhaps so long as on some tree covered hill the gods of a time older than the conquest live on. What do exist of course are rights in land. But these are of unending variety and profusion. Speaking generally the rights of the tribe are concerned solely with forbidding alienation to aliens and with deciding conflicting rights

of members arising out of marriage and inheritance. Also as a rule
grazing and forest land are definitely communal. Second, the family
or clan has rights in land. Often family rights are saleable, though
transfer by adoption is more common. Finally the individual cultivator, be he man or woman, has rights in land. These result of course
from his labour, and as some crops grow for years—fruit trees for
many years—these individual rights are often the chief. Over most
of Africa the slave wars, mainly the work of Europe, led to the evolution of monarchic institutions out of primitive tribal democracy.
When some circumstances had allowed a democracy to persist,
individual rights to land so overshadowed the others as to lead some
authorities to describe the system as one of freeholds. In the old days
land hunger was immediately followed by migration. Now that
migration has ceased, that tribal lands have been cut down and
hundreds of thousands have no homes as of tribal right, and that
the power of the chiefs, aggrandised and sometimes even invented
by European governments, is largely freed from control by tribal
opinion, it would certainly not be always just to leave allocation of
land to the kind of "chief" the political system of the last generation
has set in authority. One of the fundamental difficulties of the situation is that chiefs cannot both be mouthpieces of a growing and
changing tribal opinion and be the agents of a European Government. By all means leave land and other tribal affairs to tribal authorities vivified by intimacy of relation with the general will and
wholly free from influence from other quarters. Unfortunately the
spirit of some tribes is so broken that no public opinion exists. It will
be a long time before tribal authorities obey tribal opinion. That is
why in my draft mandate I made the right to free land the statutory
right of every tribesman. And it is also the reason why I would include in the Questionnaire an enquiry as to what is being done to
revive tribal feeling and will, and, above all, to make it a will in
which all, as once long since, have a share.

The second misconception is regarding the room for immigration.
There is plenty of room, thanks to two centuries of slaving and half
a century of exploitation of Africans in Africa. But how is that room
filled, how total production increased, by giving away land by the
square mile to Europeans, who can only make the profits they seek
by inducing governments to force Africans to leave the land they still

have to work on land given to aliens? Is it usual for trustees to take part of their wards' land, make the wards work on it for their profit and then blame them for not making use of the land left to them? Nor does it help us to distinguish between land that is fit for Europeans to occupy and what they cannot use. The morals of the distinction apart, the fact is that Europeans can live anywhere in Africa, and can make most money just where they have least right to own land, where Africans are thickest because soil is most fertile, in places like the Kavirondo plain and the lower Zambesi. In actual fact of course it makes little difference to whom African Governments grant land, provided always both that plenty of land is left for the natives of the area and that they are undisturbed in the use of it. Hitherto nowhere except in British West Africa have these conditions been fulfilled. There they have been fulfilled only because the Courts made a decision which future executives had to obey.

I am heartily in favour of Mr. Harris' opinion that in districts where land has been alienated to non-Africans there should also be available for sale to Africans, on the same money terms as land is sold to Europeans, holdings where ex-employees and others who have grown out of tribalism may form settled communities.

To sum up, Europe has hitherto failed, in four-fifths of tropical Africa, to protect native land rights from spoliation. Nothing has been done or is being done to render impossible the alienation of such land as Africans still occupy.

Before the measures necessary to protect native land rights and to stimulate the development of native lands can be rightly conceived, a full statement of fact and circumstance for each political area must be acquired and published.

Meanwhile it is most necessary that until the needs of Africans can be first measured and then secured, no African government should be allowed to alienate any land in its control. Also, since we in this country can ask nothing from mandatories that we have not first persuaded our own colonial office to carry out, it is necessary first to elicit the whole facts of land rights, ownership tenures, alienations, etc., in British Tropical Africa by questions in Parliament, publication of official reports, statements in the press, and then, when the proved facts have made their inevitable impression on the British Public, then and then only formulate the measures for bringing about a policy based on justice, on political wisdom and on sound economics, for application first to British Tropical Africa and then to mandatory areas. That is the only course open to reformers who intend reform and are not content with declamation of principles and worthless paper guarantees.

Leys to Miss Marion J. Hunter[106]
18 February 1923

The three points in dispute as between European and Asiatic in Kenya Colony are 1. Powers of land acquisition in the Highlands. At first sight it seems strange that the law should forbid both Asiatics and Africans to own land in the middle of Africa. The explanation is that the Govt. is the sole original landowner, and, having embarked on an artificial and difficult "colonisation" scheme is unwilling to allow it to be wrecked. And it would be wrecked if it allowed a free market in land. On the other hand there is no reason to believe that a free market would lead to true colonisation by Indians. So far, both races go there to make money out of the labour of the third race. Some day, no doubt the surplus population of Indian villages will overflow into half empty Africa. *Then* a different situation will arise. But *now* the demand for land by Indians is merely, in the minds of most, a consequence of the claim to equality of status and in the minds of the few, is due to jealousy of opportunities to make fortunes out of Africans' labour—opportunities that Asiatics have as little right to as Europeans.

ii. The second point in dispute is immigration regulations. The original motive of these was purely to prevent immigrants from becoming a public charge. A European had to have money enough to pay his passage back to London, an Indian to pay his passage back to Bombay. True the regulation proved useless. Immigrants spent their money. Every year Govt. has to pay for a number of passages to London. Now, however, it is proposed to adjust the regulations so as to keep out all Indian immigration except rich merchants and their agents, obviously so as to bolster up the European Community. I strongly oppose. Indian artisans and small farmers (when they come) are more valuable to African society than shopkeepers. Furthermore, the whole conception of judging people by their wealth is wrong. The regulations proposed would have kept out all the apostles and early missionaries. I don't deny that the problem of what restrictions to place on immigration is difficult.

iii. The Franchise. The Indian Community has accepted, as a temporary settlement, the purely communal representation giving them half as many members as unofficial Europeans. (They would of course prefer a single electoral roll based on franchise qualifications either educational or depending on property, as in India.) The official scheme is objected to by the Indians because it would exclude clerks and workmen from India: by the Europeans because it would give them one third of the elected members of the Legislative Council.

The settlement will probably go through but nobody expects it to last long. The struggle will continue. During that struggle the simple fact that the church as a body recognises racial distinctions in its organisation will make Xtian propaganda among Indians in Africa impossible.

The differences in opinions and feelings that, as Mr. Oldham well knows, have taken place in the minds of most missionaries in India have scarcely begun to happen in Africa. The laws of India are in process of being changed so as to eliminate nearly all the privileges of her conquerors. The opposite process is going on in Kenya. It seems inevitable that such processes should be reflected in the machinery and work of the Christian Church.

Assuming that the influence of Indian & Chinese nationalism in breaking down racial barriers in these countries is regarded as entirely good, would it not be possible for the church in India to write a fraternal letter to the church in East Africa? Either a conference resolution or a letter signed by representative Indian Xtians (meaning by "Indian" Europeans in India as well as Indians by race) would help to bring the African Church into a movement that, as I hope Mr. O. agrees, has revealed God's will for mankind. It is as unfair to blame missionaries in Africa for opposing the political claims of Indians as to blame German missionaries for supporting the war. "Religious" people breathe the air of the secular society they live in. In Kenya Colony that air is so thick that people cannot see across the ocean—and across the centuries. Why shouldn't the church in India help the church in Africa to avoid its own past mistakes?

The only trouble I foresee is that the Indian church would, I imagine, urge none but the uncompromising policy of obliterating distinctions of status due to race, whether among congregations or within the Xtian society in communal life. Kenya Europeans would probably demand the repudiation of that view, even as an ideal not now to be acted on. It might reduce—such a proceeding as I suggest—the adherents of the church among Kenya Europeans from, say, 15% to 5%. But would there not also be greater gain in the church's acting, for once, in advance of the opinion of the community it lives among?

Leys to Miss Gollock
8 May 1923

I am very sorry to hear of Mr. Oldham's ill health. He is badly needed in this Kenya controversy. Race feeling seems to make people morally and mentally blind. I hear confidentially that the Cabinet has by a majority rejected the Indians' claims. I think I have ensured a pretty full statement of the facts in the House of Commons when the inevitable debate on the subject comes on. (I don't mean of course that I alone have done anything particular.) But what kind of explosion will there be in India?

Oldham to Leys
9 May 1923

. . . I am very much interested in the Kenya controversy and should have been a good deal more in it had it not been for the fact that I have been off work for a month as the result of a severe attack of influenza. It came at a most annoying time. I have got to try to keep the pace from becoming too fast and am involved in several important matters, including an approach we are making to Government about education in Africa.[107] I believe that we shall never get things right in Africa merely by the negative policy of protecting the African peoples from exploitation. We must do something constructive to give them the chance of standing on their own feet. This, however, is a large subject about which some time we can have a talk. At the moment, however, it is absorbing a good deal of my time.

We cannot do anything official in regard to Kenya as it is too political. I am personally, however, in touch with a good many of the people who are dealing actively with the subject and am doing what I can to help. If you will look at the letter in to-day's Times by Bishop [Henry] Whitehead [Bishop of Madras] and others you will see my general view of the situation. I had a hand in the preparation of the document, though it does not express all that I should have said if I had been writing myself. Of course many many questions arise in the application of the principles laid down and I am not indifferent to these. They are too intricate, however, to discuss in a letter. . . .

Leys to Oldham
20 May 1923

. . . I too have had influenza!

I entirely concur with your opinion that protecting people from exploitation is a futile business. It isn't easy to sit quietly and see people robbed but it doesn't seem to do any good to shout about it.—Still less to raise the hue and cry about the robbers. I have been asked to examine the white slave convention and see how far it could be applied to E. Africa. Why is it so easy for non Africans to abuse the bodies of African women and why have they so little scruple about it? Why, when the same state of affairs prevailed between domestics in England and masters and sons of the house 100 years ago, are things so greatly different now? Partly because the girls have been at school & Sunday School, partly because their parents have votes, partly because nobody thinks it creditable nowadays in a poor girl to have a child by a rich man—in short because domestics have risen in status. Is there any other way to stop the traffic in the bodies of African women? The trouble is that the Church in Africa doesn't undertake what the Church in Asia Minor did. It doesn't provide Onesimus & Co. with a completely adequate for life society. Nowadays Onesimus has to go to work for Gallios or idolaters. But anyhow one must wait for *Africans* to resent the sale of African women. They won't resent that alone of course.

I still hope for your African Royal Commission. The first Labour Govt. is sure to have recourse to it when it finds reform blocked by local interests. Indian agitation will help by preventing the exploiters from securely establishing themselves. There cannot possibly be any

settlement of the Indian question in Kenya now. It isn't mainly a
political question so it cannot be solved politically.

I am just realising, of late, that what I really want is £1000 a year.
It's horrible to find new vices growing on one.

Leys to John H. Harris
(Secretary of the Anti-Slavery and
Aborigines Protection Society)
30 June 1923
[Rhodes House, Anti-Slavery Society
Papers, MSS Brit. Emp. s. 19, G134]

. . . I broke my thigh in an accident a month ago and am still in
hospital. I won't be on duty for a couple of months yet.

I don't believe Oldham is capable of an anti-Indian policy. Remember he always instinctively looks for a middle way—or to put it
otherwise, persists in attempting to reconcile incompatible views. I
don't at all agree with him in the way he relates religion and politics.
But as nobody with my view could hold his job and do his very useful
work I am not altogether sorry. It is more important for Oldham to
carry people with him than to move fast himself. I am sure he is not
anti-Indian. His policy is delay until a Royal Commission reports.

Arthur's case is the common one of a man who has never been
trained nor trained himself to think for himself, suddenly faced with
an alternative without steady principles to guide him. Inevitably he
decides in accordance with prejudices until then unperceived by
himself. Then he perceives them and is distressed and bewildered. I
know that both Oldham and Andrews[108] have dealt truthfully both
with Willis and Arthur. I am not sure that Willis' mind is capable
of adhering to a course based on reason and principle. He will
always I fear obey in the long run his instinct & oppose whatever dis-
turbs ideas and plans made 20 or 30 years ago. But I have some
hopes of Arthur. He has greatly changed in the 18 years since he
first went to Africa and is, I think, too honest ever to forget the
glimpses of other worlds of thought such as Andrews would give
him.

I don't think it matters much what Govt. decides now. What matters is to keep the whole subject open. I don't mean that we should

give up public discussion. That would only mean boredom. I suppose you know the Govt. of S[outh] A[frica] has promised new Anti-Indian legislation.

Oldham to the Rev. Donald Fraser
(Church of Scotland Mission in Nyasaland)
3 January 1924
[IMC (Geneva), Box 93]

I often have doubts whether the book I am trying to write on *Christianity and the Race Problem* is going to be a success or of much value to other people. But the writing of it is teaching me a great deal.

One revelation that it has brought to me is the extent to which doctrines utterly hostile to all that you and I believe in are being propagated. From American universities, of all places in the world, there is issuing quite a stream of books repudiating in the name of modern biological and psychological science Christian ethical ideals and openly defending a policy of exploitation. This kind of literature, especially when it appears in the guise of scientific doctrine, is capable of poisoning very quickly the public mind.

Then, as regards the African Continent, we have the prevalent South African view of native questions which is apt to be contagious. The situation in Kenya I regard as very serious. The decision of last summer contained in the White Paper[109] has been openly repudiated by the "East African Standard." The most recent action of the Legislative Council, if the information that has just come to hand from Kenya is correct, has been to cut off all grants from native education in the reserves and divert the money to technical training, having as its object the providing of the European community with the menial help which it requires.

Quite apart from the theory and practice of exploitation, the more I study conditions in the African Continent, the more I become impressed with the way in which the economic factor is operating with ceaseless energy. I am referring now to its operation where it is morally neutral, in so far as such a thing is possible. Even at its best, its influence, in a constructive sense, is small. One feels how comparatively weak are the moral and constructive forces in the Continent and how inadequate they are to direct or control the tremendous changes which are in progress.

The whole situation has taken a most powerful hold on my mind. There is nothing to which I desire more to give any strength I have in the next few years than to help in rousing the conscience of this country to its responsibilities in Africa. If that can be done, the influence will in the end extend to other parts of the Continent than those under British rule. . . .

The appointment of the Advisory Committee on Education is a development that may be important. But it will be so only if we can rally to it an adequate measure of support.

My reason for writing to you these thoughts which for weeks and months have been constantly in my mind is that I assume, though I have no definite information, that you may be asked to allow your name to be proposed as secretary of the [Church of Scotland] Foreign Mission Committee. If such a proposal is made to you, I earnestly hope that, in considering it, you will take into consideration the situation which I have tried to describe. In my view there is no man who could do more to help to meet this situation than yourself. It is not merely a question of what you could do as an individual. There is a good deal of combustible material lying about that could be used to make a good fire. What we need is somebody to kindle it and you are the only man I see who can do this. I have no concrete programme in my mind. I think it will only take shape bit by bit. If you were here, what I should like would be that a few of us should get together and ask ourselves, what are the ways in which we can best serve the needs of Africa at the present time? I can imagine several quite different answers. Each would have to be considered in order to decide which way was the best. I believe, however, that if a few of us, holding firmly together, could set ourselves over a period of years (if God spares us) to getting this country (and, in so far as we have international links, the Christians in other countries) to realize their responsibilities a good deal might be accomplished. Humanly speaking, I look on you as almost indispensable to the kind of effort I have in view.

I am not thinking at all of a campaign. I am thinking rather of the kind of thing that might be accomplished over a period of years by a group of men, clear in regard to their object and working together, though each of them at the same time be engaged in other tasks.

It seems quite clear that the only hope of gaining some measure of control over the tremendous developments that are proceeding so rapidly in Africa is to have some kind of constructive educational policy. For this the committee at the Colonial Office provides the opportunity. Personally I am certain that the policy will not amount to much unless it is very largely inspired by the Christian spirit and carried out on a Christian basis. This means that the missionary societies have got to conceive their responsibilities in a larger way and make a definite move forward. Without this, the work will pass increasingly into other hands and will not be done as well as the Christian forces might do it if they see their opportunity and seize it. At present, there is a quite inadequate realization of the magnitude of the call. It cannot be responded to without the offering in con-siderable numbers of the right kind of men and women and of the gifts from Christian people that will make their work possible. It is waste of strength to make good plans unless at the same time we are setting ourselves to stir up the Christian Church to put them into operation. You can be our leader in this effort as no one else can.

If I have at all succeeded in expressing my real mind you will see that I am viewing the whole question from the standpoint of Africa. I cannot help thinking that in the conditions I have tried to describe you can render the biggest service to Africa at home. It is doubtful whether you have many more years of service there in any case. In such a movement as that to which I believe we are called you might be able, under God, to bring to the Continent, in East and West alike, the accession of strength which is so greatly needed.

For this you need a platform and I think that the secretaryship of the Foreign Mission Committee would provide it. The object of my letter is to ask you to consider the opportunities of that position, not in the narrow limits in which the office is generally regarded, but in relation to the possibility that I have indicated. I think it would be possible once you were in office, with the friends you have behind you, to secure for yourself sufficient assistance to enable you to dis-charge the business side of your duties with no excessive demand on your time, leaving you free for a large measure of co-operation with the other missionary bodies in Great Britain (and it may be in other countries also) in a combined effort for the expansion of Christ's Kingdom, more particularly in the African Continent. I should be ready to co-operate with you at any time if you wished it, in putting before the Foreign Mission Committee the claims of this larger service. In order to render it, however, you need some platform from which to start. So far as I can see, the Foreign Missions secretary-ship would provide that.

I have had to dictate this letter in a day of great pressure and it is not what I would have liked to write. I hope, however, that it may in some degree convey to you the thoughts which have prompted me to write it and that it may be of some use to you if you are called on to make a decision. . . .

Oldham to the Archbishop of Canterbury (Randall Davidson) 30 April 1924 [IMC (Geneva), Box 93]

There is no reason why the fullest publicity should not be given to the appointment of the Advisory Committee on Native Education in Tropical Africa at the Colonial Office. An announcement on the subject was published in the *Times* of January 5th of this year. . . .

The appointment of [Alexander G.] Fraser as principal of Achimota may also be mentioned publicly as it has been confirmed by the Secretary of State. It has also been agreed to appoint Dr [J. E. Kegwir] Aggrey to a high post on the staff but owing to the fact that he is at present in East Africa I am not sure whether the appointment has been officially confirmed. If the health of Fraser and Aggrey is spared we shall have in the Gold Coast an experiment in native education which will influence educational developments throughout the African Continent. Sir Gordon Guggisberg will tell you more fully about his plans.[110]

Dr Dillard is a Virginian who has been with Dr Jones as a member of the Commission to East Africa.[111] He is one of the most influential men in the Southern States and has the confidence and respect of Southern white men while he has devoted his life to the promotion of negro education. He is an attractive man who wins the regard of almost everyone who comes in contact with him. He is accompanied by his son. I have a letter from him saying that he expects to reach London about May 6th and has to be in America by about May 15. I have had no further details. I cabled some days ago to East Africa to ask for particulars but have not yet had a reply. As soon as I hear anything further I shall let Your Grace know. At present I do not know how long he will be in London nor what his plans are. He will be able to give you a very interesting account of conditions in Kenya. I expect from Dr Jones' letter that it will be much more favourable to the settler point of view than the view we have been inclined to take during the past few years. I think this side of things should be brought forward but I a little doubt whether Dr Jones and Dr Dillard were long enough in the colony to get quite to the bottom of things. . . .

. . . I think you will find Dr Dillard an exceptionally interesting person to talk to. He is one of the best-informed men that there is on the black and white situation in the United States and his experience there will have enabled him to see a great deal in Kenya.

Leys to Oldham
29 June 1924

Congratulations on the Commission on East Africa.[112] I know that you helped more than any other man, though Harris seems to think himself solely responsible! How injurious a thing is success! I hope it is to be a proper *Royal* Commission, with fullest powers and widest terms of reference. And I hope you are to be a member of it.

Oldham to Leys
30 June 1924

. . . I had some little hand in connection with the Commission on East Africa but, so far as I know, Harris deserves the chief credit. Though I gave a push at one or two points I have been too busy to keep in close touch with what has been going on. I am not altogether satisfied with the terms of reference but I hope that the appointment of the Commission may lead to something. It certainly is the right course to take and in the hands of the right men it might mark a real turning point in the history of the East African territories. Everything will depend on the personnel. I have at present no particulars

beyond the fact that Lord Southborough is to be Chairman.[113] I
received a day or two ago an invitation from Mr Thomas to be a
member and have accepted.

It was a pleasure to see your hand-writing again. I hope that some
time we may meet and have a talk.

I have perpetrated a book on race.[114] I do not think that you will
agree with everything that is in it. In fact, I am sure you will not. No
one can be expected to do that. The whole question of race is so
complex and obscured that no two people can think alike on every
point. I think, however, that your disagreement at some points may
be fundamental. I hope, however, that on the other hand you will
feel that in some respects it helps matters forward.

I hear that you have a book on the stocks. I shall look forward
eagerly to its publication and to reading it.

Oldham to Leys
2 July 1924

Is there any chance of your being in Town during the next two or
three weeks? I should very much like to have a talk with you. If that
is not possible, there is just a chance that I might be able to come to
spend a night in Derby. . . .

I have your early paper which was frequently copied.[115] It is the
best thing that you have written so far as my knowledge goes. Do you
still stand by what you then wrote in the main? Can you direct my
attention to what you regard as your most important writings since?
I do not always agree with you but I find your writing more stimulating than that of anyone else. I shall do what I can to equip myself
for the work of this committee but at the moment I am so pressed
that I hardly know how to turn round. . . .

Leys to Oldham
3 July 1924

You simply must be on this commission, must not dream of refusing. Of the fifteen members, five are certain to come to findings
wholly satisfactory to me. So also, I am assured, will [Sir Hugh]
Clifford, whom I do not know.[116] Most of the rest are sure to be

exploitationists of different shades. In the middle are yourself and
[Sir William] Ormsby-Gore. I have tried to indoctrinate you both!
Plainly you two will be the deciding voices. Also don't forget that
African missions will be deeply influenced. [E. D.] Morel and Clif-
ford (and I think Balfour) are anti-clericals. You and Harvey are
Xtians first and last. The whole future of tropical Africa hangs on
this commission. As its pivot you are its most important member. . . .

The same day that I got your first letter I read the first review of
your book that I had seen, in the I.R.M., and ordered it. If the
review is adequate I should expect to find little or nothing to differ
from. That day I read a paper in Edinburgh House was a turning
point to me. I went back and worked over the N[ew] T[estament]
once more. I now believe the whole conception of race is an illusion,
one of the many shadows men pursue, and that Paul's statement
that racial differences inherent in people themselves, apart from
history and circumstances, do not exist is true. I now feel that I
should rejoice if my daughter married a non European if she and he
were of the same mind. I would rejoice with trembling but be proud
of her. I would only try to make sure of the man beforehand.

My book was refused by Arnold and is now being considered by
Allen & Unwin. Their only letter about it to me is a curate's egg letter. I expect I shall have to pay part of the cost of publication. The
book contains, I believe, all the important facts about Kenya policy
and history. If you know Stanley Unwin encourage him to print it,
and to print it at once. I am disgracefully afraid someone else may
bring out a book on the subject before I do! The chapter on Xtian
missions has been variously received by friends. . . .

If I may venture a suggestion it is to see that the commission takes
plenty of time. Interim report in 18 months, final report in five
years. Build for an age. . . .

Leys to Oldham
15 July 1924
[IMC (Geneva), Box 161]

I have read your book with great admiration and nearly complete
agreement. Will you forgive me for saying that I had no idea you
could write so good a book?

I am glad mine was written before I read yours. It is pleasant to think that working on different materials we have so frequently reached identical judgments on them.

My reason for writing is this. I fancy I shall come to an agreement with Allen & Unwin this week.[117] In any case "Kenya" (the title) will be published in the autumn. I have had several enquiries for information from missionary quarters in America. Could you put me in touch with somebody who would make sure that the American missionary public know about the work? Either the publishers or I would of course pay for any advertisements thought useful.

Oldham to Leys
16 July 1924

Thank you very much for your kind words about my book.

I think the best person to advise you about America would probably be my colleague, Warnshuis.[118] He will reach this country about the middle of August, and will be on this side of the Atlantic for a few weeks. You could address him at this office. This will, I think, be better than writing to America.

I am looking forward with great interest to your book and wish to read it at the earliest possible moment. Will it be at all possible to see proofs? I doubt whether I can do anything before my holiday and I am anxious to drop everything serious during August. When I get back in September, however, I want to equip myself as well as I can for the work of the new Committee and your book will be one of the things I most wish to read.

Leys to Oldham
25 August 1924

. . . The book is in the press and I hope to be able to send you a proof copy, as you wished, by the end of next month. Can you put me into touch with this American friend? . . .

Oldham to Leys
23 September 1924

I have talked with my colleague, Dr. Warnshuis, about advertising your book in America. I presume that your publisher has American connections and he would probably be the best adviser. I understand, however, that you are thinking especially of missionary circles. $5 or $10 would not go very far in advertising. A slip advertising the work might, if you desire, be posted to the foreign mission boards, the names and addresses of which are given in the Missionary Atlas. . . .

Oldham to the Archbishop of Canterbury
28 October 1924
[IMC (Geneva), Box 93]

. . . It is becoming increasingly clear to me that, on a long view, the interests of the native population, of European settlers and of the Empire, are fundamentally the same. The ultimate limiting condition of the economic development of East Africa is the question of population. The interests both of this country and of the local settlers are entirely dependent in the end on an increasing, healthy, industrious and contented population. If any of these conditions are ignored economic development is inevitably arrested. I believe we shall make more progress by demonstrating the truth of this view than by appearing to advocate native rights in antagonism to policies of economic advance. The opposition is transcended if one takes a sufficiently large view of the problem. I should like to make what contribution I can to the development and dissemination of this point of view both in the East Africa Committee and in conversations during the coming months with those who are interested. I am getting into touch with a good many people of quite different types who are interested in East Africa.

The Committee on East Africa may, I think, be a valuable means of gathering information. I do not build too high hopes on the Committee as such—partly because its personnel is not all that one would desire, and partly because I am rather sceptical of the value of reports of committees unless circumstances are favourable. I look for more from the gradual education of responsible opinion through informal conversations outside, as well as within, the Committee.

When one begins to think, however, of the question of getting things done, one is brought up against the fact that practically everything depends on those who have the power to take decisions.

I do not think that Sir James Masterton-Smith's place has yet been definitely filled.[119] This will be a very important appointment. More important still, however, if we have a Government that will last for a few years, will be the new Colonial Secretary and Under-Secretary. Conditions at the present time seem to be favourable, if we had at the Colonial Office a Secretary of State with imagination and initiative, for the adoption of a progressive, constructive policy which would both contribute to imperial development and prosperity and also do full justice to the interests of the natives and which might be expected, for this reason, to win the support both of the commercial community and of those who are specially concerned to see that the principle of trusteeship is loyally carried out. So far as I can see if the new Government can work out such a policy real prosperity might be in store for East Africa. Without it, things might easily go from bad to worse.

Of course one does not know what will happen at the General Election. I am not a party man but so far as East Africa is concerned I should hope for most from a Conservative Government. My reason for writing just now is to put the point of view which I have stated before Your Grace in case, if you agree with it, you may have any opportunity, in conversation with those who have influence to express your sense of the importance of getting at the Colonial Office someone with imagination and constructive force. I, of course, know perfectly well that no formal action can be taken in a matter of this kind. I merely wish to put the situation, as I see it, before you in case, if you think there is any truth in what I write, an opportunity may present itself of bringing home the importance of the present situation in Africa to any of those who have influence in our public life. . . .

Oldham to the Archbishop of Canterbury
December 1924
[IMC (Geneva), Box 93]

I think you will be interested to know that I had a very good talk on Saturday evening with Col. Amery about African education.[120] Steel-Maitland asked [Dr. T. Jesse] Jones and myself to dine with him to meet Amery. We had two and a half hours after dinner. I think Amery's interest and imagination have been thoroughly captured.

If Your Grace can find time I think you should not miss Leys' book on Kenya. It is a masterly piece of work whether he is right or wrong, and bound, I think, to have political consequences. You may have seen the review in the Literary Supplement of the Times. This was written by Philip Kerr.[121] Leys' terrible indictment of the system in Kenya has been a shock to men like Sir Donald Cameron, the new Governor of Tanganyika, and others who have spoken to me.[122] I am not at all prepared to accept Leys' picture as true without further investigation. On one or two points I definitely consider him to be mistaken and even if most of the facts are true, they may represent only part, and not the whole, of the truth. At the same time the book is written with remarkable moderation. Unless the facts that he states can be disproved, the existing state of things cannot be reconciled with the avowed principles of our policy. What can be done to remedy the state of things he describes is another question. I am doubtful whether public attacks on Kenya will help matters at this stage. They may only have the effect of consolidating opinion in Kenya and making a solution more difficult. I should be satisfied if the Government were willing to have a disinterested and impartial enquiry to ascertain the truth. This is as much to be desired in Imperial interests as in those of the natives. If our policy ignores realities it must, in the end, lead to disaster.

I may have an opportunity of putting this point of view before Col. Amery if, after consulting with a few other people, it seems desirable to do so.

Oldham to Leys
16 December 1924
(pencil note: "Not sent")

I have now been through your book once. I hope to read it two or three times. I think you have succeeded in your task and have forced England to face the issue. I am not surprised to find that the book is making a deep impression where it has been read. I have a good deal of evidence of its effect. You must be gratified by the notice in the Times Literary Supplement.

I think we can rely on the issues you have raised being brought to the attention of the Government. The thing to be avoided at all costs, as it seems to me at the moment, is the kind of attack on Kenya which will arouse the patriotic instincts and resentment of the average settler and put them in a state of mind in which they will not listen to reason. If this happens all sorts of complications with South Africa may arise and the Government may hesitate to take action. Very wisely you have stated the issue as not primarily one of native versus settler but as one of sound imperial policy. If the issue can be kept there I think it is possible to gain the assent of a large number of settlers through a thoroughly frank facing of the facts.

I congratulate you most heartily on a piece of work in accordance with the best traditions of the country. I have not had time yet to study the subject sufficiently to know how far I agree with you in detail. It seems to me unlikely, however, that your main assertions can be shaken.

Oldham to Bishops of
Salisbury, Liverpool, Manchester
16 December 1924

I think you should not fail, if you can find time, to read Norman Leys' *Kenya.* It is a book which may have important political consequences. It is a terrible indictment of the system in Kenya backed by the experience, study and thinking of fifteen years. I am not sure whether Leys is right in every detail and his picture does not represent the whole truth about Kenya. But I doubt whether his main contentions can be disproved and the book is one that cannot be ignored.

It is another question what action should be taken in regard to the matter. Public agitation at the moment would seem to me the worst thing that could happen. It would only have the effect of consolidating settler opinion and putting them in a state of mind in which they would not listen to reason. Attacks on Kenya can only arouse local patriotism and if Kenya is forced to put up a fight there may be all sorts of complications with South Africa. If the matter can be rightly handled I believe that the great majority of the settlers can be

got to agree that the last word always lies with the hard facts of the
situation and that any policy which ignores them must lead, in the
end, to disaster.

I think I shall have an opportunity of putting the case, as I see it,
before the Secretary of State and I hope also to have a talk with
Ormsby-Gore on his return.[123] I am not without hopes that the Government may take the situation firmly in hand. But one never knows
when issues raised by Leys may become a matter of public controversy and we ought to be prepared. I am anxious that you should
have read the book. I should deprecate much public reference to it
at present but if, after having read it, you have any opportunity of
speaking privately to members of the Cabinet it would be all to the
good.

The state of things described by Leys cannot in any way be squared
with the avowed principles of our policy as laid down in the White
Paper issued last year.[124] It is desirable that the Government should
realise that there is a strong body of opinion that is determined that
these principles should not merely be publicly proclaimed but carried out in practice, and that unless the truth of Leys' contentions
can be not merely denied but disproved this body of opinion will be
bound to assert itself.

Oldham to the Archbishop of Canterbury
17 December 1924
[IMC (Geneva), Box 93]

Thank you for your letter. Since I wrote to you I have gone more
directly into the question of Kenya. As the result of a talk which I
had with Lionel Curtis and a letter which I subsequently wrote to
him, he asked me to allow him to send the letter to Amery. I enclose
a copy of a further letter which I am sending to Amery to-day in
order to state my views somewhat more clearly. The only thing to be
done, so far as I can see (as I hinted in my letter to Curtis) is to give
Sir Robert Coryndon[125] some other Governorship, e.g. Nigeria, and
to send out a first-rate man with instructions to probe things to the
bottom, with the assurance that the Government will stand behind
him. Unless some action of this kind is taken and if things are
allowed to drift into a mess, there may be trouble of which it is

impossible to foresee the end. We shall have the settlers in Kenya on the defensive, with South Africa lining up behind them, against an indignant and suspicious public opinion in England.

Ormsby-Gore has not, I think, reached this country yet. I wrote to catch him at Marseilles. I hope very much that I may have a chance of seeing him before I leave for America at the end of this month. I think he probably holds the key to the situation in his hand. Whatever ought to be done (apart of course from the question of the Governor) ought to find a place in his report, which he will have to present almost immediately after his arrival.[126]

Leopold S. Amery to Oldham
20 December 1924

I will certainly read Ley's [sic] book at once. The whole problem is very difficult and there is a great danger of people losing their heads both ways. I much enjoyed our talk the other night.

Oldham to the Archbishop of Canterbury
29 December 1924
[IMC (Geneva), Box 93]

I had lunch with Ormsby-Gore to-day and had a long talk. I think his visit to Africa has done a good deal of good.

He has come back enthusiastic about the Kenya settlers. I do not doubt that he has good grounds. Garfield Williams took very much the same view.[127] Many of them are public school men of the best type. Ormsby-Gore attributes the undesirable state of things in Kenya to the weakness of the Government in the past. He used stronger language about Sir Robert Coryndon's predecessors than I should venture to employ.

He is going to read Leys' book. His view of the shortcomings of the Government is quite in line with what I think is needed to remedy matters. I believe we should concentrate on trying to get the Colonial Office in the next few years to send out some really good men to Kenya. Ormsby-Gore would quite agree that this is what is wanted. I am not quite so sure that he is as fully convinced of the necessity of obtaining accurate and disinterested information in regard to a number of questions on which at present there is a chaos of conflicting opinions. I may have made some impression on him and I hope to be able to follow up the point when I have more time and have got my own ideas clearer as to what is needed.

Ormsby-Gore tells me that Lord Olivier is going to raise the question of Kenya shortly in the House of Lords.[128] I rather regret this. Anything in the nature of an attack on Kenya at present will put the Europeans there on the defensive and make them unreasonable, whereas taken in the right way I believe them to be entirely open to reason. What is wanted seems to me to be the recognition that Kenya presents problems of exceptional difficulty and an attempt to explore the difficulties with a view to finding the solution which will best serve all the interests in Kenya. . . .

Oldham to the Archbishop of Canterbury
31 December 1924
[IMC (Geneva), Box 93]

I am sending you a copy of some of the advance chapters of Dr Jones' Report on East Africa,[129] which . . . seems to me to be even better than the one on West Africa. In its introductory chapters he has given us a policy of education which ought to find widespread support.

Oldham to Leys
New York, 10 January 1925

On the voyage across the Atlantic I have been able to read your book carefully. It is the only book I have read, for storms have interfered with my programme. You have produced a noble work. It leaves me with a deep sense of admiration for the mind and soul that conceived it and lived it. What will be more important to you is that I believe you have achieved your purpose. You have written a book that cannot be ignored. I believe it will influence the current of history. Accept my humble congratulations. . . .

Leys to Oldham
25 January 1925

You are far too generous and if you knew me better would think otherwise. But I am encouraged to think that you believe it would do good if some people in the missionary movement in America read the book (—and of the general public as well?) Can you help me to the best means of ensuring that the book is given some publicity? I haven't time to get [Leonard] Woolf's consent but I shall venture to guarantee personally an expenditure of £6 on advertising in any papers your American friends may advise. . . .

Oldham to Leys
16 February 1925

Your letter reached me two days before I sailed from America. I was able to arrange next day to see a man who I thought could advise me better than anyone else. He is in touch with leading newspapers in the United States. He could not advise me on the spot but undertook to get information and write to me. I expect to hear from him in a few days and will communicate with you again. . . .

Leys to Oldham
22 February 1925

(1)   A recent statement in "The London Times" predicted an early report by the "East African Commission." I hope the full Committee was not meant. Even so, I am sorry as I badly wanted to be given the chance of representing facts to the subcommittee which, as a long letter from Hooper confirms me in believing, the three visiting M.P.s were never told.[130] Hooper goes so far as to say that some of the things they were told were false.

(2)   May I rely on you to let me know in good time when and how to submit a short memorandum of three or four hundred words to the Committee? In a sense "Kenya" is my evidence. But I would like to say one or two things about the specific—and rather narrow—issues before the Committee.

(3)   The enclosed cutting shows how absurd it is for Ormsby-Gore to pretend there has been any change in either the spirit or the practice of the Govt. of Kenya. If compulsion is necessary for urgent public works why should it be applied *only* to Africans at home? Why not *also* to workers on plantations? The only

conceivable answer is that in the mind of the Government the growing of sisal, coffee &c. on plantations is something sacred, while work in the villages, whether the growing of food or of produce for export may be interrupted without either serious injury or serious injustice.

Note that this point is the very same one as you and the Archbishop rightly fastened on in the controversy over the "Bishops Memorandum."

It seems extraordinary to me that people refuse to face the most important fact of all about the country that there aren't enough workers in it to do anything like the work demanded—and expected!—of the African population. People calmly assume that no men are needed for food production. Even if they weren't there wouldn't be enough to satisfy private employers, let alone build railways. The moral is to stop all new projects for development, which must inevitably be infertile in the absence of men to make use of newly opened up areas and industries. Railway building should be confined to areas where there is already a big population. Elsewhere railways will only transfer people from imperfectly developed areas to areas not developed at all.

Oldham to Leys
23 February 1925

The reference in the Times was to the report of the Commission which went out to East Africa; i.e. the report of Ormsby-Gore, Church and Linfield. This will be out in three or four weeks. Some of it, I understand, has already gone to the press. I believe that when it comes out there will be a debate in the House.

The larger Committee has been suspended. Harris, whom I have not seen, will probably think that the cause has had a bad setback. Personally, I have no regrets. I am extremely sceptical whether a committee constituted as this was and working on the methods adopted would have produced any valuable results. My own view is that the problem will have to be tackled by other means. I can imagine a committee that really meant business and had funds at its disposal which would enable it to send out careful investigators to Africa might achieve something; but not the body as it was actually constituted. From the first I was not hopeful. In justice to the Government one must recognise that something had to be done. More than half the M.P.s who were on the Committee lost their seats at the last election so it ceased to be representative of Parliament. Three or four prominent members had for one reason or another to resign and I understand that Lord Southborough was not disposed to go on. Moreover, the Committee had been set up with very little thought and its terms of reference were not clear. Both land and education, which are vital to any effective consideration of the subject, were excluded. I am inclined to regard the abolition of the Committee as a useful clearing of the decks, leaving the way free to get the problem tackled in some more satisfactory manner; though whether the present Government will do this of course remains to be seen.

I do not think that you would gain much by sending in any document to the East African Commission. Ormsby-Gore is at present on the warpath about your book. I hear that he slated it severely at the African dinner and that his speech on that occasion was broadcast.[131] This, I am told, has had the effect of increasing the sale of your book. I do not think you need be surprised. I am informed that Ormsby-Gore's line of attack was that it was very embarrassing to the Government. I have no doubt this is what you intended. Apart from the fact that the publication of the book at this juncture makes Ormsby-Gore's position more difficult and makes it less easy for him to get things done, he is probably acting on a sound political instinct in taking up the cudgels against you. So far as getting any practical reforms is concerned it may be the line most likely to lead to results.

The more I think about the Kenya problem, the more difficult it seems to me to see how to get anything done. There appears to be no middle course between getting things done with the consent, or at least acquiescence, of the local white community, and sending out Guards. The last is not the course that the Government will adopt. I am not sure that I should adopt it if I were Secretary of State. It might mean that Rhodesia and South Africa would line up behind the Kenya settlers. Feelings would be exacerbated. It would probably end in a lot of natives getting killed and things would be left much worse. We are consequently thrown back on methods of reform that the opinion of the white community will support. That, I believe, is what Ormsby-Gore is working for. While he may slate you severely in the House of Commons, this need not mean that the Colonial Office do not intend to do anything. It may be a necessary step toward making some change that Ormsby-Gore should appear as the champion of the settlers.

I do not know whether I have succeeded in making my meaning plain. Letters are not a satisfactory means of communication, and I should very much like to have a talk with you. I am thinking about the problem as much as I can and wish I could see more daylight. The one thing that is fairly clear to me is that little or nothing has been lost by the abolition of the East Africa Committee.

From all that I hear your book is making a great impression.

Oldham to Leys
25 February 1925

It occurred to me, after writing to you the other day, that in one respect my letter was not, perhaps, sufficiently clear. I did not mean to suggest that reforms should wait until the members of the white community, who are interested parties, are willing to agree to them. I think that the Imperial Government must use the powers it possesses to the full. Unless, however, it has made up its mind that it is prepared, if necessary, to send out troops to enforce its views, the pace at which it can introduce reforms will depend on the extent to which it can get its way without forcing things to the point of rebellion. I think it is probable that with the right Governor and Secretary of State all that is necessary could be done within these limits; but the limits need to be recognised. I think this is also, in substance, your own view. I only want to guard against any possible suggestion in my letter that we are entirely dependent on the views of the local community.

Leys to Oldham
26 February 1925

I hope to see you in about a month but my experience is that such conversations are of little use unless both parties think out rigorously beforehand the special aspects of the problem seen by the other, and for that it is necessary for each to state things precisely to the other. That is why I am so glad to have your clear statement.

Before I examine your chief point let me deal with one or two minor ones. I see no reason why the Govt. had to dismiss the Committee. I believe it has scarcely ever happened before. Why should men ... suitable in 1924 be unsuitable in 1925? But I do agree that any committee of enquiry that is liable to be dismissed after an election is useless. The thing to go for is the Royal Commission you advocated long ago. I enclose a copy of extracts from a letter from Hooper. The way these three M.P.s were lied to—and successfully lied to—is even worse than I expected.

Second, O.G.'s speech didn't, so far as can be judged, help the sale of "Kenya," according to the publisher's figures of the sales. The astonishingly favourable reviews sold the book for me.

Third you are quite mistaken in thinking I meant to embarrass the Govt. I tried to tell the whole truth about Kenya and tried to keep every other consideration out of my mind except avoiding personalities whenever possible. To my mind whether a Govt. would be embarrassed or not is the very kind of consideration which should never be allowed to enter an author's mind. I had rather he considered whether what he was writing would go down well with the public. And in fact I expressly stated that governing Kenya today is a Herculean task. If the publication of the true state of affairs makes O. G.'s job more difficult that can only be because his policy is in conflict with the facts.

Now for your dilemma. You say there are only two ways of bringing about reforms, either by persuading the local Europeans to accept them or by "sending out guards" to compel their acquiescence. I don't think your dilemma is a real one, as I shall shortly explain. But even if it is you haven't stated it realistically. The real dilemma is whether 2-½ millions of Africans are to continue to suffer injustice and compulsion or several thousand Europeans inhabiting a country constitutionally subject to the will of Parliament are, if they so wish, to be allowed to prevent our country from doing justice. I admit that the compulsion of the Europeans would, if it were necessary to reform, be an evil. But why do you consider that fact rules their compulsion out of court? Do you find more tolerable the continuance of the injustices suffered by the Africans of Kenya?

Second, do you know of any occasion when any body of men in a position comparable to that of . . .

26 February 1925

I had got so far in the *third* draft of an answer to you, and now your second letter comes as a perfect illustration of the necessity of exact statement. If I had spent an hour with you last week and you had expounded the substance of your first letter until just at the end you expressed yourself in the sense of letter No. 2—then I am afraid I would have lost my temper, unjustifiably I know.

So we seem to be agreed that the problem is how to carry through certain reforms in Kenya with the minimum of violent resistance on the part of local Europeans. (The reforms are unspecified but I shall assume they are those which I define in Chap. XVI of "Kenya.") You hint at your answer in the phrase "the pace at which the Govt. can introduce reforms." I don't think time an important factor in the situation. I would ask you in turn, how are you going to make use of the delay? My answer is ready. Publicity. More and ever more publicity. The facts from every angle, as seen by every kind of person. I want Ross to publish the book he has partly written in spite of the fact that I think him wrong in thinking that the evils in Kenya are due to there being so many bad men among the settlers. I want somebody in Delamere's confidence to write a book exposing my mistakes and confounding my arguments. The British public is responsible for events in Kenya, more responsible than for events in Egypt, as responsible as for events in India. It has a right to know the facts.

The reason I wrote "Kenya" was that reform is impossible until the facts are publicly known. Do you remember what Lincoln said just before the Civil War broke out, how every drop of blood the lash had drawn from the back of a slave would have to be recompensed by those who had been responsible for the wrong, and by their children? I refuse to believe in such a necessity, not from mere shrinking from so painful an issue, but because I see a better way out. And that way out is some measure of expiation done by those responsible, that is the British public. That involves sacrifice. Justice cannot be done without it. It never can. We can say with substantial accuracy that a single act of sacrifice by our country killed the institution of slavery in the whole world. The payment of £20,000,000 to redeem the slaves in the W. Indies, an act done by the country which the world knew was more guilty than any other country and had profited most by its guilt, proved, though people at the time could not see it, to be decisive. Such an act of public expiation involves personal sacrifices. You cannot rouse the public conscience by pulling wires. Think of all that you and others did five years ago and of how at this very moment the Govt. of Kenya is again proposing to conscript village workers and leave plantation workers alone.

I hope you will forgive me for thinking that your occupation and habits dispose you to give too great importance to people in high position. You know them well, constantly meet them in many countries. You see the levers of the machinery of government in their hands. It is tempting to think that a thing is done when the hand of such a man is rightly guided. In the modern world it is not so. We are helpless unless the lever moves a powerful engine. That engine is public opinion.

If O[rmsby]-G[ore] thinks he can do anything whatever in E. Africa without the public behind him he must be even more easily deceived than I had feared. As an ex settler wrote to me the other day Delamere is as sly as a jackal. He is as determined as a buffalo as well. I know him as O. G. doesn't. With O. G. he was playing a game, exactly as he played it with half a dozen governors in succession. No wonder he won his game with O. G. (and with Major Church who actually was made to believe that Kikuyu and Kavirondo don't know what to do with what little money they get in wages!). That is why I regard O. G. as a traitor to the people of Kenya. If he has read my book he knows the truth of things. He knows that the forces at his disposal in the C.O. have over and over again tried to do what he intends. He knows why they failed. He knows that since the threat of rebellion succeeded in 1923 the C.O. is by itself even more helpless than before. And yet he repudiates the one means of getting justice done and publicly defends those who are determined to prevent its being done. You hint that he agrees with me in private while condemning me in public. How perfectly futile! What is he going to say in debate next month when he is told that Delamere and Co. threatened rebellion in 1923 and got their way? Will he tell a lie? How will that help the ends you say he is privately pursuing? Whereas suppose he frankly acknowledged the facts, making for the settlers the one excuse that is fair to offer, that a negligent public opinion in this country had allowed these men privileges which had resulted in an impossibly difficult position, from which the country can only be extricated by acknowledging past mistakes and, with all necessary care to prevent injustice to local Europeans, by resolutely and methodically undertaking the reforms that past neglect had made long overdue. Would O. G. by saying that ruin his chance of Cabinet rank? I don't think so. But if he would then all I say is that evil cannot be overcome by people who refuse sacrifice. Take Howard's work for prison reform, Shaftesbury's work, any other's. It may be career in one man's case, in another's a fortune, in a third his reputation for sensible views. But the time comes when a man has to make his choice.

In short my answer to your dilemma is that the degree of resistance to reform in Kenya depends on two factors. The wisdom with which the reforms are planned and the volume and intensity of the public demand for their execution.

That is my attitude to the chief aspect of the problem in your mind. Next week I mean to state to you its chief aspect in mine—a very different aspect capable fortunately of being quite briefly stated!

P.S. Traitor wasn't the word for O. G. When a man of fair intelligence, great kind heartedness and average moral courage comes into close contact with an abler and more determined man his amiability proves his ruin. O. G.'s job demands a very unusual kind of man, not the least like O. G. That's the trouble. But if O. G. is not a traitor, no traitor could do worse than by trying to keep the facts from the public.

My wife makes the point that we have no right to expect to see a Colonial Sec. so heroically self denying! Quite true. But I can think of men who may some day be Cabinet Ministers whose sacrifices (for the Labour Party) *prove them fit to represent an awakened public conscience and intelligence.* I don't mean people like most of the last Cabinet. Heaven forbid that we should ever see such another.

Oldham to Leys
3 March 1925

Thank you very much for your letter. I shall be very glad to learn the angle from which you approach the subject when you have time to write further.

You will understand that in suggesting that Ormsby-Gore may be more in sympathy with the need for reform than might appear from his attack on your book I was expressing an opinion based on purely general grounds. I have not discussed Kenya with him since your book appeared. I had a talk with him the other day but it was concerned exclusively with certain matters connected with my American visit and we did not touch on the Kenya question at all. . . .

Leys to Oldham
3 March 1925

The aspect of the problems of Kenya that appears to me to be fundamental is that enough people do not exist in it to cultivate much more land than is already in cultivation. Phrases like the country having "great possibilities" and needing "development" are fallacious because they don't deal with realities. Development, if the man who uses the word means anything at all by it, chiefly means men cultivating the soil and building railways. No doubt credit capital is necessary to get such work going, or rather some of it since cultivation needs little or none. But the importation of fresh capital, while existing capital is only partly being used, must be a pure evil since it must aggravate the difficulties arising from the fact that already there is work for thousands for which no one offers. The official view that what the country needs is more capital is impossible to anyone who knows the simple economy of African village life and tries to see it through the eyes of African villagers. In any country expected to feed itself without imported food the surplus of labour available for other purposes can never be large, in the absence of machinery and other devices that are useful only in civilised societies. That surplus is in Kenya already fully employed, in the development of, at most, 10% of the alienated land and in the upkeep of the machinery needed for dealing with its produce, i.e. railways, mills, shops, docks &c. If areas not now being cultivated are brought under cultivation the areas now under cultivation must suffer. Every additional £1000 of imported credit capital, every new European immigrant dependent for livelihood on getting so many scores of Africans to work for him, clogs the machinery of industry by still further stimulating to frenzy the scramble for workers who don't exist. While every additional immigrant willing to work, whether at the plough, or at unloading ships, or making earthworks, releases the capital that is now infertile because in reality it is no more than pieces of paper in a Bank.

All this I made clear enough in Chap. VIII of "Kenya." Why do people refuse to face the fact? As regards people in Kenya mainly because the fact proves the wisdom of a policy contrary to the one on which immigrant Europeans base their hopes of profit. Delamere for example is a rich man on paper. On paper he has made at least £500,000 in Kenya. Not by working. All he did was get the Govt. to give him land and pay experts, and managers, and labourers to use it. At one time or another he must have had control of nearly 300,000 acres. As soon as ever any European arrived from home prepared to buy any of it (outright or on mortgage) for £3 an acre, D. sold. By now he has got rid of perhaps 60,000 acres. (Most of that area is probably either leased or on mortgage so that D. hasn't really received most of the money yet.) If he could sell most of the rest at £3 an acre on an average, he would make his fortune and still own so much African soil as would make an English county. But that cannot happen unless a few thousand more Europeans go out to the country, each with so many thousand pounds to spend in buying land from Delamere. And all the big landowners, the people who won Ormsby-Gore's heart, are in the same position. If European immigration and the import of capital stop, farewell to their hopes of fortune. Note that the working farmer's interests are quite different. Thanks to the anti-Indian agitation and the cry that all Europeans must stand together to resist the humanitarian nonsense of the Anti-Slavery Society, these men—whose welfare should in my view be most carefully safeguarded—have allowed the group of whom D. is the most influential, to run the country.

Another reason the authorities decline to face the fundamental fact I described is that to admit the need of immigrant *workers* is to admit the need of Asiatic immigration.

I have been rereading some of your book. I see you believe that
Xtianity is to be the solution of the race problem. If by Xtianity you
mean the Xtianity of the churches then I see no ground for the belief. As reasonably give Xtianity . . . the credit for slavery abolition,
when only a few small nonconformist sects did anything to help
abolition and the leaders of the important churches opposed it. The
case is exactly the same today. The most surprising thing about your
book is that you nowhere describe or define New Testament teaching
on your subject. You seem merely to assume that professing Xtians
(including of course their leaders) accept, even if they imperfectly
follow, that teaching. The obvious fact is that they do not accept it.
What your own position is I cannot make out. In some chapters you
write as if you shared Paul's view that racial distinctions are irrelevant illusions that can be got rid of only by being ignored. In other
chapters you write as if they were very real, perhaps even so valuable
as to deserve effort to preserve them. But why not have stated the
fact that the early church successfully (in the main) sought to oblit-
erate the distinctions between Jews and non Jews? Because it would
"embarrass" your American readers? I don't believe it. I believe that
instinctively you shrank from the statement of a policy so downright
and devoid of balance and compromise.

I make this point because it is relevant to Kenya. If your influence
is going to be of any service to the people of Kenya you must reach
a clear view of certain at least of the important changes to be brought
about there (e.g. direct taxation of the richer inhabitants with some
remission of the taxes paid by the poorer) and devote such a proportion of your time and energy as you believe the case of these Africans deserves to advocating these changes and explaining why they
are wise and right. Why say it is hard to know what can be *done*?
What *you* can do is simply your share of making the facts known
and of encouraging people to think out for themselves the course the
facts prescribe. There were good men a hundred years ago who found
slavery very difficult to decide about. The reason was that they refused to try to see the facts of slavery through the eyes of slaves, and
persisted in looking at them distortedly through the eyes of those
who profited by slavery.

The real difficulty—just as in the matter of slavery and in your own
subject of race—is that the right course is too simple for compromis-
ers to believe in, too unpopular for the respectable to adhere to, too

hard for people who like you and me, want to do the right thing without depriving ourselves of any comfort. Surely the parables of the priest and Levite and of the good Samaritan were told in a vision of the Africa of the XVIIIth and the XXth century.

Oldham to the Archbishop of Canterbury
3 March 1925
[IMC (Geneva), Box 93]

. . . I have been thinking a good deal about Kenya.

I believe that the most important thing so far as the immediate future is concerned—more important even than anything that can be achieved by the debates in Parliament—is the appointment of the new Governor.

Ormbsy-Gore made a vehement attack on Leys' book at the African Society dinner, which Lugard and others very much regretted. I said to Ormsby-Gore when I saw him the other day that as a step towards getting things done I was not at all sorry to see him appearing as the champion of the settlers. That they should feel that there is a sympathetic understanding of their point of view at home is a good thing, since their co-operation is necessary to carry out reform.

Ormsby-Gore attacked the book as embarrassing the Government and as likely to injure our national reputation. It is not the book, however, that does this injury but the facts which it narrates. There are only two ways in which our good name can be re-established. One is that Leys' facts should be disproved, and the other is that what is wrong should be set right. Unless one or other of these things is done, the embarrassment is certain to become greater as the contentions of the book become more widely known.

I do not think that Leys' assertions can be disproved. He can no doubt be shown to be in error in particular statements, and it can be urged that the book is one-sided. But his main contentions cannot be easily disproved. A mere official denial will not satisfy public opinion either in this country or abroad (i.e. in America and India). The facts would have to be shown to be mistaken by some impartial and competent authority that would inspire general confidence.

The crux of the matter seems to be this. The White Paper laid down that where the interests of the native inhabitants and of the immigrant communities conflict those of the natives are to prevail.

Leys shows that in fact those of the European community invariably receive first consideration. When labour is insufficient it is native production in the reserves that suffers. When labourers are wanted for public works the call is made on the reserves and not on the labour on European estates. The natives pay the bulk of the taxation, yet the European community runs the country in their own interest. The railways serve their estates; the services of the agricultural and veterinary departments are mainly at the disposal of the same estates. At every point the scales are weighted against the natives whose interests are said to be primary. It is the contradiction between our professed policy and the actual reality that seems to me so serious and so damaging to our national reputation.

The intentions of Downing Street are excellent. Ormsby-Gore in his speech at the African Society dinner said plainly that no settler must go to Kenya thinking that he has a *right* to labour. He laid it down that the native must be perfectly free either to work in his reserve, if he prefers it, or to go out and work on industrial and commercial enterprises.

What we have to reckon with, however, is that one of the two communities whose interests have to be served has a voice so powerful that it can largely control the administration of the colony while the other is much less able to represent its point of view. The consequence is that no matter how excellent the intention, in practice the interests of the European community always prevail. It is this issue which the Colonial Office will not, I think, really face.

How this state of things can be remedied is an extremely difficult question. The Royal Commission which we suggested a few years ago might have provided the remedy, but I doubt whether the plan is now practicable. My experience on the East African Committee has convinced me that the only enquiry that will be of any use must be made on the spot. Enquiry by an outside body would probably be resented and opposed by the local European community as unjustifiable interference, while if that community were represented the controversy would probably be carried into the commission of enquiry itself and prevent a dispassionate and judicial examination of the facts. These difficulties are not insuperable, but they are real, and I doubt whether the present Government will favour an enquiry unless the debates in Parliament make it unavoidable.

Public opinion in this country is likely to insist that something must be done. If there is not to be an enquiry, the only alternative is that the Government should undertake reforms itself. That must be done through the Governor, and it can be done only if he is a man capable of dealing with a very difficult and delicate situation. If the right man can be found and the Government stands behind him, it will probably be the most effective means of getting things set right. If the co-operation of the local community is necessary to carry out reforms, as I believe it is, personal touch seems essential. A strong governor possessing tact and experience in dealing with men could get things done which could never be brought about by despatches from Downing Street.

I know that supermen are not always available when they are wanted. Lord Cromers and Lord Milners are only too rare. But I do not believe the Empire cannot provide a man with the necessary ability, resolution and gift of dealing with men, if the Government are determined to find him. If the opportunity is seized, a great improvement may be witnessed in the next six years. If, on the other hand, some one is appointed in the ordinary course of promotion, and he is not equal to the demands of one of the most difficult and critical posts in the Empire, no matter what Parliament may decide a few weeks hence the way to real reform may be effectively blocked through things being badly or feebly handled in Kenya itself.

I have been wondering whether I should say this to Ormsby-Gore. I had an hour's talk with him last week, but there was so much to talk about connected with my American visit, which was more directly and properly my concern, that we did not get on to Kenya except for a minute or two at the beginning. I hesitate to write to him, lest I should seem to be interfering in what is not my business. Moreover, I do not know how much real say he has in the appointment.

I am writing to Your Grace in case any opportunity may present itself of drawing attention to the importance of the appointment of Sir Robert Coryndon's successor in relation to the whole Kenya situation. That situation will become a matter of public interest when the debates take place in Parliament. But the opportunity of dealing with it in the most effective way may have been lost, if an appointment is made to the vacant Governorship without sufficient regard to all that is involved.

Oldham to Leys
9 March 1925.

I have read your letters two or three times with much interest and appreciation.

(1)   You must have some patience with a person who has no first-hand knowledge of Kenya and is trying slowly to master the facts.

(2)   I think that you are right that in my book I have not worked out fundamental Christian principles as fully and clearly as I should. If the time ever comes to produce a revised edition I shall have to tackle this.

(3)   I think I probably do attach a good deal more importance than you do to both race and civilization as factors to be taken into account. I do not believe that the analogy of the early Church can be pressed too far; the problem in its modern shape did not exist for the early Christians.

(4)   However much we may differ on this point, I do not think that we are far apart in regard to what needs to be done in Kenya. So far as I can follow your statement, I think I agree with it.

(5)   I have no doubt that cowardice, dislike of unpopularity, the desire to be thought sane and respectable, are real temptations to which we too often succumb.

(6)   After all necessary allowance has been made for these influences, the particular contribution any man makes to a cause is determined in part by the position he holds. So long as I am secretary of the International Missionary Council I cannot entirely separate myself from my office and act as a free lance. As you will see from what follows this is not meant to be an excuse for doing little or nothing. An occasion may arise in which it would be my duty to chuck my job and gain complete freedom. So long as I retain it, there are limitations in regard to the kind of things I can usefully do.

(7)   I agree with you entirely as to the primary importance of publicity. To the best of my ability I am trying to get the facts in

your book before people who might help. I have discussed your
book with dozens and taken every opportunity of doing so. I
think if you were able to make a list of those who were doing
propaganda, the order being determined by the amount of time
given to it, I should stand reasonably high in the list.

(8) Publicity is a comparatively clear issue. I agree, as I have said,
that it is the first thing and I am trying, so far as time and
strength permit, to assist in it. But what I wrote to get your
mind about is what political action, following on knowledge of
the facts, should we aim at bringing about now? I am presump-
tuous enough to think that I know what I should do if I were
Secretary of State. But I am not Secretary of State, and the
question is what in the existing political situation is the practical thing to aim at. It is in regard to this that I am in per-
plexity. It is fairly plain to me that unless in the last resort you
are prepared to send out troops, which this Government won't
do, you are shut up to getting as far as you can without antago-
nizing local opinion or at least driving it to extreme lengths. For
this reason I don't much mind Ormsby-Gore appearing as
champion of the settlers, if it creates a more favourable atmosphere for an attempt by the Government to give effect to the
policy you advocate or as much of it as they can.

What I asked you was whether, apart from a sustained campaign of publicity, you had any ideas about inducing the Government to take some action in the right direction in the
reasonably near future.

What line is the Labour Party going to take in the debate in
the House of Commons when it comes off? Have you any hope
from the Liberals? What demand, if any, are the Opposition
parties going to make? Is it to be a Royal Commission? I am
not clear that as a matter of political strategy or tactics this is
the best proposal to put forward? I mean that I doubt whether
it would be carried. If this is so, is there an alternative? And, if
so, what? These are the questions that are perplexing me.

Publicity with a view to ultimate reform, certainly. But in
addition to this, is any immediate action by the present Government within the range of practical politics? I don't know.

(9)   I put several weeks of work a few years ago into mobilizing
      public opinion to support the demand for a Royal Commission.
      I am not averse to doing it again. I do not know whether I can
      give that amount of time just now on account of other com-
      mitments already entered into. But one could contemplate it
      only if there was at least a fighting chance of getting something
      done. Assisting in publicity is a continuous job and I am doing,
      and will continue to do, all I can find time for. But the more
      intensive work means setting aside other responsibilities and
      this can be justified only if there is a fairly clear immediate ob-
      jective. Do you see one? I don't.

(10) The most immediately practical thing I can think of is that the
      Government should appoint a really strong and big Governor
      and stand behind him. But will they? Or would the last Gov-
      ernment?

Leys to Oldham
10 March 1925

. . . Your letter has just come and needs digesting. But I want to
try to define what I suspect to be the origin of the difference between us. You speak of pressing the "analogy of the early church"
too far. Is the fact not rather that modern ideas, which you share,
are in conflict with New Testament teaching taken as a whole? According to Jesus' definition I am not a Xtian. But I find it impossible
to escape the conviction that his plan of life is not only the remedy for
specific human evils and miseries but is absolutely right in a sense
similar to the law of gravity being right. But it is an organic scheme.
I grant you it is incapable of adequate definition since definition
must follow experience and not even St. Francis expressed the whole
of Jesus' plan of human relations—far from it in fact. But so far as I
can comprehend the plan it is a coherent one, incapable of being
treated eclectically. I at least cannot understand how without doing
violence to my intelligence I can imagine any exception, whether due
to differences between 1st and XXth centuries or to anything else
whatever, rendering partially invalid the practice of equal fraternity.
The scheme may be wrong. Most people, including most Xtians,
obviously don't believe in it. But I cannot imagine it to be sometimes

right and sometimes wrong. When Paul asked what could hinder
him from the door of Christ I take it he partly meant what I mean,
that for him it infused every human contact. He expressed his mental revolution at his conversion by substituting for his belief in the
superiority of the Jew the dogma that in so far as Jesus' plan were
followed every hindrance to free fellowship whencesoever derived
would disappear.

I see nothing "analogous" between the problem before the early
church and our problem. It is the same problem. If the early church
interpreted the mind of Christ aright in any matter, such as this of
race feeling, it is only open to us to enrich the interpretation. Where
it went wrong, as we belive it did about women, we expect to explain
the error by tracing it to the influence of the age rather than to Jesus'
influence. In fact it is obvious from the records that Jesus behaved
to women in a way quite inconsistent with some things Paul said
about them. I should say, generally, that it is the task of the church
in every age to remove the hindrances to Xtian relations between its
members. The form they take will vary with the age. But the same
impulse must always be their solvent.

One more point. I don't think it is ever of much consequence to
work for right measures to be taken when the time is ripe for them.
The work is done by then. Fox passed the Act abolishing the slave
trade.[132] But the achievement was not his. Neither was it theirs who
prompted him. The real work was done by thousands who with common conscious aim ripened public opinion. That is what is needed
for Kenya. That is why O. G.'s policy of reform by confidential dis-
patches is futile. Publish the facts and get people to lay them along-
side their consciences and their intelligences and the question what
should be done will answer itself.

I shall bring your letter and go over it with you if you can give me
the time.

Leys to Oldham
13 March 1925

. . . I wasn't thinking about you when I mentioned the need of
sacrifice. Kenya is not a primary concern with you. But everyone to
whom it is must either be ready to suffer loss, serious or trifling, or
play at best a futile, at worst a cowardly part. . . .

Leys to Oldham
26 March 1925

I have surprising news for you. Major [Archibald G.] Church turned up (uninvited!) to that meeting in the H. of C. yesterday. I read my statement advising concentration in the debate on the two points of imposing direct taxation on non-Africans and discouraging further development because labourers are already too few for what development exists. Then Major Church bowled me out by saying that on both these points the Committee agreed with me and were reporting accordingly! But there you are! The strategy you spoke of is discovered in the opposite camp.

There are of course important points remaining for the Labour Party to urge, mainly criminal prosecutions for breach of labour contracts and the contents of the dispatch in "The Times." But I think you ought to hold your hand meanwhile until we know not only what the report contains but *what people in Kenya say to it*.

I fully expect Delamere & Co. to be very angry and I doubt if they will be able for prudential reasons to contain themselves. If they do protest and threaten resistance my task with M.P.s will be easy, almost superfluous. You must remember that these people had every reason to believe, when the three M.P.s left the country, that they had been won over completely. I have no doubt that, indirectly rather than directly, my book has induced a change of policy. O. G. told a friend that he had intended to support fresh European colonisation.

Thank you very much for giving me so much of your time. . . .

I have just read your review.[133] *All* the missionaries I have heard from and seen are better pleased with Chap IX than you are. As for Jesse Jones, if he doesn't mean what he says he ought to be silent.

Oldham to Leys
30 March 1925

. . . Thank you for your letter. The information is of great interest. We must wait for the Commission's report, which should be out in a week or two.

I think that the reference to your chapter on missions in my review of your book has conveyed to you a different impression from what I intended. I was not attempting to appraise the chapter but to describe it. You are, so far as I can judge, both from your book and from what you said in my office the other day, rather distrustful of organized Christianity. So far from condemning this attitude I have a great deal of sympathy with it. I wanted to let readers know that your attitude, as it seems to me, is deeply interesting and challenging since you believe that the Christian view of life provides the way out and at the same time have, to a large extent, lost hope in the Church as an adequate expression of that way of life. I do not agree with everything in your chapter but I think it is one of the most stimulating discussions of missions that I know and my intention was to say this in the review.

Oldham to the Archbishop of Canterbury
2 April 1925
[IMC (Geneva), Box 93]

I am of opinion, and I think Your Grace agrees, that a royal commission being out of the question the key to the Kenya situation lies in the new Governor. I have had no clear conviction with regard to any particular appointment, though there are several men who I think might fill the post successfully, such as Colonel Schuster of the Sudan[134] and Sir Graeme Thomson, the Governor of British Guiana.[135] I have now come to think that the man who could most certainly render the service which the Empire needs is Mr R. Feetham, the Chairman of the Irish Boundary Commission.[136] He is a member of the Round Table Group and I have long known that they regarded him as their ablest member. This would not, however, be a recommendation in the eyes of the present Government. The following facts, which are intended only for your own eye, will let Your Grace know how I have been led to the view that he is the best man. . . .

Feetham has been a South African judge and before that was in Parliament. He holds what one may call the South African point of view in regard to native questions to a greater extent than Curtis or I do. I do not think, however, that this would be a disqualification in Kenya. The appointment would probably be extremely acceptable to the settlers. The important thing about Feetham, however, is that he has an essentially just and constructive mind. . . .

Leys to Oldham
16 April 1925

. . . Ormsby G's theory of a [settler] change of heart is founded
not on fact but on his strange simplicity in believing he had a vast
influence over the planters and merchants of Kenya.

I greatly fear that the delay in publishing the report by the 3
M.P.s is due to protests from Kenya on its contents being learned
there. That day I saw you Church told us it was then in the printer's
hands and would be out by April 1st. Once more I fear the C.O. is
going to surrender.

Leys to Oldham
25 April 1925

I had no idea you and your friends would take so much trouble
over "Kenya." . . . I expect I shall, in the end, send half a dozen
copies to American papers for review, stock an agent with 50 copies,
and, perhaps, spend £10 in advertising. Woolf thinks it would all
be mere waste of money.

More and more plainly there are evidences that the report of
Ormsby Gore's Committee has been objected to in Kenya. I vividly
remember how, to my great joy, Harcourt put his foot down in 1910,
only to be defeated later by his own agents. Ormsby G. has announced in advance that he will stand by the "settlers." I have no
doubt in Parliament he will allege that they have changed hearts.
The whole thing is a pitiful tragedy. I sometimes wish I had taken no
concern in it.

Oldham to Leys
27 April 1925

. . . I should urge you on no account to waste ten pounds advertising in America. It would simply be money thrown away.

The essential thing is to arrange with an agent to stock the book
and then to have him send review copies to the most important
American papers. I think you could send a good many, more than
half a dozen. I believe review copies will do much more for the sale
of the book than advertising. . . .

**Leys to Oldham
28 April 1925**

Delighted to know you may come here. . . .

I am most grateful for your advice about circulating Kenya in America which I expect I shall entirely follow. . . .

I hope you noticed a dispatch in The Times from Nairobi in which proof was given—out of Lord Delamere's mouth!!— both that officials giving evidence unpalatable to the authorities were censured and that the evidence of native witnesses was prepared for them beforehand.[137] I hope Ormsby G. read the dispatch.

**Oldham to Leys
5 May 1925**

. . . I sent you a message yesterday to let you know that I am sorry I cannot come to Brailsford for to-morrow night. I am very pressed just now with a number of matters and not least with the situation in regard to Kenya. I am trying to write a memorandum on the subject. If I find that I can manage to get to Brailsford for a night I shall wire to you to find if it is convenient. I am not very hopeful, however. . . .

**Oldham to Archbishop of Canterbury
13 May 1925
[IMC (Geneva), Box 93]**

At the meeting of the Royal Colonial Institute last night, Lugard threw out the suggestion of earmarking a proportion of the [East African] loan for education. The suggestion about earmarking a proportion of the loan is not, of course, a private one. It has been brought up several times during the last year or two at the Advisory Committee [on Education] by Sir James Currie.[138] I do not think, myself, that "education" is quite the right description of the object, but that is a detail. Ormsby-Gore in his reply conveyed the impression that he was, personally, in favour of a plan of this kind, but that he had to recognise that he was not only Chairman of the East African Commission, but also a member of His Majesty's Government. He went on to say that it would be quite unprecedented in

British practice to use a loan for such purposes and that such a proposition would have to come under the severe scrutiny of the Public
Accounts Committee in the House of Commons. I told him afterwards that the proposition, as I conceived it, was one for which I
thought a very good defence could be made. . . .

I think that it is necessary that the Government should be made to
understand clearly, either publicly or privately, that we are not satisfied that the principles of the White Paper are being carried out in
Kenya; and that, while we shall be content if a serious effort is made
to get a firm hold of the economic problem, we cannot rest with
things as they are. If the proposition of earmarking a portion of the
loan for this purpose is not feasible, what alternative is there that
gives real hopes of getting things set right? So far as justice to the
natives is concerned, it will not be achieved by declarations of policy,
however excellent in intention, but by giving them practical effect.

If the earmarking of part of the loan is the best way of going forward, we may have to make a strong effort to convince public opinion. I am willing to do anything to help that I can. Will it be possible for Your Grace, if you are convinced as to the rightness of the
course proposed, to try to convert Geoffrey Dawson[139] and Lord
Astor[140] to the idea. I shall try to see Ian Colvin[141] of the "Morning
Post." I also, probably, can get into touch, after the debate in the
Lords, with H. A. L. Fisher,[142] who is speaking on the Liberal side,
or if necessary with J. H. Thomas or Ramsay MacDonald. There are
other people like the Prime Minister[143] and Lord Salisbury,[144] who
might be influenced as well as, of course, Amery himself. I do not
know where the chief obstacle is likely to lie. A good deal may turn
on the attitude of the Chancellor of the Exchequer. . . .[145]

P.S. I have no disposition at all to make a public attack on the
Kenya settlers. I do not believe that they mean a half or quarter of
what they say. I am certain that they are very much better than their
speeches. But I question whether many of them have emerged intel-
lectually from the school-boy stage or have any real understanding
of economic or political matters. Hooper says that few of them have
ever seen the inside of a reserve. They are not fitted to decide Imperial questions of the first magnitude and some means must be
found of providing so clear and authoritative a statement of the
facts that the ascertained facts will be allowed to determine policy.

Oldham to the Archbishop of Canterbury
21 May 1925
[IMC (Geneva), Box 93]

I thought your speech last night was splendid.[146] It presented the whole matter with admirable balance. I hope that the effort did not prove too exhausting.

Lord Balfour's plan for a central committee to deal with civil problems of the Empire, as the Committee of Imperial Defence deals with the military problems, is excellent.[147] It goes entirely in the direction that we want and I expect much from it, more especially as I believe that the secretarial work will be in the hands of Tom Jones. But it is supplementary to the plan of earmarking a portion of the loan for research and not a complete substitute for it. To gain an intelligent control over the economic forces in East Africa we need both a co-ordinating and directing mind, which it may be hoped Lord Balfour's organization may supply, and also an immense amount of detailed research in East Africa itself into diseases, soils, agricultural methods, and, above all, the labour problem. The latter will need lots of money and I think a very strong case can be made out for the view that the return from the proposed development loan will be much larger if a proportion of the money is spent on research. The essential point is that the railways are not an end in themselves, but are intended to lead to increased production, that in production many other features are involved, and that the best results from the development of transport cannot be hoped for unless account is taken of these other factors. I learned this morning from my friend in the Treasury that the mind of officials at the Treasury is definitely turning in this direction and inclining to the view that research is necessary if the transport loan is to be justified.

Lord Balfour's defence of the present state of affairs in Kenya seemed to me entirely unconvincing. He made some good points but ignored almost entirely the real grounds for anxiety. He left the way open for a devastating reply from a well-informed and able opponent.[148] The essential points in the case of those who fear that the principles of trusteeship are not being carried out in Africa have never yet received an answer.

I think there is still need to impress on the Government that there is a strong body of opinion in this country which is genuinely concerned that our public declarations of policy should be made a reality and is by no means satisfied that this is being done at present. Probably in the actual circumstances this can best be said privately rather than by way of public attack. If the Government is prepared to undertake a disinterested enquiry with a view to ascertaining in the interests of all parties, including the settlers, the real economic facts, we may hope that this will result in a rational control of the situation which will eliminate abuses. But if things are allowed to drift there is nothing left to those who want our professions of trusteeship to be taken seriously except to protest against a state of things which we believe to be incompatible with these professions. . . .

Oldham to the Archbishop of Canterbury
27 May 1925
[IMC (Geneva), Box 93]

. . . (1) We can accept the main contention of the Ormsby-Gore Report that there is a moral obligation resting on Great Britain to develop these rich territories for the benefit of mankind as a whole, and if this is accepted a loan for development purposes seems the inevitable practical consequence. On this ground we can sympathize with the proposal contained in the Report and the support given to it by the Empire Cotton Growing Association.

(2) It is essential that this economic development should take place in ways that are consistent with native welfare. The way to secure this is by obtaining a real control of the situation through knowledge. Lord Balfour's announcement is for this reason to be cordially welcomed. In order that it may be made really effective, however, research in various directions in East Africa itself is necessary and this requires money. We, therefore, believe that the ear-marking of a portion of the loan for this purpose is a real key to the solution of East African problems.

(3) Action on these lines would simply be the application to our immensely important territories in East Africa of that policy of constructive Conservatism which the Prime Minister has been so splendidly advocating in his recent speeches. (I may add that

I have this morning received a letter from Dr Abraham Flexner of the General Education Board in the United States, who is one of the acutest and most far-seeing men in America, and to whom I sent a copy of the Ormsby-Gore Report and of my paper.[149] He writes, "Up to this time almost all social development has been haphazard, accidental and, therefore, blundering and wasteful. It would seem to be high time that we endeavoured to learn the facts first and to act afterwards. I sincerely wish you may succeed in persuading the Government to try this form of procedure. You will introduce a new era in colonization.")

(4)   It might do well to add that it is, of course, essential in providing for research to ensure that the study will include those human and moral aspects of the problem which are as essential to sound economic development as to the carrying out of the responsibilities of trusteeship.

Ormsby-Gore told me confidentially—the appointment will not, I understand, be made public for a week or two—that Sir Edward Grigg has accepted the Governorship of Kenya.[150] This is excellent news. I do not know him personally but from all that I know about him he is just the kind of man we want.

With Lord Balfour's Committee, with money for research, if we can get it, with Grigg in Kenya, Cameron in Tanganyika, and Gowers in Uganda, and with Ormsby-Gore and Amery at the Colonial Office, the prospects of East Africa seem brighter than we could have hoped for some time ago.

Leys to Oldham
30 May 1925

I thought the debate in the Lords very satisfactory. Of course Lord Balfour made several quite false statements but one expected that. The one disappointment was the Archbp. Ecclesiastics live on fences. They simply cannot come off and join wholeheartedly in any battle over a living issue. Things are moving so fast about Kenya that victory is almost in sight. Will it be won without the church's help? If you ask what I mean by help I would instance this. Lord B[alfour] said that compulsion was being applied only to those Africans in the reserves who did no work. Could you write to Owen and suggest that

Kenya missionaries should unanimously issue a statement, sending copies to Govt. in Nairobi, to Downing St., to Nairobi press, to The Times and to the Manchester Guardian, to the following effect: that there is no appreciable number of unemployed in the reserves: that already there are too few left in the reserves for the work of food growing, house building, road making &c: that this levy is injuring the work of the Church.

If missionaries did issue such a statement they would make forced labour impossible in future. No others can do what they could do.

... Your review ... was certainly not too critical of the book [i.e., *Kenya*] as a book. But it lacked, just as your book did, any frank advocacy of any definite things which the church should work for. As with the Archbp. one comes away feeling things are not all they should be: the right course is very difficult to find, so difficult that ordinary people can't hope to find it. When you write again on the subject, write for publication I mean, I beg you so to state facts, especially the known facts of early Christian beliefs and practice in the matter, as to compel the reader to discover where his duty lies.

I know quite well my fault is in the other direction. I see things all too clearly. And don't imagine I fail to value all you have done and are doing. I value it immensely. Remember this is the real end of my life. You and others do many successful things. This is my one job that may redeem my life from failure. If my demands on my friends lead to the sacrifice of their friendships then so be it....

Leys to Oldham
2 June 1925

I am sorry I sent you that letter and sorry that I wrote as I did myself. I suppose my judgement is apt to be affected by the anxiety of my mind for so long continued, about Kenya affairs and the situation being so critical now. You have always generously offered help. The *only* thing between us, except my recent rudeness, is that I would have you, when you do write about the subject, as when you reviewed my book, say boldly, this and this and this are what every Xtian ought to work for in Kenya, giving your readers no excuse for ignorance of the main issues. Please forgive me for going beyond any such criticism as I fear I did myself.

P.S. It is difficult to write a personal letter on such a subject without exaggerating its personal aspect. I could understand your saying "Godspeed to the venture: I cannot join in, having much else to do." But I cannot understand your saying "I think I ought to help but fail to see what can be done, either by myself or by the authorities."

Oldham to Leys
2 June 1925

Thank you for your letter. I was going to write to you to-day to say that I hope when you next come to Town it may be possible for us to meet for a talk.

I have been putting in a lot of work in regard to Kenya. I have been keeping clear of the Labour Party because if we are to get anything *done* just now, which seems to me the thing that matters, ideas have got to initiate with the present Government. The practical question, so far as I can see, is how much of a step forward in the right direction it is possible to get taken in this particular year of grace. Having done a certain amount of spade work in that quarter, however, I think that in view of the debate on the Colonial Office Estimates those of us who care about East Africa ought to lay our heads together and see what is the best thing to aim at in present circumstances. . . .

I shall leave other matters, including a defence of the Archbishop, until we meet.

. . . [In the review] I tried to write the truth as I see it. I think that society needs both the radical and the conservative type of mind. I find myself having a great deal of sympathy with both. Or, to put the matter in another way, an army if it is to win a campaign needs both pioneers and camp followers. Some of us perhaps belong only to the latter class but we may be able, by doing our bit, to contribute something to make advance possible. However, all this is a matter for a talk and not a letter. . . .

Leys to Oldham
3 June 1925

Very glad to find you have so charitable a heart as not to be annoyed.

I have the greatest difficulty in fitting people in when in London. You are sure to be in Swanwick soon. Why not let me go there and fetch you here in my car—a little over an hour? . . . You could spend a few hours, a night, or a weekend.

Oldham to Archbishop of Canterbury
5 June 1925
[IMC (Geneva), Box 93]

. . . It is, I think, important to watch developments in connection with the new Committee announced by Lord Balfour. Everything will depend on the way it works out. A mistake in detail might very easily deprive us of the results we are seeking, though this consequence might not in any way be intended. I do not think that the Government have as yet given much thought to the question how the plan is to be made to work, unless Lord Balfour has done so himself. The Colonial Office, I think, are quite hazy on the subject. Lord Balfour is probably giving a good deal of thought to the plan as a whole but I doubt whether he is sufficiently informed about East African conditions to think out the application to that particular area. Tom Jones has gone to Italy for three weeks and I do not think there will be any further formal consideration of the matter till his return . . . .

Oldham to Archbishop of Canterbury
10 June 1925
[IMC (Geneva), Box 93]

I had the opportunity on Sunday night of introducing the subject of the colour question at the meeting of the Ralegh Club at Oxford. I dealt principally with the East African problem. Amery was at the meeting and so I had an opportunity of expounding at some length in his presence the ideas contained in my paper. He took part in the discussion which followed, and said that there was a precedent for the suggestion, as Lord Milner had spent a substantial portion of the loan of thirty million pounds for the reconstruction of South Africa on the kind of objects to which I have referred. He added that if there were a loan for East Africa a portion of it would certainly be

spent on research and that research must unquestionably be interpreted to include not merely the study of raw materials, but very
particularly of the human factor on which I have laid stress.

This is very good as far as it goes.

I lunched yesterday with Sir Edward Grigg and am greatly encouraged by his attitude.

Sir James Currie tells me that he has discussed matters with the
Chairman of the Empire Cotton Growing Association and that he is
quite prepared to back the 7½% for research.

The two fences that have still to be got over before we reach our
goal are, first, that the money is got and, secondly, that the enquiry,
when undertaken, includes the objects to which we attach importance and approaches the whole question from the right point of
view.

As regards the first, I gather from a friend in the Treasury that
there are certain technical difficulties that might upset calculations.
Grigg does not attach much importance to this. I am to see Amery
next Tuesday at the Colonial Office and will talk to him about this
point.

The second matter needs a good deal of thought. I am taking
every opportunity of discussing it with those whom I meet.

I think what we need to impress on Amery, Grigg and others who
are involved in a decision is that we believe conditions in East Africa
to be far from satisfactory, that we have deliberately preferred the
method of trying to get them set right through a more scientific control and better organization rather than by agitation, but that we
cannot be satisfied unless they are set right, and unless the situation
is brought under control there is nothing left to those who want the
principle of trusteeship to be made real except to raise their voices in
protest.

I put this quite plainly to Grigg who, I think, entirely agrees. I
shall also put it to Amery.

The illustration which I used at Oxford was that of a business
which is making small profits and paying its work-people less than a
living wage. It is possible to spend one's energies in denouncing the
moral wrong of stunting human development in this way but such
denunciation may accomplish very little in setting matters right. If
through more scientific management and better organization one

can make the business yield larger returns and so make better wages possible, one has accomplished one's purposes more effectively. Similarly, our hope is that by bringing trained intelligence to bear on East African problems it may be possible both to develop these territories economically and at the same time to do this with full regard to native welfare. But if we place our hopes in this course of action we cannot rest content until things are actually set right in Africa. We have to guard against every risk of failing in our object through the setting up of committees which either fail to operate through lack of the necessary funds or which operate wrongly through leaving out of account essential and vital factors. . . .

Leys to Oldham
21 June 1925

I am sorry I expressed an adverse opinion on Lugard's proposal to withdraw reserves and their affairs from control by the Legislative Council.[151] I realise now that I don't know enough of practical administration to have the right to an opinion, one way or other.

I am quite fascinated by the other idea. I am not sure how far I grasp it. I can imagine its being a new social organ. As you said the whole trouble would be personnel. I should say the commission should at first be 1. small, so that later additions would be easy. 2. its members should be as independent as judges and paid like first class civil service clerks. 3. *should completely represent the country*, i.e. 4 Conservatives, 3 Socialists, 2 liberals in rough proportion: also 1 Catholic, 2 Anglicans, 2 nonconformists, 2 non Xtians, again in rough proportion. If it is not thus representative it will not carry the public. 4. should contain few or none over 60. First class men (e.g. Haldane, Sidney Webb, Balfour) who are past their best are far worse on such a job than second class men at their best. But how on earth to find first class men when at their best? The only ones I know of are T. Jones and Roden Buxton. Of course I know few people who are not Socialists.

I fancy T. Jones is working the scheme out.

One objection to it is that if such a commission proved a real success it would in some degree be a rival to Parliament.

I suppose you wouldn't object to the idea being described as the scientific method applied to politics. I feel sure that, now or later, the idea will become real.

Oldham to Leys
22 June 1925

Thank you for your letter. The plan you suggest for giving effect to the idea would, in my judgment, kill it. The moment you start representing parties, whether political or ecclesiastical, as such, you make the thing political, while its very essence is that it should be scientific. As soon as you talk of putting on a Tory because he is a Tory, or a Socialist because he is a Socialist, you immediately make it important that he should be a pronounced Tory or a pronounced Socialist and the whole emphasis gets thrown on to "views" instead of the disinterested scientific attitude of mind. So far as I understand Lord Balfour's announcement, the idea is that the new committee, like the Committee of Imperial Defence, should be a body which advises the Cabinet of the day and the Cabinet of whatever party takes full responsibility for decisions. This seems to me to fit in much better with our constitutional system than the attempt to create a new body representative of different parties. The body, if created, should be like the Civil Service in which no one asks questions about the political views of its members. A tradition has been established by which Civil Servants work loyally with any Government or, if they are conscious of difficulty, resign.

Another fatal objection in my mind to your suggestion is that the body proposed is far too large. I have no counter suggestion to make at the present moment. I am trying to let my mind work on the problem, what kind of a machine will produce facts which, when properly presented, may be expected to have their due influence on the opinion both of Government and of the public. It is an exceedingly difficult problem and may prove impossible of solution at the present stage. It is worth, however, all the thought one can give to it.

I greatly enjoyed my stay with you.

Leys to Oldham
23 June 1925

It is quite impossible that men should exist capable of dealing with political matters wholly without prejudice. The most prejudiced of all are those who are unconscious of the assumptions they hold. Nine tenths of the well to do are anti Socialists. Put these facts together and your commission appears as entering party politics in the sense that all Socialists would urge its destruction. I for one should do so, if the commission were not made representative of types of mind.

But my reason for writing is a more serious one. Please read the enclosed from my brother.[152] You will no doubt repudiate the version he reports. But I assure you I always hear the same view of what you write and say in public. When you were here you seemed, and I believe you are, convinced that cruel unwisdom prevails in Kenya and that you agree in the main with my remedies. But that is never the impression your hearers and readers get. Other people say I am mistaken in explaining the public Oldham by your constitutional aversion to any view or statement that contains no compromise.

But I beg you to realise that if you leave on your hearers the impression that the things you definitely urge are railway construction and scientific research you are really in the enemy's camp. As things are, both these things are injurious. New knowledge is wasted on men who do not act on old knowledge. New railways in the absence of political reform do great harm. I cannot of course expect you to share in the experience that people like Cripps and me have had, of hearing thousands of Africans express their minds. But I want you to remember that if they cannot see what statesmen see statesmen are blind too. I know I convinced you of the necessity of certain measures designed to do justice. Won't you, on platforms, stick to these? In any such struggle, side issues are devices of the enemy.

Oldham to Leys
24 June 1925

Thank you for your letter. I don't agree at all. I believe there is such a thing as a scientific attitude of mind as distinct from a political. I know both Tories and Socialists who have got it. My object at present is to try to get some machinery for getting at facts. I believe that the facts, when got, will support your position; that, however, is not my immediate concern. If we can get some machinery which is constituted for getting facts in an unbiased way and is not political it will, if it is efficient, give us the facts we want. I admit the thing is difficult, but the whole essence of the thing is that it should not be political. We have an analogy in the Committee of Industrial and Scientific Research and in the Medical Research Council.

As regards the other matter, I am not responsible for what other people convey of what I say. I should not expect an undergraduate to be able to answer on my behalf the conumdrums which your brother probably propounded to him. It would take too long to try to clear matters up and it is not worth while. You are constitutionally inclined to mistrust your friends. You have at different times re- garded McGregor Ross, Curtis, Tom Jones and myself as unfaithful to the cause and have little use for the Archbishop and the mis- sionaries. I work with a different philosophy. I believe that, if we are to win in a big cause like this, we need the aid of all types of mind and that we are doing something to help things forward if we can get people at various stages of enlightenment to move a little further in the right direction. I do not for a moment think that what I am try- ing to do either expresses the whole truth or will bring about the millennium. I think it may advance the cause a little bit and I shall go on making the effort according to my lights.

I know this matter is a question of life and death to you and that you are naturally full of anxiety in regard to the issue. I do most honestly wish to help things forward. You are thinking in terms of the ultimate issue. I am occupied at the present moment with the question what particular thing can be done at the present moment which will help in the end to decide that issue in the way we want. Both points of view seem to me necessary to success. Each by itself has its own limitations and dangers.

Do not trouble to write in reply. I have no faith in correspondence as a means of clearing up differences. I have written at this length merely because I know how much the whole thing means to you and want to offer such explanations as I can, though I am very sceptical whether they will do much good.

Leys to Oldham
27 June 1925

Apparently the only way of convincing you about anything is by writing a book of 400 pages. You say you don't believe in correspondence as a method of clearing up differences. Unless I completely misunderstand you the differences between us are far greater than you imagine.

You give a list of people whom I have at various times regarded as unfaithful to the cause. Please listen to the facts. 1. Tom Jones—My *only* complaint of him—*ever*—was that he gave himself no time to read my book.[153] And nobody who does not know the facts can forward reform in Kenya. 2. Curtis. Years ago he was informed of the main facts. He could have given them to the public. He shared in the production of a journal which is written to give the facts about political and social and industrial affairs in the Empire to the public. He deliberately suppressed the facts about Kenya. I believed his motives to be good, far better indeed than those he confesses in a recent letter to me, in which he says he is convinced now that things really are as I described them. He certainly has forwarded my aims by booming the book. But I doubt whether he will ever, in his speeches and writings, advocate what I advocate. But I don't call that being "unfaithful." His aims aren't mine. That's all there is to be said. It's true I expect little help from him. I have many friends from whom I expect no help at all. Why should I complain? 3. The Archbishop. I regard his speech in the Lords as valueless except for his reference to affairs on the Congo which I now know he owed to you. 4. Ross. He and I agreed to write a book together. Each man's part was to be in draft by a certain date. Mine was. He hadn't written a single chapter. I sent him all I had written—no, nearly all. He violently disapproved. I was astonished to find that his *interpretation* of the facts in Kenya was quite different from mine.

I still think Ross missed a big chance when he spent the second half of 1923 holidaying instead of writing half a book. If his forthcoming book is mainly an impersonal record of fact it will help immensely. Twice recently I have written begging him not to be afraid of telling the *whole* truth so far as he sees it and to publish it as quickly as possible. 5. Yourself. How can you say you are not responsible for what people think you say? On the contrary what you intend them to hear matters nothing. The impression you convey is everything. I have given you two separate proofs that when you write and speak on the subject of affairs in Kenya your readers and hearers come away unconvinced that the specific things I advocate are necessary and just. If you don't think them necessary and just, all right. But I know you do. Then why not say so in such terms as will leave people in no doubt of your meaning? The proofs I gave you of your being misunderstood do not stand alone.

The confounded thing about you and Curtis is that you admire the book instead of regarding it as conclusive proof that serious injustice has been done to helpless people, is being done, and will continue to be done until remedied by certain specific measures. The only merit of my book is that it offers these proofs fully, candidly, fair-mindedly. I have no unusual abilities beyond what are needed for industriously compiling and arranging a mass of data.

As I told you before I can understand you saying "God speed you in your work. My job is to stick to mine." I cannot understand you saying as you do, that you feel a duty to the natives of Kenya, and then acting so as to encourage the infliction of further injury upon them. Several years after certain political reforms have been in operation expenditure on railways in Eastern Africa *may* prove to be beneficial. Now, I am certain, every mile of new railway construction (except probably from Nyasa northwards) is bound to increase human loss and suffering.

I suppose it is useless to tell you you think absurdly highly of my character and abilities.

Leys to Dr. Jesse Jones
29 June 1925
enclosed in Jones to Oldham,
14 July 1925
[Edinburgh House, Box 233]

I am afraid I am unconvinced though I appreciate your kindness in writing. It is true that in one passage you admit that the educational ideal for Africans is the same as for Europeans.[154] But in most of the book you assume the contrary. Would Paul have welcomed the idea of different schools for Europeans and Asiatics among Ephesian Christians?

Second, I think your "cooperation" idea is as foolish and as imperious as preaching Cooperation between Slaves and Slave owners in Alabama would have been 80 years ago.

Third, I think it is ridiculous to attempt to educate people for "leadership." The leaders of the future are as unlikely to come out of the Special Schools you suggest as are the future leaders of this country to come out of Eton and Harrow.

There is no special educational problem in Kenya today. There is a special political and industrial problem, similar to the one that forced Abraham Lincoln. To cover it up with smooth phrases as you do is to increase the danger of a violent resolution of that problem.

I read the "Crisis" and share Du Bois' views. Affairs in Howard and Fisk don't seem too prosperous. I imagine you would or could do immense good in Africa by sending trained agricultural organisers out to work with men like Hooper. Perhaps, however, such men's success would be impossible unless political and industrial reform preceded them.

If your feelings to the natives of Kenya were fraternal you would write very differently.

Oldham to Leys
30 June 1925

. . . The point where I think we differ seems to me to be indicated in your remark about Curtis—"His aims are not mine: that is all there is to be said." In my view this does not in any way affect the way that Curtis and others like him are in their own way contributing to the achievement of the end we all desire. The end is so great that to reach it the help is needed not of one group of people alone but of all who, however much they may differ, do genuinely desire and seek a common end.

For myself I see one particular contribution that I think I can make and I am putting what strength and time I have into trying to make it. I do not for a moment suppose that it is the only path to the goal: possibly not even the most direct. All I hope is that, if it succeeds, it may prove to be a small contribution to a better state of things.

I do not think I gave you a copy of my paper.[155] I printed only a few copies and they ran out. Several people have asked for it and so I have had a few more copies printed.

Leys to Oldham
1 July 1925

You have repeatedly assured me that *our aims* were the same and I felt bound to take that as meaning that your aims agreed with mine, though I found the statement increasingly difficult to square with what you wrote and said.

The difference of aim was shown me definitely in your big book for the first time, in which, among many admirable descriptions and statements of matters of fact you did not include any statement of New Testament doctrine and practice. Then you concluded by urging that the solution of the problem lay with Christianity though your own conceptions and assumptions (common as they are to most Xtians of the time) were the very opposite of New Testament conceptions and assumptions.

I raised this vital point both in conversation and in letters, but without success. From that time I felt compelled to regard the agreement of aim you alleged as partial at best.

Then you came here—and most welcome you were and always will be—and told me that you considered the main theses of my book to have been established. I hoped I had to some extent convinced you. Now comes this pamphlet, which in tone and substance, in its ideas and assumptions and in its practical proposals is totally at variance with all that I have written and with all my aims for Africans. I cannot imagine why you should wish to be thought in agreement with me. You say you are not on the other side yet you fight on it. Coming from an avowed friend of native interests I can imagine nothing more injurious to my aims than this tract of yours.

Don't imagine I am blaming you or accusing you of hypocrisy, because I think your fundamental attitude is wrong. And don't imagine that I think everybody wrong but myself. That tract of Buxton's is exactly right, far better than anything I have ever written.[156] So is what the Manchester Guardian so frequently writes on the subject. You mention Curtis' name. He assures me I have convinced him. I shall know of what he is convinced when I read what he says about Kenya affairs to others.

Oldham to Leys
3 July 1925

I give it up.

This does not lessen my regard and admiration for you and for what you are doing or my desire to help, according to my lights, to further the ends you are seeking.

Leys to Oldham
7 July 1925

Have you any copies of that tract of yours you could let me have for sending to missionaries mainly? I want to know what they make of it. I mean the one marked "Private" that you sent me last week.

Oldham to Leys
9 July 1925

The paper I sent you was a memorandum intended in the first instance only for Ormsby-Gore. I had it printed in order to make it easier to read and also because I thought I might wish to show copies to some of my friends. I printed only a small number of copies. I hardly think I have given a copy to anyone with whom I have not had the opportunity of talking over the matter. It was written in a particular context and not with those in view to whom this context might not be familiar. I am therefore reluctant to have any general use made of it and in any case would like to retain the few copies that are left in case occasions may arise, in the course of conversations that I have, to put a copy in the hands of the man with whom I am talking.

Oldham to Leys
30 September 1925

Miss Latham has shown me the enclosed which I suppose I am meant to return to you.[157] I have read it with much interest. I agree that the utmost vigilance is necessary, but I do not think that the official world is altogether blind to what is involved. I am told that your book has woken up the Colonial Office, though none of the officials have spoken to me about it. I had a talk with Maxwell, the Commissioner for Native Affairs, and formed the impression that he is putting up a stronger fight than might appear on the surface.[158] I also have a good deal of faith in the new Governor. He will go cautiously, but I think he is a genuine believer in the Liberal tradition and when he is sure of his ground will put his foot down where this is necessary.

Leys to Oldham
4 October 1925

It has just occurred to me that it may seem rude if I don't answer your letter.

I know of no instance in which the Colonial Office has ever got its way in any controversy with the European Colony in Kenya. Instances of the contrary kind are always occurring. So I cannot think that events are likely to support your strangely confident prediction.

I don't know Maxwell. All I really know about him is that I once was given a private letter from him to read. In it he claimed credit for the recent change in the law whereby the police are in future to be free from the obligation to arrest "deserters" without warrants. My informants tell me that the legal change is quite without any practical effect. A slight change in procedure allows everything to go on as before. Maxwell may of course have been excusably deceived by some lawyer. But I cannot forget that it is the regular custom, and indeed a chief requisite for promotion, to be able to say one sort of thing in London to men like you, and do quite other things in Kenya. Maxwell's unpopularity with Europeans in Kenya proves nothing. Hollis was as unpopular but he got Laikipia for them from the Masai and was promoted. Ainsworth was also unpopular but he devised the Registration (—his story to you that he was not really responsible is so far as I can learn quite baseless) and though over age was given lucrative employment by the C.O.

The issues, fortunately for the Africans in Kenya, are perfectly clear. And so long as you and those you influence support the existing system on every one of them, you are, whatever you call yourself, an enemy of justice.

P.S. As I explained before I don't say for a moment that you *intend* injustice. All I do say is that the words you use have the result of making it more difficult for justice to be done.

Leys, Letter to the Editor
Manchester Guardian
26 October 1926
"The Education of the African."

Important political issues have a way of imperceptibly changing their shape and even their substance. A hundred years ago, for example, one could argue against slavery simply by citing the golden rule. In the end slavery was abolished because enough people in this country had come to feel the tie of a common humanity with the slaves. So that when it was proved that slaves were often cruelly treated, and that under slavery the cruelty was irremediable, people with consciences knew it to be wrong that any human creature should suffer as slaves suffered. By this time, however, something has happened to blunt the edge of this simple, direct, and effective appeal to conscience. It is suggested that common humanity is a misleading phrase. It is alleged nowadays that differences of race are so many and so deep that the golden rule is inapplicable to Asiatics and Africans. If one asks a woman how she herself would enjoy the conditions of life endured by the women who work underground in the coalmines of India, or a man how he would like to be treated as labourers in Kenya are, one is told that these people don't feel things as we do. If you prick a negro he doesn't bleed, or at least he can stand the loss of blood without injury and scarcely feels the prick. He is quite happy, in fact, in conditions which we should feel intolerable. There is just enough truth in this theory to make it the most cruel of falsehoods. People do vary in their capacity for suffering, and cultural level is perhaps the chief cause of differences in sensibility. But these differences exist among ourselves, and among ourselves they are not regarded as justifying cruelty or loss of liberty. As events in South Africa inform us, the motive of oppression by the dominant race is not the alleged incapacity of the subject race for cultural development, but its very ability to rise in the scale of human development, to show greater skill, to acquire greater knowledge, to enjoy life more wisely. The black man's offence is that he is proving himself to be fully human in spite of having been treated for generations as sub-human. So, to prevent him from thinking and feeling and behaving like a European, he is to have forced on him the culture Europeans desire him to have.

To those who are familiar with colonial opinion in such matters there will be nothing surprising in all this. But it is quite another matter to find that certain missionary bodies are beginning to act on these ideas. A certain American education expert,[159] of whom, by the way, educated negroes in America are by no means enamoured, toured Africa, East and West, and discovered the horrifying fact that African children were being taught just what European children are taught. They even have to learn about the boy upon the burning deck and the lamb that little Mary had. Well, why not? To which the answer is that Africans ought to be taught their place in the world. Certain eminent persons in the religious world seized upon this new theory of Christian propaganda. So popular did they find it with the Colonial Office that all over British tropical Africa it is now the accepted basis for educational work. In many parts Governments bear half the cost of mission schools, so that in future missions will be bound to teach what Governments tell them to. In some countries the missions have been deliberately given a monopoly of the education of Africans. It is highly questionable if by any means possible Africans can be prevented from getting what is a passion with them, the knowledge that has enabled Europeans to subjugate them and to conquer the world of nature.

Meanwhile subscribers to missions would do well to inquire what mission boards are doing with their subscriptions, since only if missions act on the faith that the best things in the world are to be shared with all men, barbarian, Scythian, bond or free, will the Christian Church have any future in Africa.

Oldham to the Editor
Manchester Guardian
29 October 1926.

My attention has been called to a letter from Dr Norman Leys in your issue of the 26th instant, in which the attitude of the missionary societies towards African education is seriously misrepresented.

Dr Leys has, presumably, in view the International Conference on the Christian Mission in Africa which met in Belgium last month.[160] The Conference was attended not only by missionaries but by members of the African race. The African members included the Rev. John Dube[161] and the Rev. Z. R. Mahabane[162] from South Africa. One is a former and the other the present President of the National Native Congress. Dr Leys will probably agree that two more outstanding representatives of independent native opinion in South Africa could hardly be found. The Conference was attended also by several distinguished leaders of the Negro community in the United States, such as President Hope of Morehouse College, Atlanta.[163] It may be taken for granted that these prominent representatives of American Negro and native African opinion would not have assented to any educational policy of the nature described by Dr Leys.

Dr Thomas Jesse Jones, to whose influence on educational policy in Africa Dr Leys refers, though he does not mention him by name, has always insisted that the educational ideals which he advocates are just as applicable to education in Great Britain and America as they are in Africa. His latest book, *Four Essentials of Education* is concerned with the application to western systems of education of the principles which he has advocated in regard to education in Africa.[164] The elements in education on which Dr Jones would lay the primary emphasis, whether in Great Britain or in Africa, are health of body and mind; understanding of the environment and ability to control it; building up of sound and healthy homes; and the right use of leisure and recreation as part of the rhythm of living. Which of these elements in education does Dr Leys regard as inimical to the welfare of African peoples?

Dr Leys attacks in his letter the policy not only of missionaries but of the colonial governments with whom they are co-operating. The most important experiment in African education is that which is being undertaken in the Prince of Wales' College at Achimota. If Dr Leys will take the trouble to examine the facts, he will be able to convince himself that the aim of this institution is to give to Africans the very best education, judged by western standards, which it is possible to give, and that the staff of the institution includes a number of the very best products of our universities, both men and women. At the same time, no one is more insistent than Mr Fraser, the Principal of the College, and Dr Aggrey his African colleague that it is necessary to build a bridge between the western knowledge, which it is the object of the institution to impart, and the African's own heritage from the past. The policy of the Prince of Wales' College at Achimota, of Dr Thomas Jesse Jones and of the missionary societies is, on the one hand, to open to the people of Africa the treasures of western knowledge and, on the other, to encourage them to appreciate, value and develop what is distinctively and characteristically their own.

The charge which is being brought at the present time against missionaries in India and China by educated Indians and Chinese is that education has been too western in character and had denationalised the people. Nationalist and educated opinion in India and China is in fact demanding that adaptation of education to the distinctive national conditions and needs in these countries which Dr Leys in his letter condemns, which the missionary societies, taught by the lessons of the past, are attempting to carry out in Africa.

No doubt there are people to be found who desire that the African should remain permanently a hewer of wood and drawer of water and who do not desire that the door of progress should be opened to him. But this is not the view of the Advisory Committee on Native Education at the Colonial Office, nor of Dr Thomas Jesse Jones, nor of the missionary societies. What these are concerned with is the broadening of the basis in education and its increasing adaptation to the social needs of the community, on which progressive educational thought in Great Britain and in America, as well as in Africa, is laying increasing emphasis.

Nothing is more to be desired than that not only the subscribers to missions, but that all who are interested in the education and advancement of the human race should act upon Dr Norman Leys' suggestion and enquire what the mission boards are doing with the funds which they receive. They will find that, notwithstanding many inevitable shortcomings and failures, the missionary societies are making a serious endeavour to give to the peoples of Africa, who have been suddenly swept into the fierce currents of western civilisation, an education which will enable them to meet these new conditions and which is more and more being brought into harmony with the best and most progressive educational ideas.

In support of what has been said in this letter about African education, I may be allowed perhaps to call attention to the chapter on African education in Sir Michael Sadler's recent little book *Our Public Elementary Schools.*[165] The inclusion of such a chapter in a book dealing with English elementary education is a recognition how much education at home may gain by the new conceptions regarding the fundamentals of education that are taking shape in the minds of the best educators in Africa in their effort to cope with the new and difficult educational problems of that Continent.

Leys to the Editor
Manchester Guardian
6 November 1926.

The point on which I am at issue with Mr. Oldham is as to the aims, social and educational, of the people with whom he thinks missions ought to co-operate. He writes that "there are people to be found who desire that the African should remain permanently a hewer of wood and drawer of water," but that he and his friends have no such view. That is a separate point. What I assert is that the representatives of the Europeans of Kenya, official and non-official, who are the people to whom Mr. Oldham and his friends have given partial control over mission schools in Kenya, are only in favour of opening "the door of progress" to Africans in so far as that door is believed by them to lead to the advantage of Europeans. The whole history of the Colony proves that to be the case beyond dispute. I am aware that Mr. Oldham and his friends have convinced themselves that opinion and policy have changed during the last few years. Let me adduce what was said less than a fortnight ago by the Colonial Secretary in the Legislative Council, in answer to complaints by planters that the relaxation of the efforts by Government to induce the natives to leave home to work on the plantations was threatening their prosperity. In the London "Times" of October 25 he is reported to have "declared that the Government believed that the attitude of hostility or neutrality on the part of administrative officers hindered the flow of labour. Therefore they were now definitely instructed to do their utmost to promote the flow of labour from the Reserves." What I assert is that the kind of government in Africa with which Christian missions ought to co-operate in education is one that follows resolutely and permanently the policy of neutrality as between village and plantation agriculture, which the spokesman of the Government of Kenya has definitely repudiated. Any other policy is a slave policy, however disguised, and whether the disguisers call themselves Christians or Atheists.

But Mr. Oldham raises another matter of even greater importance. He summarises the educational policy of his friend Dr. Jesse Jones and asks me which of its items I object to. I confess I do not understand what "rhythm" in education means. The rest seems to me to consist of all but one of the usual platitudes. The excluded item is the training of African youth to be the free citizens of a free society. This omission explains why Mr. Oldham and his friends are so popular with men of the type of Sir Edward Grigg, who has told us Cecil Rhodes is his hero, and Lord Delamere. Here I am at issue with Mr. Oldham and his school, not merely in our estimates of the aims of those with whom he would have missions co-operate, but as to what we regard as Christianity. He repeats the phrases so often in the mouths of those who are responsible for so many African wrongs—the "distinctive national conditions and needs," his wish that Africans should be encouraged "to appreciate, value, and develop what is distinctively and characteristically their own." When Paul preached in Antioch he did not warn his Jewish hearers not to be "denationalised"; nor did he urge the Greeks of Corinth to "develop what was distinctively their own." Instead he urged the abandonment of whatever in any man's heritage hindered full association in a free fraternity, so that all the members of the fraternity might share, to the fullest extent of which they were capable, all that was best in the ideals of both Asiatic and European thought and practice. The apathy of the Church (though not of its missionaries in Africa) and its subservience to Mammon have rendered that ideal excessively hard to conceive, and even harder to attempt, in Africa. All these fine-sounding phrases of Mr. Oldham's amount in practice in Africa to Africans being forbidden to aspire to control their own destinies. Who would guess from reading Mr. Oldham's letter that the Government with which he has persuaded missions in Kenya to co-operate is one that denies legal rights in land to individual Africans unless they undertake to work for some European master for such 180 days in the year as their masters may choose, and that exacts from the average African, whose wages are 14s. a month, as much in direct taxation as the richest European in the Colony pays?

You will not expect me to follow Mr. Oldham into West African affairs. I do know that, to the eternal glory of our country, we have made Africa for the Africans our motto in West Africa, and I fully expect that Governments there are ready to support a more liberal educational policy than is pursued in Eastern Africa, where concessionaires are allowed to call the tune though they do not pay the piper. But it makes me uneasy to know that educated West Africans are gravely mistrustful of this new mission policy. Most of these men were educated in the poorly equipped bush schools of which Dr. Jesse Jones wrote so contemptuously in his book, and many of them have earned his disapproval by being denationalised by being educated in Europe. I confess I would give to these men's opinions more weight in educational policy and practice than to the opinions of men like Mr. Oldham, whose short visits to Africa have been spent mainly in the company not of Africans but of Europeans of importance.

This crisis in African missions reminds one tragically of similar crises in the past, from the time of Constantinople onwards. The alliance of the Church with Governments based on some authority superior to the mass of the governed has always been ruinous. In India and China to-day the younger missionaries find it hard to fight down and to disprove by their actions the current belief that missions are the advance guard of Imperialist exploitation. Your other correspondent, Mr. Hutchings, quotes with approval the view that irreligious education is the danger to be dreaded. I would suggest to him that the danger to true religion never lies in irreligion but in sham religion. The Voltaires and Tom Paines of our day are, like their prototypes, the friends, not the enemies, of the religion of the

New Testament, the religion of justice and compassion. The worst enemies of the Church in Asia and Africa to-day are not the secularists, but those who for the sake of gaining for the Church an illusory control over the education of the young condone and defend those distinctions of race, whether in Church or in State, which are being used in Eastern Africa to sustain an unjust and oppressive racial dominance.

Leys, "Christianity and Race:
A New Policy for Missions"
The Scots Observer (Glasgow)
13 November 1926

As we know, our age is witnessing the revival of one of the original elements or features of the Christian ideal. The early Church provided its members, in a makeshift fashion, with the social and economic arrangements that were necessary in that simple age. The Church educated the children of its members and supported their widows and found work for any who could not find it themselves. The Church was, in fact, to some extent, a self-governing state. The first Christian missionary, in some moods at least, envisaged the future of the Church as a universal conquest, of society as well as of individual consciences. His faith was boundless, and for that reason the victorious Church he foresaw was one that absorbed or supplanted all the kingdoms of the world, or as we should say, Christianised all the institutions of human society.

Fifty years later, as the last book of the Bible tells us, the seeming failure of these hopes dissipated that ideal in the Church. The nearly desperate faithful few had no hope of victory save beyond the grave or by the world's destruction. Three centuries later still and world conquest seemed to the Church to be in its very hand. Ever since, the centuries have seen the Church pass from hope of triumph to despair of the world's future, and again from despair to hope, at times raising the banner of some solemn League and Covenant as symbol of the Kingdom of Heaven on earth, at others content with the evident necessity of conforming with an unredeemed world's usages and obeying its laws until in heaven they might learn and obey the law.

The Older Missionary Ideal

Protestant Missions began at a time when the latter view almost universally prevailed. The missionaries themselves were a minority despised by the Church at large, and they believed as a rule that all who had never heard of Jesus would be eternally damned. Their aim was the gathering of a minority, of a company of brands plucked from the burning. That the country they lived in, like all the kingdoms of this world, should ever become the Kingdom of Heaven was to them a forgotten ideal. Though they no longer expected, as the first Christians did, the last trumpet to sound in their ears at any moment, they as little hoped to found a society in Asia or Africa, with all the functions that a social [society?] can perform, industrial, political and the rest, as in their native land. To them Christianity was not a solution of all the problems of life so much as a means of escape from them, and many of them definitely believed, as the explanation of the powerlessness of the Gospel to transform society, that God had handed the world to the devil.

We have moved far since then, and to us the missionary of the illustrations in old missionary magazines, eternally preaching in tall hat and frock coat under a palm tree, is as strange a figure as a rope-girt friar. But we need to be reminded how great a work these men did. The best of them soon broke away from the narrow ideals they were brought up to. It is to these men, and to their strange allies the rationalists, that the world chiefly owes the abolition of slavery and infanticide and many another evil institution. To those men the fact is due that in many countries where the Church itself is weak the influence of the Christian ethic is as wide and deep as it is with us, perhaps sometimes even greater. They began to care for the sick, and in many ways reached out into life, long before the Church saw these activities to be the Church's duty. All over the world outside Christendom the best of the liberators of their peoples, the creators of nations out of oppression and anarchy, have been the men these early missionaries trained.

Religion and Economics

The secret of their success was simply their devotion. They were no doubt mistaken in many of the things they confidently preached. For real Christianity is the apprehending of the eternal, by men and

women of grievously imperfect sight. And the inward eye's lack of
clearness and imagination is due, not only to sin, to love for its own
sake, but also to there being much in the thought of every age that
makes it almost impossible to grasp some part or other of what Jesus
taught. Thus it was not the fault of these early missionaries that the
Church they came from thought economics and industry had nothing to do with religion, though Jesus had more to say about these
things than any other. So when they found the peasants they were
preaching to were suffering from poverty so extreme as to be de-
grading, they did not at first seek for its causes, nor did they feel it
to be their duty to teach improved methods of agriculture. The very
fact that they escaped from this kind of atheism long before the
Church at home did proves them to have been the saints of their age.
So that, while they were blind to much that God offered them—and
who is not?—of all his gifts of which they were aware, there was not
one which they were not eager to share. These gifts they knew were
not theirs to measure but God's, who gives men liberally without up-
braiding them for making poor use of the gifts, and they saw themselves not as superior beings conferring boons on inferiors, but as
the honoured instruments for transmitting God's boons to people
who for so long had been denied them. That is not to say that all the
early missionaries acted up to that ideal. But it certainly was their
ideal.

New Testament Teaching

Perhaps the greatest of these boons was the New Testament in the
languages of common speech. Few even now realise how much that
involved. For one thing, it meant that the taught could discover for
themselves what the teachers had failed to find. The most conspicuous of such discoveries was that being a priest before God involves
being a king before men. And when Protestant missionaries reinforced the teaching of the book by the doctrine that all Christians
are priests, then the inevitable result was nationalism of the democratic type. Few missionaries welcomed this development of their
teaching, since they themselves looked for God's kingdom to come
in heaven rather than on earth, and set little store by their own political liberty. But true religion, like some pot-bound plant, shows its
true habit of growth when transplanted to new soil, and blossoms as

it scarcely ever does in the stifling air of the compromises of Christendom.

Some will demur to this theory that the doctrine of social equality is derived from the doctrine of the equality of all men before God, and will truly urge that the spread of democratic ideas has not always followed the preaching of Christianity. But historical Christianity has not always given the common people the New Testament to read. In fact, it has rarely done so. Is it mere accident that the theory of democracy was first formulated when the Book was first translated into the languages spoken at the time? Or that the working-class in England began to demand the franchise at the same time as free and compulsory education enabled the poorest to read the New Testament? And could the ethic of the book be better stated in three words than it was by the people who first attempted to set up a democracy—the words liberty, equality and fraternity?

Political Aspirations

Nationalism in the East is the child of the Protestant missionary movement, in spite of the fact that the parent has long disowned its offspring. Indeed, even now younger missionaries often find that lack of sympathy with popular aspirations among the older missionaries hinders fraternal relations with those they live among. This hindrance to mission work will no doubt soon pass away. But a new danger is threatening the movement. It is chiefly to be met with in Africa, where in most parts aspirations after political liberty have scarcely arisen as yet. Alien governments never think they can be superseded, and naturally discourage the preaching of democratic ideas. Also it is obvious that the Europeans who are engaged in industry in those countries, where they have a practically complete monopoly of political rights and an effective control of industry, should do all they can to preserve their position of dominance. These are the circumstances in which certain leaders of the missionary movement are advocating a much closer co-operation with both governments and planters and merchants than was ever known in former times. This closer co-operation has, indeed, already taken place. Even its advocates will not deny its dangers. It is here suggested that so great a change in mission policy as it involves demands the most careful examination by the Church, in the fullest light that can be got from the directions of its Founder.

Leys, "Missions and Governments:
Objects of Christian Education"
The Scots Observer (Glasgow)
27 November 1926.

Nearly everywhere in the world education is mainly or entirely the
business of the State. But in tropical Africa practically all the
schools belong to Christian Missions. Probably most of the cost is
borne by the parents of the children, but the missions themselves
nearly always bear part. Until recently Governments confined their
help to small grants, sometimes accompanied by inspection. But the
only duty of the inspectors was to make sure that the taxpayers'
money was spent on real instruction in the ordinary subjects of a
primary school. Some missions, such as the large Universities Mission to Central Africa, fearing even the smallest interference from
Governments, refused these grants. But most people have always
thought it right for missions to accept them. And the Government
certainly made good bargains in giving them, since they could not
have done the work themselves for a fraction of the cost. The salar-
ies usually paid by missions, both to Europeans and Africans, are
about half what other agencies would have to pay for men with the
same qualifications. That was how things stood a few years ago.
Then the Colonial Office began to urge on its agents in Africa a
larger expenditure on education, and the problem arose whether to
set up Government schools, to increase the subventions to Mission
schools, or to go into a kind of educational partnership with missions. Under the influence of a certain group, of which it is not too
much to say that Mr J. H. Oldham is the moving spirit, the Colonial
Office has definitely adopted the last of these alternatives. In Kenya,
for example, the cost of running the schools for Africans will, except for school-fees, be borne equally by the Government and the
missions.

Superficially, this policy offers great advantages to the missions.
It saves them much expense, and saves them from having to com-
pete with Government schools with much more expensive equipment
and better-paid teachers. But there are other aspects of the question
to be considered. It is pertinent to ask, and important that subscribers to missions should ask, what kind of Government it is with
which missions are to enter into an alliance so unprecedently close,

what its general aims and policy are, since it is with them that its educational policy must conform.

European and African Education

The key to this new mission policy is the doctrine that African children should be given an education different in kind from what European children are given. Hitherto the only differences have been due to the fact that missions are poor, and African parents poorer still. Critics of missions have always objected to this "literary" kind of education. If we define the purpose of education among ourselves as being to prepare children to be free men and women, able each to take his part in controlling the forces of nature and his share in the ordering of human society, we might have to criticise the older type of mission school in Africa for fulfilling that purpose very inefficiently, even less successfully than our schools at home do. But the missionaries did the best they could with what they were given. Their aim was, in one word, enlightenment, and they did enlighten.

Education for Wealth-Production

But not even the friends of the new policy would claim that the chief educational purpose for Africans entertained by the Government of Kenya is enlightenment. Its chief aim is wealth production of a special type. It has given half the best land in the country to Europeans, and its avowed purpose is to induce the natives of the country to leave the land that has been left to them to work for wages for Europeans. Wages in Kenya average fourteen shillings a month. The average adult African male pays in direct taxation alone as much as the richest European has to pay. These facts are proof— and they might be multiplied indefinitely—that the Government of Kenya intends its African inhabitants to be the servants of its European inhabitants. It is claimed, of course, that they learn by working for Europeans. They certainly do. So did the slaves in slavery days. But West African experience proves—for in British West Africa the land is still in native ownership—that an independent native peasantry can learn more quickly than a society of wage-earners, and produce more wealth as well.

Already it is plain that the kind of instruction most favoured officially is not of the kind that will be of any use to the people in the

villages. It is not so much that vocational rather than liberal education is predominant. What is significant is the type of vocational
education given. Boys are trained to make, in wood and stone and
steel, the kinds of furniture and tools and houses that Europeans
use. Such articles are far beyond the means of men paid from ten to
twenty shillings a month. Be it observed that this criticism is not
directed against the Educational Department. It would be useless to
teach boys to make things they could use in their villages, partly because every Government agent is officially instructed to "encourage" the able-bodied males to leave their villages to work on the
plantations, partly because, in the absence of any organisation, the
produce grown in the villages fetches so little when sold that those
who, in spite of official discouragement, remain in the reserves, are
miserably poor. Every missionary knows that village life is far better
for the natives and far more favourable to the growth of the Church
than plantation life. But the efforts made by the Government to
satisfy the demands of the planters for labourers have killed village
industries. And the Government knows that a genuine attempt to
revive them would result in organised rebellion by the planters.

Implications of the New Testament

That is one side of the situation. The other side is what Africans
think about it, particularly those under mission influences. We give
them the New Testament, and tell them it is the key to the universe.
There are large parts of Africa where the people do regard it as the
key to life, to all life, social, industrial, and political, far more really
than we do. At first, of course, they nearly all interpret it as the missionaries tell them to. But some soon begin to reflect, and African
life is so closely shared, so largely communal, that thinking once
begun spreads fast. That thinking results in a reaching out for just
those things that we regard as the best things in life. That reaching
out is not the result of encouragement by the missionaries. They are
too busy with getting the people to grasp the chief doctrines and to
conform to the chief precepts of the Church. What Africans find for
themselves in the New Testament are that they may become kings
and priests to God, that he is the greatest who gives most service,
not he who gets most service—and in Africa it is the African who
serves and the European who is served—and that the humble and

meek will one day inherit the earth and sit on thrones beside the
Judge of the world. To give any people the New Testament and tell
them it should be their guide in life is to teach them these as well as
other doctrines. Whenever they are understood by people who live
under political subjection, especially if they live under economic
subjections as well, they are enthusiastically embraced.

Restrictions

In India and China most of the younger missionaries now recognise
all this. They see that it is sheer hypocrisy to ordain "natives" to be
presbyters and bishops, as being men to whom the divine wisdom
has been specially imparted, and deny them the rights and privileges that the most ignorant European may enjoy. But in Kenya
missions have gone into partnership with a Government that refuses
any rights in land to any individual native of the country except on
condition of his working for a European for such 180 days in the
year as the European may choose. In Kenya every school must be
registered, and the authorities may close any school merely because
they disapprove what is taught in it. If, whether owing to close co-
operation with a Government of this type, or for any other reason,
the natives of Kenya find in the Christianity the missions offer them
something less than the best and fullest life they can realise, they
will as the years pass increasingly turn elsewhere than to the Church.
They will be right in so turning, since a Church that refuses to the
least of its brethen the best of God's gifts has lost its Christianity.

Oldham, "African Education:
Missions and Governments"
The Scots Observer (Glasgow)
18 December 1918

Many of those who sympathise with Dr Norman Leys's sincere
desire for the welfare of the native peoples of Africa and admire his
courage in fighting their battles will regret his article in your issue of
November 27, in which he seriously misrepresents the attitude both
of the missionary societies and of the Colonial Office towards African education.

Dr Leys asserts that the missionary societies have entered into an

unprecedentedly close alliance with Governments, and implies that
in so doing they have compromised their principles. The policy of
the Colonial Office in regard to co-operation with missions in education is substantially the same policy as has prevailed in India for the
last seventy years. In the famous educational dispatch of 1854 the
Government of India laid it down that in undertaking the task of
diffusing the benefits of education among the peoples of India it
would avail itself of the help of voluntary agencies, assisting them
with grants-in-aid. A similar policy has now been approved in Africa.

Consultation and Co-operation

It has, however, always been felt by missions to have been a defect in
the working out of the policy in India that the opportunities of consultation between the Government educational authorities and those
responsible for the management of aided schools were not as frequent or full as was desirable. Provision for such consultation has
been made in African education by the setting up of Advisory Committees in the different Colonies and of an Advisory Committee at
the Colonial Office, and on these bodies the missions, and in several
Colonies the African peoples themselves, are represented. The fact
that missions are permitted to have a share in the formulation of
policy renders it far less likely that the educational policy of government will conflict with their distinctive aims and purposes than if
the policy were framed by the education departments alone and
handed out to the missions ready-made. There is nothing in the existing co-operation between missions and Governments in African
education which differs from the co-operation of which the missionary societies have had long experience in India, except that the conditions are, from the missionary point of view, more favourable.

Africa's Educational Needs

Dr Leys goes on to say that the key to the new mission policy is the
doctrine that African children should be given an education different in kind from what European children are given, and, using
Kenya as an illustration, suggests that the difference necessarily involves some kind of inferiority. There are no doubt people in Africa
who desire that the education of Africans should be different, because they would like to see Africans condemned permanently to an

inferior status. But any emphasis that may be laid in mission policy on the adaptation of education to African conditions, so far from being due to any desire of this kind, is prompted by the wish that the African peoples may make the most rapid progress possible. It is dictated solely by educational considerations. Education in Africa must differ to some extent from education in Scotland, because Africa is different from Scotland, and because leading educators in all countries are coming more and more to recognise that sound education must have regard to the pupil's environment. Missions in China have in recent years been forced to recognise that the position and future of their schools and colleges have been gravely prejudiced by the fact that they are in the eyes of the Chinese foreign institutions out of touch with Chinese life.

Nothing could be further from the truth than to suggest that either the missionary societies or the Colonial Office desire to bar the door of progress to the African peoples in any sphere. The recent International Missionary Conference in Belgium, which was attended by representatives of every leading Protestant missionary society working in Africa, declared in one of its resolutions that "in classes beyond the primary stages the teaching of an European language should be begun in order to enable the pupils to meet the situation arising from the rapidly-increasing contacts with European civilisations, to profit by them, and on their part to make a full African contribution to the shaping of a developing society." And the Memorandum of the Advisory Committee at the Colonial Office on Educational Policy states that, so far as resources permit, "the door of advancement must be increasingly opened for those who by character, ability, and temperament show themselves fitted to profit by such education."

That this is no mere pious aspiration is shown by the establishment at Achimota in the Gold Coast of an institution designed to become a West African University, at which the aim is to impart an education that will not fall below the highest Western standards. A similar higher institution, though necessarily on a smaller scale, has recently been started in Uganda.[166] When Dr Leys's attention has been called on a previous occasion to the work at Achimota, he has replied that he is not concerned with West Africa. But in the article in your issue and elsewhere he has brought charges against the general educational policy of the missionary societies and of the Colonial Office, and to such charges Achimota and similar efforts elsewhere are a valid answer. The missionary societies and the Colonial Office have work in both West and East Africa, and their general educational aims were the same for the Continent as a whole.

Correcting the Bias

After bringing a general charge against the educational policy of missions and of Governments, Dr Leys goes on to discuss the quite distinct and separate question of administrative policy in Kenya. This is too large and complicated a matter for me to attempt to discuss in the space at my disposal. My only reason for writing is to correct the misrepresentation of the educational policy of missionary societies and of Government in Africa. But it is, of course, obvious that general administrative policy must react on educational policy, and I think it is true that in education in Kenya at the present time there is a disproportionate emphasis on the production of the masons and carpenters required by the European community. But efforts are being made to correct this bias, and it is only fair to point out that the new Jeanes School for the training of visiting teachers, which is receiving the strongest backing from the Government, is concerned wholly with the improvement of the conditions of the natives in the reserves. In this institution, under the leadership of the Rev. J. C. W. Dougall,[167] who was recently ordained by the Scottish Churches for his present work, one of the finest attempts in the whole of Africa is being made to improve the little village or bush schools, which are the fundamental problem at the present time in African education and offer the chief opportunity of laying secure foundations for the advancement of the peoples of Africa.

Leys to the Editor
The Scots Observer (Glasgow)
25 December 1926.

... Mr Oldham accuses me of misrepresentation, and says the new policy is not new at all. Mr Calderwood describes it as both new and good.[168] In my time in Africa missionaries were never classed by Africans with "all Europeans." Other Europeans, in the universal opinion, went to Africa to make what they could out of Africans. Missionaries gave as well as took. In my time the Government was feared and detested. If Missions come to be regarded by the natives as a department of State, their influence in the future will be totally destroyed.

Mr Calderwood is too humble. He knows that I believe that the men and women who actually work in foreign Missions are the best people in the world, and the most valuable to the world. He also knows that this new educational policy is not of their devising at all, but is the invention of people who have neither taught Africans, nor listened to them, nor had intimate acquaintance with them.

The differences between Mr Oldham and me are too profound to be suitable for controversy in the Press. The people of Kenya have suffered, and still suffer, injustice and oppression. Mr Oldham has publicly deprecated exposure of the facts. I am afraid I call that the policy of the priest and the Levite in the parable. Subscribers to Missions who wish to know the facts can get my book in any public library. If they care to read Hansard for December 9, 1926, they will learn that things have got worse since I wrote my book, instead of better, as Mr Oldham has it.

We all regret the fact that most of the leaders of the Church a hundred years ago defended or condoned slavery. (The Society of Friends, and the smaller Presbyterian bodies in Scotland, were conspicuous exceptions.) The motive of slavery is not dead. The spirit of domination and avarice will never die. That motive, and that spirit, have resulted in a new sort of slavery in Kenya.

Mr Calderwood asks me for my alternative policy. I cannot expound it here. But I may say how heartily I agree with Mr Jameson's article in last week's "Scots Observer." We are all apt to ignore, in the ethics Jesus taught, what is in conflict with the ideas and practices of the age. What is wanted, in Scotland as in Kenya, is for the Church as a whole to preach and to practice the code of conduct Jesus taught.

Appendix

J. H. Oldham "A Note on the Report of the East African Commission" (privately printed by W. H. Smith), encl. in Oldham to Ormsby-Gore, 6 May 1925, CO533/344/ 20779.

The Report of the East African Commission is an imperial document of the first importance. [1] It brings together a most valuable body of information, not hitherto easily accessible, about the vast territories which constitute our East African empire. One of its great merits is that it envisages East Africa as a whole and presents particular problems in their proper setting, true perspective and relation with one another. It sets forth a policy and makes positive recommendations which, if acted on, must contribute greatly to the well-being and progress of these territories. It would be regrettable if the opportunity created by the publication of the Report were allowed to pass without decisions which will mark a turning point in the history of our East African Empire.

I. The Significance of the Report

The governing idea of the Report is that there is a moral obligation resting on Great Britain to develop the vast productive areas in East Africa, for the administration of which it is responsible. Their potential wealth, as the Report makes plain, is prodigious. Dr. Shantz, of the Agricultural Department at Washington, who accompanied the Phelps-Stokes Education Commission in its recent visit, estimates that the area of East Africa (including Abyssinia and Portuguese East Africa) capable of being brought under profitable culti-

---

1.   PP, 1924–25 [Cmd. 2387].

vation is equal to that in the United States.[2] He considers that ninety million acres could, if desired, be put under cotton, as contrasted with the thirty-four million acres on which cotton is grown in the United States.

It is plain from the facts set forth in the Report that, if these rich territories are to be developed, improvement of transport facilities is a primary necessity. Without this, progress in other directions is impossible. The conclusion to which the facts set forth in the Report inevitably point finds expression in the main proposal of the Commission that Parliament should authorise a loan of ten million pounds, guaranteed by the imperial Government, for the construction of harbours, railways and roads.

Along with the moral obligation to make available the potential wealth of these territories, there exists a parallel and equal obligation, as is fully recognised in the Report, to promote the physical, mental, moral and social advancement of their native inhabitants. To this responsibility His Majesty's Government is committed by many public pronouncements, and notably by the Kenya White Paper of 1923, as well as by its adhesion to various international treaties. It is stated in the Report, with reference to Tanganyika Territory, that since this is a "mandated" area, "Great Britain has a special responsibility before the world for ensuring its good government and development." It will, however, be generally agreed that the responsibility which we owe to our own imperial traditions, public professions and sense of duty is not less weighty

2.   Homer L. Shantz (1876–1958). Botanist with the U.S. Department of Agriculture; with the Smithsonian Expedition to Africa, 1919–21, and the Phelps-Stokes mission to East Africa, 1924. Mildly critical of Dr. Jesse Jones for views he thought too favorable to settlers. See King, *Pan-Africanism and Education,* p. 139.

and exacting than the obligations arising out of international engagements.

The object of this paper is to urge (1) that in the endeavour to carry out this twofold responsibility the crucial problem for which a solution has to be found is that of population; (2) that the basis of any attempt to deal successfully with this and other problems that find a place in the Report of the Commission must be an unprejudiced and scientific study of the facts and, in particular, of the human factor on which everything else depends; and (3) that the best results from the proposed loan for development will be obtained if a small proportion of the sum voted is put at the disposal of the Secretary of State for expenditure at his discretion for the purposes of research and educational experiment.

II. The Question of Population Crucial

A careful perusal of the Report makes clear that the fundamental problem is that of population. On this depends the supply of labour for the economic development of the territories.

The area of the territories under British rule in East Africa is approximately 1,000,000 square miles and the population is estimated at about 12,000,000. The relative sparseness of the population is the dominating fact in the situation. As the Governor-General of the Congo recently remarked with reference to the Belgian Congo, where conditions are analogous—an area of 900,000 square miles with an estimated population of 10,500,000—"the population is manifestly too small, much too small; the exploitation of the known wealth of our colony and of the resources of which the existence may be presumed will demand an abundant supply of labour."

From the standpoint of the economic development

of these areas account has to be taken not only of the
fact that the people are for the most part ignorant,
untrained, unaccustomed to continuous effort, and
undisciplined in habits of regular work. These deficiencies have to be remedied before the existing supply of
labour becomes efficient. According to the Report
(p. 40) there is already a shortage of labour in Uganda
and Kenya and Tanganyika. In Nyasaland and Northern Rhodesia there is a surplus, but this is due to the
lack of transport facilities which at present stand in
the way of the economic development of these territories.

If a shortage of labour already exists in three of the
most important territories, it is all the more important
to look ahead and to prepare for those increased demands that will be made by the economic developments which the Report contemplates as the result of
the opening up of fresh areas by new railways and
roads.

A still graver issue arises if there are reasons for
thinking that the population as a whole is decreasing
rather than increasing. The facts necessary for a decisive judgment are lacking. Reliable vital statistics do
not exist. The Report holds that there is no conclusive
evidence as to whether the population of East Africa is
increasing or decreasing (p. 46). At the same time it is
important, as Mr. Linfield points out in a supplementary memorandum, to note that in Nyasaland the
Census Report for 1921 asserts that the indigenous
population is declining and gives reasons for this decline; that in Kenya the Chief Native Commissioner
considers that, when every allowance has been made for
defects in his estimates, it is difficult to avoid the conclusion that the population has lately shown a tendency
to decline [Dr. Norman Leys, in his recent book,
Kenya (p. 282), expresses the opinion that the population of Kenya has declined since the European occupation 33 per cent.]; and that in Uganda until recently

the population has been declining rather than increasing (p. 144), and it is only now, thanks to the heroic efforts that have been made to combat disease, that the corner seems to have been turned and the population has begun slowly to increase (pp. 184–85).

It is perhaps worth while to note in passing the conditions in the Belgian Congo, where the subject appears to have received closer attention than in British East Africa.

The Commission for the Protection of the Natives, which is a permanent body in the Congo itself, established under the Colonial Charter, in its Report for 1919 stated that there was no difference of opinion among its members as to the fact of depopulation, which was "real, rapid and alarming." It quoted with approval a memorandum by one of its members in which it was estimated that the population of the Congo had since the European occupation fallen by half. (*Rapport au Roi de la Commission Instituée pour la Protection des Indigènes*, pp. 18, 26.) After citing opinions and evidence on both sides apart from the devastation wrought from sleeping sickness, regarding which there is no question, it is possible to affirm with certitude that among the native population generally there is a decrease. While exact data for an authoritative and final judgment are not available, they find themselves compelled to state that it is extremely probable that depopulation is taking place in the Congo. (*La Question Sociale au Congo*, p. 41.)

In the present state of our knowledge, controversy as to the facts of increase or decrease of population would be futile. It is sufficiently serious that the healthy, natural increase of population, on which the economic development and prosperity of these territories entirely depend, should be a matter of doubt. Moreover, whether an actual decrease in the population of East Africa is taking place or not, there can be no question that the forces tending to produce such a

result are active, powerful and dangerous. They may
be divided into two classes.

First, there are the ravages of disease following in
the wake of the European occupation. Sleeping sick-
ness is said to have carried off 300,000 people round
Lake Victoria in the epidemic of 1901–5, and the
Commission point out that in the past year cases of
sleeping sickness have been recorded in all the five
territories visited, and that since the tsetse fly is ad-
vancing in most parts of East Africa, there is abundant
cause for anxiety (p. 56). In the district of Bunyoro in
Uganda practically the whole population is said to be
infected with venereal disease. The spread of the same
disease is a real danger in other territories and the in
fection of the population must inevitably result in the
decline of the birth-rate, which has only now been
overcome in Uganda through the energetic and costly
efforts of the medical department over a period of
years. Ankylostomiasis is stated to be second only to
syphillis in its bad effects on the community; investigations in specimen districts in Kenya showed that between 60 and 80 per cent. of the population were infected with some kind of worm disease (p. 55). Plague
exists in Kenya and Uganda, and constitutes a danger
which may at any time become a scourge. Malaria,
yaws, dysentery, tuberculosis, influenza, leprosy, and
spirillum fever are among the other diseases which are
a menace to the health and increase of the population.

The second group of causes adverse to the growth of
population are those connected with the disturbance
of native life as a result of contact with a more advanced civilisation. The effects of this contact on native
life call for more exact study than has yet been given
to them. The gravity of the situation in the Congo has
led to increased attention being given to the subject by
Belgian students of Colonial affairs and its great importance is recognised in the Report of the Standing
Committee of the National Colonial Congress which

has already been quoted (*La Question Sociale au Congo*).

Prolonged periods of absence from wife and family for work at industrial centres; disease contracted at such centres and brought back to infect the reserves; social conditions in labour centres unfavourable to the setting up of a home and the birth of children; changes in habits of life resulting in a greater susceptibility to disease and lessened power of resistance; conditions of life at labour centres and in the journeys to and from them prejudicial to health; excessive drain of the male members of a tribe leading to the neglect of the cultivation of food crops or imposing an excessive burden on the women, and resulting in under-nourishment of both adults and children—these and other similar causes operate in greater or less degree to prevent the healthy growth of population. In addition to these more directly adverse influences there are also operative, in the opinion of some students of the subject, certain more subtle psychological and social causes, resulting from maladjustment between the inherited mentality and habits of the people and the new environment into which they have been suddenly introduced. These influences undermine the social stability which is conducive to the natural increase of population.

The Belgian Government recently appointed a strong commission to examine and report on the labour situation in the Congo. The Report of the Commission, which is in process of publication, accepts as a basal fact that "native societies brought into contact with civilisation exhibit an extreme fragility," and holds accordingly that the starting point of any consideration of the labour problem must be an attempt to determine the proportion of labourers which can be safely withdrawn from native society without disturbing the economic, political or social equilibrium of tribal life. (*Rapport de la Commission pour l'Etude*

*du Problème de la Main-d'oeuvre au Congo Belge.—
L'Essor Colonial et Maritime*, April 18th, 1925.) This
seems to be the right approach to the problem. Measures designed to ensure a healthy increase of the population are an indispensable foundation for the
economic development of the territories.

If this point of view is adopted and the problem is
taken firmly in hand there appears to be no need for
pessimism. The results already achieved by the medical departments in combating disease are full of encouragement. Recognition of the danger makes it
possible to devise measures for dealing with it. The
hearty co-operation of the administration, the medical
departments, the education departments, and the
missionaries in carrying out a constructive policy may
be expected to bring about a great improvement in the
situation. But success can be hoped for only if the increase and health of the native population and their
increased efficiency as producers are seen to be the
fundamental economic problem of East Africa, and
the attainment of these ends is made a primary object
of administrative policy.

III. A Plea for the Scientific Treatment of East African Problems

The Report contains an admirable and illuminating
chapter on the importance of scientific research in relation to the development of East Africa.

The Commission point out that anthropology is a
subject having the most important applications in the
sphere of administration. Attention is called to the
paucity of systematic records regarding rainfall and
crop production. The need for scientific and technical
experts in connection with crop production, animal
husbandry, the exploitation of minerals and forests,
the conservation of water supply, the improvement of
existing industries and the development of new ones is

strongly emphasised. Scientific investigation of human, animal and plant diseases is indispensable if
these are to be successfully combated. Yet in almost
all these directions the Commission found the existing
provisions quite inadequate for the work to be done.
Additional scientific workers are urgently required in
every colony. The increase is needed alike in the agricultural, veterinary and medical departments. The
Commission are of opinion that one of the chief methods by which Great Britain can assist her tropical possessions and her own trade is by increased provision
under this head (p. 94).

Valuable and important as are the recommendations of the Commission in this chapter of the Report,
it seems necessary, if they are to yield the largest practical results, to carry the matter a stage further and to
consider whether the particular proposals put forward
in the chapter can be co-ordinated in some comprehensive and unifying plan.

If the local governments and the Imperial Government are to initiate and give effect to a considered and
progressive policy directed to the economic development of the territories and the advancement of their
inhabitants, they must have at their disposal fuller
information than is at present available regarding the
forces at work in East Africa in order that they may
bring them increasingly under intelligent control,
combat tendencies of a destructive nature and direct
the course of development to wise and beneficent
ends.

The enquiry that is wanted would need to be scientific in the sense that it would be a disinterested attempt to ascertain the facts and would enlist the aid of
the best expert knowledge obtainable. The use of the
term scientific research is apt, however, to be misleading, inasmuch as it does not immediately suggest two
aspects of the enquiry that are of fundamental importance.

In the first place, as ordinarily used, it tends to convey the suggestion of enquiry related to natural products and physical forces. These must, of course, be included in the enquiry, but if, as has been contended, the question of population is fundamental, it is essential that the approach to the subject should be from the human side. The primary questions are how native life may be protected from disintegration, how the health of the people may be promoted, and how they may be trained in habits of industry and taught to make the fullest use of the natural resources of their environment. In recent Belgian discussions of colonial questions the vital relation of these questions to the economic future of the Congo is clearly recognized.

Scientific research is apt, secondly, to suggest exclusively the work of specialists, whereas the main point of the suggestion that has been made is the need of co-ordinating the work of specialists and relating it to administrative policy. The services of specialists in the various sciences are indispensable, but the largest return from their labours will be obtained only if the investigations undertaken are related to a constructive policy aiming at the most advantageous economic development of the territories and the health and progress of their inhabitants. For this task of co-ordination the qualities required are not so much exceptional proficiency in a particular department of knowledge, as a broad outlook on human affairs, width of sympathy and a sense of proportion. It is an interesting fact in this connection that the survey of Medical Education in the United States and Canada, which has led in the past fifteen years to a transformation in the conditions of medical education in North America, was made by Dr. Abraham Flexner, who was not himself a medical man.

It would be premature at this stage to consider what kind of machinery is needed for the kind of survey that has been suggested; whether, for example, some

permanent machinery is required or whether the end
in view could be achieved by a Commission which
would report within a definite period. Such questions
as well as the composition of the body undertaking the
enquiry can be determined only after a careful study
of the existing situation with the aid of expert advice.
It is obvious that no single body could undertake
directly the whole of the enquiry. The greater part of it
could doubtless best be provided for by strengthening
the scientific staffs of the medical, veterinary and
agricultural departments, as is proposed by the Commission. Moreover, as the Commission point out, a
great deal of valuable information could be assembled
not by instituting new independent enquiries but by
bringing together knowledge already possessed by
administrative officers, missionaries and others, and
by enlisting their co-operation in obtaining information which could be utilized by specialists. But to set
on foot these various lines of investigation and direct
them towards a common end, there is need of some
central driving force and co-ordinating mind or minds.
The range of possible enquiry within each department
of knowledge is practically unlimited. The essence of
the problem is to know what in view of the total requirements of Government policy should come first. A
primary qualification in those directing the enquiry
would be the ability to recognize what amount of information at any particular stage is enough. The value
of the survey would depend more than anything else
on an appreciation of the relative value of facts.

   In order to give more definite content to the suggestion that has been made, it may be desirable to
indicate the kind of matters with which a survey might
deal. The following tentative suggestions are offered
for the purpose of making clearer what is intended
and not as in any sense an adequate exposition of the
subject.

   (1) Since the question of population is crucial, an

endeavour might be made to find out how present
estimates of population are arrived at, how far they
may be regarded as approximately correct, and
whether any improvement can be effected in the
method of arriving at results. Conditions in Africa will
no doubt for long make it impossible to obtain exact
statistics corresponding to those in European countries, but it may be found possible to obtain estimates
sufficiently accurate for practical purposes. It might
be considered further whether by carefully conducted
investigations in selected areas it would be possible to
obtain information that would shed valuable light on
questions relating to the increase of population.

(2) It should be possible with the help of the experience of administrative officers, missionaries and
others to arrive at an estimate of the proportion of
adult males which can be safely withdrawn at any
given time from the life of a tribe for employment outside. The percentage would doubtless vary according
to the circumstances of the tribe. The estimate could
be revised from time to time, since with the progress
of education, increase in efficiency and the introduction of improved and labour-saving methods into the
reserves, a larger supply of labour would be released
and become available for work outside. This method
of approaching the labour problem is a distinctive feature of the recently published report of the Labour
Commission appointed by the Belgian Government,
and determines the lines of the Report. (*Rapport de la
Commission pour l'Etude du Problème de la Main-
d'Oeuvre au Congo Belge.*)

(3) An enquiry might be instituted into the more
economical use of existing labour. This would include
such questions as the progressive elimination of por-
terage through the improvement of communications
and the increase of mechanical means of conveyance;
improvements in organization which would prevent
wastage of labour; the encouragement, wherever pos-

sible, of the introduction of labour-saving machinery in industrial enterprises; and the reduction of the amount of manual labour required in the reserves through the introduction of better tools and labour-saving methods of various kinds.

(4) It should be possible, as has been done by the Belgian Labour Commission, to obtain estimates of the present and prospective demands for labour in the various colonies, and to regulate the pace of development by the supplies of labour that are available, or that can by improved organization and the introduction of labour-saving methods progressively be made available.

(5) Much fuller information than is at present available is needed, as is pointed out in the Report of the East African Commission, regarding the conditions of life, customs and beliefs of the various tribes. In such enquiries the assistance of anthropologists is indispensable. But while every fact relating to the life of a people has both a scientific value and a human interest, it will doubtless be found that for the purposes of successful administration, with which we are here concerned, there are certain facts that are of primary importance—the facts, for example, which relate to customs that affect the health and physical efficiency of the people or to beliefs and tabus that hinder production or to the industrial organization of the tribe and the division of labour between men and women. Measures might be taken to collect and relate information of this nature, which for the most part is already in the possession of administrative officers, missionaries and others, but which needs to be assembled, co-ordinated and made available for administrative use.

(6) Questions of health, which are of vital importance, are for the most part the concern of experts, and the primary necessity is no doubt to strengthen the medical departments, not least on the scientific

side. But there are many points where such questions touch, and need to be definitely related to, the subjects dealt with in preceding paragraphs.

(7) A special Advisory Committee has been set up at the Colonial Office to consider the question of education, but at every point educational policy needs to be related to the general policy of Government for the advancement of their peoples.

(8) It has been recommended by the Commission that provision should be made to obtain systematic records of rainfall and temperature. This important information can be obtained at relatively small cost, but unless definite provision is made for securing it, there is danger of the matter being neglected.

(9) Consideration should be given to the question whether it is desirable or possible to co-ordinate and extend the information at present in the possession of the agricultural departments regarding the possibilities of the soil. In this matter valuable advice and help could probably be obtained from the Agricultural Department at Washington, which has had to undertake soil surveys on a large scale and has had experience in dealing with the question of soils as a geographical rather than a chemical problem. Such investigation would supply additional information regarding the economic possibilities of the country and the most effective use to be made of the different types of land.

(10) Enquiry could be made whether present information regarding crop production, area under cultivation and yield is adequate and presented in the most convenient form to provide a basis for a policy of economic development. The same question might be asked in regard to information relating to stock and industries.

(11) Dr. Shantz, of the United States Department of Agriculture, in his chapter on "Agriculture in East Africa," in the Report of the Phelps-Stokes Commis-

sion, lays great stress on the importance of the study
of native methods of agriculture. He is of opinion that
it would be a great mistake in many cases to interfere
with their established customs until a thorough and
unprejudiced study of these methods and their results
has been carried out. (*Education in East Africa*, pp.
365–71.) The suggested study of native agriculture,
which would include the crops raised, the amount of
the yield, the unit of cultivation by each individual,
the implements used, the amount consumed per head,
etc., would not only lead to improved methods and increased production, but would also have an important
bearing on other matters dealt with in preceding paragraphs.

(12) Land tenure and transport are subjects of
which the importance is obvious.

It is not intended to suggest that a comprehensive survey should be immediately instituted embracing all
the matters touched on in the foregoing paragraphs.
This would be an undertaking beyond the capacity of
any body that might be constituted for the purpose
and would inevitably break down under its own weight.
Much of the information required can best be obtained through the normal activities of the agricultural, veterinary and medical departments. It may be
found that the best way to deal with certain matters
will be to start experiments in selected areas, and, if
the results are found to justify it, to extend such efforts to other areas.

The essential thing is to determine whether there is
at present available the information which is necessary
to enable the local and Imperial governments to frame
a wise policy of economic development that includes in
its purview the well-being and advancement of the native peoples, and, if this information is lacking, what
kind of information is required and how it may best be
obtained. The wisest course may be to make a begin-

ning with the examination of some one subject of
pressing importance, such as the question of labour,
on which economic progress entirely depends. It is
important, however, that each particular enquiry
should be viewed in relation to the main objective and
to the other factors in the situation. A survey of the
soils and the potential production of the territories,
for example, would lose a large part of its value if account were not taken of the human element by means
of which alone the agricultural potentialities can be
realized. So long as the ultimate end is kept clearly in
view a beginning can safely be made at some point.
The attempt to deal with the problems of East Africa
in a scientific spirit and to base policy on a thorough
and progressive study of the facts, even if it is only a
beginning, may be expected to exert a stimulating and
vitalizing influence in many unforeseen directions.

IV. Advantages of the Suggested Method of Dealing with East African Problems

(1) The suggestion that has been made is in line with
important tendencies which are manifesting themselves in our industrial life at home. Public attention
has recently been directed to an investigation that is
being undertaken by the Industrial Institute with a
view to preventing unemployment. *The Times*, in a
leading article on the subject (April 20th, 1925),
pointed out that the Institute is not committed to any
political theory and has as its sole object "to study
things as they are and in the light of ascertained
knowledge to reach conclusions that will minister to
the improvement of industrial life." It has the "single-
minded purpose of examining the industrial system,
with a view to the development of a descriptive science
of its working, especially from the point of view of the
human relations, and ethical conditions involved."
Attention is called in the same article to the fact that

in launching out on a purpose so wide, the Institute "has seen the wisdom of fixing upon certain definite and relatively circumscribed subjects of enquiry in order to harness and concentrate its energies."

The investigation undertaken by the Industrial Institute is only one indication of a growing recognition that the chief hope of finding a solution to the industrial problems which constitute so serious a menace to our civilisation lies in a dispassionate and unprejudiced study of the facts. Problems of a similar character are beginning to emerge in Africa, with the added complications of racial differences. We have in East Africa to deal not merely with difficult economic problems arising from the introduction of western capital, but with racial issues that may have a profound influence on the future of the Empire. The wise course would seen to be to apply to them in the early stages that unbiased study and scientific treatment which we are coming to recognise to be our chief hope of dealing with economic problems at home, in order that we may be able to gain through knowledge a rational control of forces that may later become much more difficult to direct and manage.

(2) A scientific treatment of the problems of East Africa would help to avert, or at least greatly to mitigate, the conflict which is apt to arise between those who are concerned primarily with the exploitation of the natural resources of the country and those who from humanitarian motives are interested primarily in the welfare of the native peoples. Both points of view have their legitimate place, and there is no necessary antagonism between them. It is not desirable that the perfectly legitimate endeavour to make available for the good of all mankind the potential wealth of our East African territories should, through lack of a policy which takes account of all the factors, give rise to abuses which are incompatible with our declared aims and which can be redressed only by public agitation.

Such agitation is an unnecessary and wasteful expenditure of energy, and our national reputation is apt to suffer discredit as a result of the exposures which have to be made. These undesirable results could be to a large extent prevented by the adoption of a constructive policy based on an unprejudiced study of all the factors and giving to the human element that primary consideration which is demanded as much by sound economics as by the dictates of morality.

(3) It is only by this method that a solution can be found for the fundamental problem of the development of East Africa—namely, the supply of labour. Unless Government is prepared to accept the responsibility of regulating the rate of development in accordance with the supplies of labour that are available, or that can be made available, by taking appropriate measures, shipwreck on the rock of unalterable facts cannot be avoided. There is bound to come, as the Belgian Labour Commission insist throughout their Report, a rupture of the equilibrium between the demands of development schemes and of European enterprises and the existing supply of labour. When that point is reached either development schemes must be held up and European enterprises allowed to go bankrupt, or recourse must be had to methods of obtaining labour which are injurious to native welfare and which can therefore only have the effect of reducing the population and making the situation worse. The means of averting such disaster is to be found in a far-sighted policy based on an accurate knowledge of all essential facts.

(4) If as a result of the Report of the East African Commission this country were to initiate a policy of bringing scientific study to bear on the problems of our East African Empire, she would gain a position of leadership in methods of colonial administration which, in virtue of the magnitude of her responsibilities in the African continent, ought to belong to her.

Reports on colonial subjects published in Belgium in
recent years show how much systematic thought is
being given in that country to the problems of its colony in the Congo. With our larger responsibilities
there is the greater need for such study. A serious
attempt to lay the foundations of a large constructive
imperial policy in scientific investigation and knowledge would undoubtedly make a favourable impression on public opinion in the United States, and in
particular on the small but influential section of opinion which is beginning to recognise that the future of
the African continent is a world problem and to take
an interest in the progress of its peoples. The line of
treatment suggested here is in accord with ideas which
have inspired some of the most successful leaders in
American life to grapple with their own problems. In
South Africa at the present time there is an increasing
body of opinion which recognises that scientific study
is indispensable if a solution is to be found for the
many difficult and pressing problems connected with
the native question. Significant efforts are being made
in the South African Universities to provide for such
study. A strong move in the same direction by the
Imperial Government might be of great assistance to
South Africa and would open up many lines of fruitful
co-operation between that Dominion and this country. Any action on the lines suggested, in addition to
the advantages which it would bring to East African
territories, would have a wider international significance and influence.

V. Practical Proposal

The most effective means of achieving the objects set
forth in this paper would appear to be that, if Parliament in accordance with the recommendation of the
Commission authorizes the issue of a loan of ten million pounds for the development of the territories in

East Africa, the Secretary of State should at the same time be authorized to expend a proportion of this sum, not exceeding, say, five per cent., at his discretion for the purposes of research and of education.

A very small part of this sum would suffice for the expenses of a special Commission, or central organizing and co-ordinating body, which appears to be essential for the purpose of surveying the whole field and advising how the rest of the money available for research can be used to the largest advantage. But in addition to any more general survey there is urgent need of provision for investigation along particular lines in connection with the work of the medical, veterinary and agricultural departments. The Commission state that the outstanding example of neglected opportunities in research work in East Africa is the once-famous Amani Institute which they found lying derelict.[3] They recommended that Parliament should make provision for the restoration and upkeep of this essential undertaking. For the solution of many of the problems which have been touched on not only research is needed but the training and education of the natives. Generally speaking, education ought to be a charge on the ordinary revenues of the colony; but in relation to the problems which have been discussed there appears to be urgent need for educational experiments. The term education is used here in the widest sense to include the introduction of improved agricultural methods, of labour-saving devices and of sanitary and health measures. Hand in hand with scientific research must go the advancement of the natives in all that makes for true human efficiency. From the economic standpoint the one is as important as the other. In many directions what is needed is experiment. Local governments with their very mea-

3.   A biological-agricultural research institute founded by the Germans in German East Africa, one of the symbols of their scientific approach to imperialism.

gre resources may be reluctant to embark on expenditure on such experiments. Capital funds may be legitimately used to initiate such experiments at selected centres, which, once their value has been demonstrated, may be given a place in the programmes of the governments of all the territories.

It is respectfully submitted that if five per cent. of the proposed loan were placed at the disposal of the Secretary of State for the purposes which have been described, both the East African territories and this country would obtain a far larger return for the loan than if the whole of it were spent exclusively on the development of transport. Merely to open up new areas by railways will not yield results of the same value, even from the economic standpoint, as may be looked for if measures are taken simultaneously to deal with those other factors which as well as transport are involved in production.

It might be thought that the question of scientific survey is one which concerns the Empire as a whole and that the best means of providing for it would be to create some general body having a purview wider than East Africa. Experience, however, seems to show the superior advantage of demonstrating the value of a new method in a limited area. The problems of East Africa are of exceptional urgency and have recently engaged a large share of public attention. Parliament is being asked to grant a loan of ten million pounds. Even if it be true that the need for scientific survey is not limited to East Africa, it may be the more practicable course to make a beginning in connection with the developments which are expected to take place in East Africa. If the methods tried there prove to be a success they can easily be extended to other parts of the Empire. If Parliament were to earmark a proportion of the proposed loan for expenditure on research and education in the territories concerned, and if careful thought is given to the most fruitful use to

which these funds can be applied, the experiment may
lead to valuable results in the evolution both of the
African continent and of the British Empire.

Notes

Introduction

1. Margery Perham and Elspeth Huxley, *Race and Politics in Kenya: A Correspondence* (London: Faber and Faber, 1944).

2. See Kenneth Robinson, *The Dilemmas of Trusteeship: Aspects of British Colonial Policy between the Wars* (London: Oxford University Press, 1965).

3. Ralph A. Austen, *Northwest Tanzania under German and British Rule: Colonial Policy and Tribal Politics, 1889–1939* (New Haven: Yale University Press, 1968), and "The Official Mind of Indirect Rule: British Policy in Tanganyika, 1916–1939," in Prosser Gifford and William Roger Louis, eds., *Britain and Germany in Africa: Imperial Rivalry and Colonial Rule* (New Haven: Yale University Press, 1967), pp. 577–606.

4. Responsible government had in fact been conceded for years, and the question during the 1920s was whether Rhodesia would remain a separate colony or join the South African union. See Lewis H. Gann, *A History of Southern Rhodesia: Early Days to 1934* (London: Chatto and Windus, 1965), chap. 6. Even John H. Harris, secretary of the Anti-Slavery and Aborigines Protection Society and, with Arthur S. Cripps, the principal defender of African interests, thought that direct opposition to responsible government would be pointless and framed his strategy accordingly. See particularly Harris to Lord Olivier, 18 October 1920, Rhodes House, MSS Brit. Emp. s. 22/G162.

5. On the company see John S. Galbraith, *Mackinnon and East Africa, 1878–1895: A*

Study in the New Imperialism (Cambridge: Cambridge University Press, 1972), and Marie de Kiewiet Hemphill, "The British Sphere, 1884-94," in Roland Oliver and Gervase Mathew, eds., *History of East Africa,* 2 vols. (Oxford: Clarendon Press, 1963-65), 1:391-432.

6. See Frederick J. D. Lugard, *Diaries,* ed. Margery Perham and Mary Bull, 4 vols. (London: Faber and Faber, 1959-63), 1:316, and *The Rise of our East African Empire,* 2 vols. (London: Blackwood, 1893), 1:392-94, 397.

7. On this early period see Gordon H. Mungeam, *British Rule in Kenya, 1895-1912: The Establishment of Administration in the East African Protectorate* (Oxford: Clarendon Press, 1966), and Donald Anthony Low, "British East Africa: The Establishment of British Rule," *Oxford History of East Africa,* 2:1-56.

8. See for instance Sir Charles Strachey's criticism of Oldham's economic development pamphlet of May 1925, CO 533/344/20799; the negative reaction of the agricultural expert Sir Frank Stockdale and other officials to settler efforts to resist native coffee growing, May 1933, CO 533/3040; and the minutes on further white settlement in CO 533/474/38232/1 (1936). For the economic history of this period see Richard D. Wolff, *The Economics of Colonialism: Britain and Kenya, 1870-1930* (New Haven: Yale University Press, 1974).

9. Sir Charles Eliot, *The East African Protectorate* (London: Arnold, 1905).

10. That this supposed emptiness was a myth is made clear by Maurice P. K. Sorrensen, *Origins of European Settlement in Kenya,*

Memoir Number Two of the British Institute
of History and Archaeology in East Africa,
(Nairobi: Oxford University Press, 1968), pp.
28–29. What gaps existed were the temporary
results of smallpox, famine, and rinderpest.

11. See the report of the Economic Commission of
the East Africa Protectorate, 1919, in CO
533/210.

12. Robert G. Gregory, *India and East Africa:
A History of Race Relations within the British
Empire, 1890–1939* (Oxford: Clarendon Press,
1971), pp. 372–74.

13. The best guide to white politics is George
Bennett, *Kenya, A Political History: The
Colonial Period* (London: Oxford University
Press, 1964), and "Settlers and Politics in
Kenya, up to 1945," *Oxford History of East
Africa*, 2:265–332.

14. See Robert I. Rotberg, "The Federation Movement in British East and Central Africa, 1889–
1953," *Journal of Commonwealth Political
Studies* 2 (1964): 141–60; Elspeth Huxley,
*White Man's Country: Lord Delamere and the
Making of Kenya*, 2 vols. (London: Macmillan,
1935), 2:213–34; and Margery Perham,
Lugard, 2 vols. (London: Collins, 1956–60),
2:675–92.

15. Glasgow, 13 January 1900, Bodleian Library,
Gilbert Murray Papers, Box 32.

16. Norman Leys and T. A. Joyce, "Note on a
Series of Physical Measurements from East
Africa," *Journal of the Royal Anthropological
Institute of Great Britain and Ireland*, 43
(1913): 195–267. Biographical information
from Leys' daughter, Mrs. Agnes Avery.

17. Leys to Murray, Karonga, British Central

Africa, 14 February 1905, Murray Papers, Box 32.

18. Same to same, Chinde, 7 February 1902, ibid.

19. Same to same, Karonga, 18 June 1905, ibid.

20. Circular letter, Nakuru, British East Africa, March 1908, ibid. It must be added that the Colonial Office was more disgusted than Leys by the expedition. Minuted Churchill, the parliamentary undersecretary: "I do not like the tone of these reports. No doubt the clans should be punished; but 160 have now been killed outright—*without any further casualties* on our side, & the main body has not yet been encountered. . . . It looks like a butchery, & if the H. of C. gets hold of it, all our plans in E.A.P. will be under a cloud. Surely it cannot be necessary to go on killing these defenceless people on such an enormous scale" (Minute of 3 February 1908, CO 533/41/3648).

21. The skeptical secretary of state, Sir Lewis Harcourt, minuted: "Sir P. Girouard must have telepathically inspired Lenana's dying speech"! (On Girouard to CO, 15 March 1911, CO 533/85/8416).

22. Leys to Murray, Nakuru, 3 February 1910, Murray Papers, Box 32. Copy in CO 533/72. On the Masai incident see CO African Confidential Print, No. 1011, CO 879/112, and Mungeam, *British Rule in Kenya,* chaps. 11 and 12.

23. 4 *Hansard's Parliamentary Debates,* 28 (20 July 1911): 1325–31; 37 (16 April 1912): 181.

24. Norman Leys, *Kenya* (London: Hogarth Press, 1925), p. 121.

25. Leys to Murray, Nakuru, 24 April 1910, Murray Papers, Box 32.

26. Same to same, Nakuru, 18 June 1910, ibid.

27. See F. G. Butler memorandum (3 February 1911) of C.O. discussions with Girouard in 1910, CO 533/72.

28. The case of Galbraith Cole, who was tried for shooting and killing an African suspected of stealing sheep.

29. Leys to Murray, Mombasa, 23 April 1911, Murray Papers, Box 32.

30. Same to same, Mombasa, 27 December 1911, ibid.

31. Mungeam, *British Rule in Kenya,* p. 261, and Bennett, "Settlers and Politics in Kenya," *Oxford History of East Africa,* 2:284, follow contemporary Colonial Office opinion in presuming that Leys' role in bringing the Masai into court must have been stronger than he admitted, and that he must have engineered the whole affair. George S. Shepperson, in his introduction to the recent fourth edition of *Kenya* (London: Frank Cass, 1973), p. xiv, has already cast doubt on this interpretation. I believe that the Murray correspondence makes it necessary to revise it entirely. Leys told Murray (Fort Hall, 14 July 1912, Murray Papers, Box 32) that a friend of his had suggested to the Masai chief Legalishu that counsel be retained. Leys' own part had been restricted to contacting the lawyer. He had not, then, stirred up opposition to the government's policies himself. He told precisely this same story in his letters of defense to the Colonial Office (e.g. Glasgow, 16 February 1913, CO 879/112), in *Kenya* (p. 113), and in his application of 1930 for reinstatement to the colonial service (Leys to Secretary of State, Brailsford, 25 July 1930, Murray Papers, Box

32). Leys was clearly not acting alone. There are three anonymous letters of 1911–12 in the files of the Anti-Slavery Society (Rhodes House, MSS Brit. Emp. s. 22/G131) which urge the Society to capitalize in its propaganda upon the losses in people and cattle the Masai suffered during their move, a line Leys was explicitly discouraging in his letters to Murray and Ramsay MacDonald (Mombasa, 6 October 1911, Murray Papers, Box 32) on the ground that it would be impossible to obtain supporting evidence. My conclusion is that Leys did precisely what he admitted, no more. Candor perhaps to excess, not dissimulation, was his characteristic. Above all he would not have lied to Murray.

32. The dismissal grew out of his own admission (Leys to Acting Governor Bowring, Fort Hall, 22 July 1912, CO 879/112) that he had contacted counsel. CO minutes in CO 533/105–06.

33. Leys to Secretary of State, Fort Hall, 16 September 1912, CO 879/112.

34. In the same year, ironically enough, that the CO became convinced that Girouard after all had misled them about the wishes of the Masai. See minutes on Acting Governor Bowring to Secretary of State, 29 January 1913, CO 533/116.

35. Leys' continuing ambiguity found its way into his testimony before the East Africa Protectorate Economic Commission of 1912–13 (p. 274), in which he accepted compulsory registration by finger-printing of African males for labor recruitment. So long as they were going to have it, he argued, it ought to be improved.

36. Leys to Murray, Zomba, Nyasaland, 30 June 1914, Murray Papers, Box 32.

37. Same to same, Fort Hall, B.E.A., 27 June 1912, ibid.

38. Same to same, Karonga, Nyasaland, 24 November 1914, ibid.

39. Same to same, Glasgow, 17 March 1918, ibid.

40. Same to same, Mombasa, 22 March 1912, ibid.

41. Edmund D. Morel (1873–1924). Secretary of the Union of Democratic Control; founder of the Congo Reform Association; member of the West African Lands Committee, 1912–14. Author of *Red Rubber* (New York: Nassau Press, 1906), *The Black Man's Burden* (Manchester: National Labour Press, 1920), and other books. See William Roger Louis and Jean Stengers, eds., *E. D. Morel's History of the Congo Reform Movement* (Oxford: Clarendon Press, 1968).

42. Letter of Mrs. Avery to the editor, London, 22 September 1972.

43. Leys to Lady Mary Murray, Brailsford, 17 October 1930, Murray Papers, Box 32.

44. Leys to Murray, Glasgow, 25 February 1918, ibid.

45. Cf. the obituary in the *New Statesman*, 28 (2 September 1944): 149, presumably by Leonard Woolf.

46. Ormsby-Gore to Sir Edward Grigg, 24 August 1930, cited by E. A. Brett, *Colonialism and Underdevelopment in East Africa: The Politics of Economic Change, 1916–1939* (London: Heinemann, 1973), p. 60.

47. Leys to Murray, Karonga, 14 February 1905, Murray Papers, Box 32.

48. On the prevailing anthropological theories see Raymond Firth, ed., *Man and Culture: An Evaluation of the Work of Bronislaw Malinowski* (London: Routledge and Kegan Paul, 1957), and Marvin Harris, *The Rise of Anthropological Theory: A History of Theories of Culture* (New York: Crowell, 1968), pp. 514-67.

49. See Elizabeth Colson's important article on the stereotyping of African land law. "The Impact of the Colonial Period on the Definition of Land Rights," in Lewis H. Gann and Peter Duignan, eds., *Colonialism in Africa, 1870-1960,* 5 vols. (London: Cambridge University Press, 1969—), 3:193-215.

50. Leys to Murray, Mombasa, 19 March 1911, Murray Papers, Box 32.

51. *Kenya,* p. 334. Leys liked to shock people. His letter of 19 March 1931 to Winifred Holtby, his closest friend, is not untypical: "I don't know if I ever told you that I don't particularly like Africans. In fact I don't like uneducated people who won't give straight answers to plain questions. Occasionally some pious old woman tells me I must have a great love for Africans. When he or she hears my answer she moves swiftly to the other end of the room and I become 'that dreadful man' " (Holtby Papers, Hull Public Library).

52. "The Place of John Chilembwe in Malawi Historiography," in Bridglal Pachai, ed., *The Early History of Malawi* (Evanston: Northwestern University Press, 1972), p. 423.

53. "The Colonial Situation: A Theoretical Approach," in Immanual Wallerstein, ed., *Social*

Change: The Colonial Situation (New York: Wiley, 1966), pp. 34-61.

54. Balandier makes this point. See also Dorothy Gregg and Elgin Williams, "The Dismal Science of Functionalism," *American Anthropologist* 50 (1948): 594-611.

55. Leys to Murray, Brailsford, 18 August 1930, Murray Papers, Box 32.

56. Leys to Fraser, 29 June 1936, Fraser Papers, Rhodes House, MSS Brit. Emp. s. 283/11/1.

57. George Shepperson makes this same observation in his introduction to the fourth edition of *Kenya*, p. xv.

58. See for instance John Middleton, "Some Effects of Colonial Rule among the Lugbara," in Gann and Duignan, *Colonialism in Africa*, 3:6-48.

59. The best case study I know is by A. L. Epstein, *Politics in an Urban African Community* (Manchester: Manchester University Press, 1958).

60. Bronislaw Malinowski, *A Scientific Theory of Culture* (Chapel Hill: University of North Carolina Press, 1944); and "Introductory Essay: The Anthropology of Changing African Cultures," in Lucy Mair et al., *Methods of Culture Contact in Africa* (London: Oxford University Press, 1938), pp. vii-xxxviii.

61. Monica [Hunter] Wilson, "Contact between European and Native in South Africa," Mair, *Methods of Study*, pp. 9-24.

62. On this point see Philip Mayer, *Townsmen or Tribesmen: Conservatism and the Process of Urbanization in a South African City* (Cape Town: Oxford University Press, 1961).

63. For the comparison see Keith V. Thomas,

Religion and the Decline of Magic (New York: Scribners, 1971), and Alan Macfarlane, *Witchcraft in Tudor and Stuart England* (New York: Harper and Row, 1970).

64. The literature is surveyed in Robert I. Rotberg and Ali A. Mazrui, eds., *Protest and Power in Black Africa* (New York: Oxford University Press, 1970).

65. See, however, the valuable article by Donald Savage and J. Forbes Munro, "Carrier Corps Recruitment in the British East African Protectorate, 1914–1918," *Journal of African History* 7 (1966): 313–42.

66. On the theory of Indirect Rule see Frederick J. D. Lugard, *The Dual Mandate in British Tropical Africa,* 5th ed. (London: Frank Cass, 1965), and his *Political Memoranda,* ed. Anthony H. M. Kirk-Greene (London: Frank Cass, 1970); Margery Perham, *Native Administration in Nigeria* (London: Oxford University Press, 1962); and I. F. Nicolson, *The Administration of Nigeria, 1900–1960: Men, Methods, and Myths* (Oxford: Clarendon Press, 1969). For Leys' reaction to Cameron see *A Last Chance in Kenya* (London: Hogarth Press, 1931), pp. 68–77.

67. Leys' reaction to the Thuku incident, even then sometimes regarded as the first stirring of African nationalism, is in *Kenya*, p. 197 and chap. 13. Leys disapproved of Kenyatta not, as one might have thought, because of financial irresponsibility or his well-known sexual prowess, but because he became convinced that Kenyatta was indeed a Communist being subsidized by Russian gold. Leys to Winifred Holtby, 12 September 1933, Holtby Papers.

68. Letter to the Kikuyu Central Association from

Josiah Wedgwood, W. McGregor Ross, and Leys, 23 January 1930, McGregor Ross Papers, Rhodes House, MSS Afr. s. 1178.

69. On Owen and these associations see John M. Lonsdale, "Some Origins of Nationalism in East Africa," *Journal of African History* 9 (1968): 119–46; "European Attitudes and African Pressures: Missions and Government in Kenya between the Wars," *Race* 10 (1968): 141–51; and "Political Associations in Western Kenya," in Rotberg and Mazrui, *Protest and Power,* pp. 589–638.

70. Terence Ranger, "African Reactions to the Imposition of Colonial Rule in East and Central Africa," in Gann and Duignan, *Colonialism in Africa,* 1:293–324; "Connexions between 'Primary Resistance' Movements and Modern Mass Nationalism in East and Central Africa," *Journal of African History* 9 (1968): 437–53, 631–41.

71. *Kenya,* pp. 122–23.

72. It is a measure of the cooperation I have received from Norman Leys' family that I owe this reflection to his daughter.

73. Shepperson, "The Place of John Chilembwe," in Pachai, *Early History of Malawi,* p. 421.

74. For this interpretation see Robert I. Rotberg, "Psychological Stress and the Question of Identity: Chilembwe's Revolt Reconsidered," in Rotberg and Mazrui, *Protest and Power,* pp. 337–73; George S. Mwase, *Strike a Blow and Die: A Narrative of Race Relations in Central Africa,* ed. Rotberg (Cambridge, Mass.: Harvard University Press, 1967). See also the refutation by Jane and Ian Linden, "John Chilembwe and the New Jerusalem," *Journal of African History* 12 (1971): 629–48.

75. For recent studies see John S. Trimingham, *Islam in East Africa* (Oxford: Clarendon Press, 1964), and I. M. Lewis, ed., *Islam in Tropical Africa* (London: Oxford University Press, 1966).

76. German missionary groups urged such a policy but without effect. See Austen, *Northwest Tanzania,* pp. 69–70, 135, and John Iliffe, *Tanganyika under German Rule, 1905–1912* (London: Cambridge University Press, 1969), pp. 199–200.

77. Richard H. Tawney, *Religion and the Rise of Capitalism* (New York: Harcourt, Brace, 1926).

78. PP, 1929–30 [Cmd. 3573].

79. Leys applied through Lady Murray's good offices with Beatrice Webb (Lady Passfield), 31 August 1930, Murray Papers, Box 32. His letter to the secretary of state was not registered in the Colonial Office, and Beatrice simply replied that the job was not on.

80. Leys to Murray, 25 July 1930, ibid.

81. He was careful to exclude the parliamentary undersecretary, Dr. Drummond Shiels, from his indictment. *Last Chance,* p. 141. Robert G. Gregory, *Sidney Webb and East Africa: Labour's Experiment with the Doctrine of Native Paramountcy* (Berkeley: University of California Press, 1962), shows that Passfield's performance fully deserved Leys' attack.

82. Leys to Harris, 21 September 1930, Anti-Slavery Society, Rhodes House, MSS Brit. Emp. s. 22/G145.

83. See the file of correspondence between Lord Francis Scott and the Colonial Office, along with minutes, CO 533/436/3198/2 (1933).

John E. Flood argued that Byrne was the first
"really strong governor" in Kenya's history
and that his unpopularity was a measure of his
effectiveness. Leys hinted at this in *Last
Chance*, p. 151.

84. PP, 1934 [Cmd. 4556].

85. Leys to Murray, Yalding, Kent, 1 April 1942,
Murray Papers, Box 32. One of the critics who
can be compared to Leys was Edward J.
Thompson, who was inspired by *Kenya* to
publish *The Other Side of the Medal* (London:
Hogarth Press, 1925), which described British
atrocities during the Indian Mutiny. See
Thompson to Murray, Oxford, 23 January
1925, Murray Papers, Box 51.

86. On Oldham's place in the rise of the ecumenical movement see Ruth Rouse and Stephen C.
Neill, eds., *A History of the Ecumenical Movement, 1517–1948* (Philadelphia: Westminster
Press, 1954), especially Kenneth S. Latour-
ette's chapter in that book, "Ecumenical Bear-
ings of the Missionary Movement and the
International Missionary Council," pp. 353–
405; and William R. Hogg, *Ecumenical Foundations: A History of the International Missionary Council and Its Nineteenth-Century
Background* (New York: Harper, 1952).

87. Hogg, *Ecumenical Foundations*, p. 136.

88. Ibid., pp. 178–201; Marcia Wright, *German
Missions in Tanganyika, 1891–1941: Luther-
ans and Moravians in the Southern Highlands*
(Oxford: Clarendon Press, 1971), pp. 137–81.

89. It was, indeed, never registered, and there is
no copy of it at the Public Record Office.

90. Leys himself had called Ainsworth without
question the best administrator in East Africa.

Leys to Murray, Mombasa, 19 September 1911, Murray Papers, Box 32. See F. H. Goldsmith, ed., *John Ainsworth: Pioneer Kenya Administrator, 1864–1946* (London: Macmillan, 1955).

91. See for instance Governor Northey to CO, London, 26 March 1920, CO 533/253.

92. The texts of the Ainsworth circular, 23 October 1919, and of the bishops' memorandum are printed in Leys, *Kenya*, pp. 395–404.

93. See CO 533/248, 249.

94. Oldham's Negotiations with the Colonial Office are in CO 533/249, 272.

95. Leys to Harris, Brailsford, 30 June 1923, Anti-Slavery Society, Rhodes House, MSS Brit. Emp. s. 22/G134: "I don't believe Oldham is capable of an anti-Indian policy. Remember he always instinctively looks for a middle way—or to put it otherwise, persists in attempting to reconcile incompatible views. I don't at all agree with him in the way he relates religion and politics. But as nobody with my views could hold his job and do his very useful work I am not altogether sorry. It is more important for Oldham to carry people with him than to move fast himself. I am sure he is not anti-Indian. His policy is delay until a Royal Commission reports."

96. Ronald Hyam, *The Failure of South African Expansion, 1908–1948* (New York: Africana, 1972), p. 35 and passim.

97. There were race riots in nearly every port city in England in 1919, as veterans returned to find their jobs and sometimes their women had been taken over. On the race question within Britain between the wars see

Kenneth L. Little, *Negroes in Britain: A Study in Racial Relations in English Society* (London: Kegan Paul, Trench, Trubner, 1948), and Eliot J. Rose, *Colour and Citizenship: A Report on British Race Relations* (London: Oxford University Press, 1969).

98. Joseph H. Oldham, *Christianity and the Race Problem* (London: Student Christian Movement, 1925).

99. Robert A. Huttenback, *Gandhi in South Africa: British Imperialism and the Indian Question, 1860–1914* (Ithaca, N.Y.: Cornell University Press, 1971).

100. Telegram, Gov. General, Union of South Africa, to S. of S., 10 July 1923, Cab 24/161/325.

101. For the argument that the Government of India was fully capable of such a Machiavellian policy see Donald Anthony Low, "The Government of India and the First Non-Cooperation Movement 1920–1922," in Ravindar Kumar, ed., *Essays on Gandhian Politics: The Rowlatt Satyagraha of 1919* (Oxford: Clarendon Press, 1971), pp. 298–323.

102. See Gregory, *India and East Africa,* especially chaps. 5–9; J. S. Mangat, *A History of the Asians in East Africa, c. 1886 to 1945* (Oxford: Clarendon Press, 1969), pp. 120–31; and Roland Oliver, *The Missionary Factor in East Africa* (London: Longmans, 1952), pp. 255–62.

103. Dyarchy was a severely restricted form of responsible government in which power was transferred to provincial ministries on certain subjects, while being retained in the hands of the governor and his executive council on others. It was introduced under the Government of India Act of 1919, and was offically

ended by the Act of 1935. See R. R. Sethi and Vidya D. Mahajan, *Constitutional History of India* (Delhi: Chand, 1956), pp. 116ff., and Arthur B. Keith, *A Constitutional History of India, 1600–1935* (London: Methuen, 1936), pp. 245ff. It was against Dyarchy that Gandhi's first noncooperation campaign of 1921–22 was launched. The usual interpretation is that the system failed miserably. Low, "The Government of India," in Kumar, *Essays in Gandhian Politics,* argues that it succeeded brilliantly in its main object, which was to delay Britain's relinquishment of power for as long as possible.

104. Oldham to Archbishop of Canterbury, 25 May 1923, Edinburgh House, Box 241.

105. See Harris to Oldham, 19 May 1923; Arthur to Harris, 19 June; Harris to Arthur, 20 June. Rhodes House, Anti-Slavery Society, MSS Brit. Emp. s. 22/G134.

106. PP, 1923 [Cmd. 1922].

107. Archbishop of Canterbury to Duke of Devonshire, 29 May 1923, CO 533/305/27303.

108. Oldham to Archbishop of Canterbury, 25 May 1923, Edinburgh House, Box 241.

109. *The Times,* 28 January 1922.

110. There were persistent rumors, which affected government thinking. See the minutes on Acting Gov. Bowring to CO, telegram, 25 April 1923, CO 533/294.

111. See John W. Cell, *British Colonial Administration in the Mid-Nineteenth Century: The Policy-Making Process* (New Haven: Yale University Press, 1970), chap. 3.

112. See Roger B. Joyce, *Sir William MacGregor*

(Melbourne: Oxford University Press, 1971).

113. See David Kopf, *British Orientalism and the Bengal Renaissance: The Dynamics of Indian Modernization, 1773–1835* (Berkeley: University of California Press, 1969).

114. Claude Lévi-Strauss, *Tristes Tropiques*, Trans. John Russell (New York: Atheneum, 1968), p. 59.

115. Jane E. Harrison, *Prolegomena to the Study of Greek Religion*, 3d ed. (New York: Meridian, 1955), and *Themis: A Study of the Social Origins of Greek Religion* (Cambridge: Cambridge University Press, 1912); G. Gilbert Murray, *Five Stages of Greek Religion* (Oxford: Oxford University Press, 1925).

116. This is the real point of Malinowski's diary, which recorded not the findings of a detached scientist but his explicitly confessed shortcomings. See Bronislaw Malinowski, *A Diary in the Strict Sense of the Term* (New York: Harcourt, Brace, World, 1967).

117. See Charles G. Seligman, "Presidential Address; Anthropology and Psychology: A Study of Some Points of Contact," *Journal of the Royal Anthropological Society* 54 (1924): 13–46; Ernest Jones, "Psycho-Analysis and Anthropology," ibid., 47–68.

118. Oldham to Sir Edward Grigg, 7 July 1926, Grigg Papers, Microfilm in Queen's University Library, Kingston, Ontario.

119. As Oldham and Betty D. Gibson were to put it in *The Remaking of Man in Africa* (London: Oxford University Press, 1931), p. 18: "Africa is a single battlefield in a conflict that is being waged on a world-wide front. The issues that are being decided there are those between the

Christian understanding of man and of the purposes of his existence and standards and values of modern secular civilization."

120. Thomas Fowell Buxton, *The African Slave Trade and its Remedy* (London: John Murray, 1840). See John Gallagher, "Fowell Buxton and the New African Policy, 1838-1842," *Cambridge Historical Journal* 10 (1950): 36-58.

121. John E. Flint, "Nigeria: The Colonial Experience from 1880 to 1914," in Gann and Duignan, *Colonialism in Africa,* 1:220-60.

122. H. Alan C. Cairns, *Prelude to Imperialism: British Reactions to Central African Society, 1840-1890* (London: Routledge and Kegan Paul, 1965).

123. Oldham and Gibson, *Remaking of Man in Africa,* pp. 49-50.

124. Gustave Spiller, ed., *Papers on Inter-racial Problems* (London: P. S. King, 1911).

125. Oldham to Ormsby-Gore, 10 May 1923, Edinburgh House, Box 219.

126. Same to same, 13 March 1923, ibid.

127. See Ronald E. Wraith, *Guggisberg* (London: Oxford University Press, 1967).

128. See William E. Frank Ward, *Fraser of Trinity and Achimoth* (Accra: Ghana Universities Press, 1965).

129. Aggrey deserves a new biography. But see Edwin W. Smith, *Aggrey of Africa: A Study in Black and White* (London: Student Christian Movement, 1929), and Kenneth J. King, "James E. K. Aggrey: Collaborator, Nationalist, Pan-African," *Canadian Journal of African Studies* 3 (1969): 511-30.

130. Ernest F. Spanton (Chancellor of St. Andrews College, Zanzibar) to Oldham, 8 June 1924, Edinburgh House, Box 266.

131. Oldham to Guggisberg, 14 January 1924, ibid.

132. Journal of Dr. Jesse Jones, 16 October 1920, Edinburgh House, Box 263.

133. Oldham to Guggisberg, 14 January 1924, Edinburgh House, Box 266.

134. See Guggisberg to Oldham, Accra, 5 March 1924, ibid.; Fraser to Major Ralph Furse (recruiting officer for the British colonial service), 1 February 1924, Fraser Papers, Rhodes House, MSS Brit. Emp. 2. 283/4/1.

135. A disappointment shared, incidentally, by Charles Strachey of the Colonial Office, who received the news "with a growing feeling of depression." (Minute on Acting Gov. Maxwell to CO, 4 December 1924, CO 96/650/59770).

136. This last took place in 1931. See the amusing minutes, including the comment that Ward's statement that the Gold Coast and Nigeria were "young nations" looking toward dominion status was "simply tripe of the very worst kind," in CO 96/700/7119.

137. Kwame Nkrumah to Fraser, Accra, 6 September 1954, Fraser Papers, Rhodes House, MSS Brit. Emp. s. 283/11/1.

138. Kenneth J. King, *Pan-Africanism and Education: A Study of Philanthropy and Education in the Southern States of America and East Africa* (Oxford: Clarendon Press, 1971).

139. For the rise of this establishment see C. Vann Woodward, *Origins of the New South, 1877–1913* (Baton Rouge: Louisiana State University Press, 1951), chap. 13.

140. Thomas Jesse Jones, *Negro Education: A
      Study of the Private and Higher Schools for
      Colored People in the United States,* 2 vols.
      (Washington, D.C.: Government Printer,
      1917).

141. Thomas Jesse Jones, ed., *Education in Africa:
      A Study of West, South and Equatorial Africa*
      (New York: Phelps-Stokes Fund, 1922), and
      *Education in East Africa: A Study of East,
      Central and South Africa* (New York: Phelps-
      Stokes Fund, 1925).

142. In addition to King's book see his article,
      "Africa and the Southern States of the U.S.A.:
      Notes on J. H. Oldham and American Negro
      Education for Africans," *Journal of African
      History* 10 (1969): 659–77.

143. Loram to Oldham, Rondebosch, 18 November
      1925, Edinburgh House, Box 1229. By 1929
      Loram no longer regarded Hertzog as a poten-
      tial friend to the African, though he still
      believed the African could expect fairer treat-
      ment from him than from Smuts.

144. On the "triumvirate" see Jones, Memorandum
      on Oldham's Plans, 8 June 1926, Edinburgh
      House, Box 233.

145. Oldham and Gibson, *Remaking of Man in
      Africa.*

146. See Murray to Oldham, Birmingham, 20 July
      1931, Edinburgh House, Box 275.

147. Oldham and Gibson, *Remaking of Man in
      Africa,* p. 61.

148. Edinburgh House, Box 216.

149. Edwin W. Smith, *The Golden Stool: Some
      Aspects of the Conflict of Cultures in Modern
      Africa* (London: Holborn, 1926).

150. Smith Memorandum, August 1924, Edinburgh House, Box 216.

151. See Westermann to Oldham, Cleveland, Ohio, 26 December 1925, Edinburgh House, Box 204.

152. See the Malinowski-Oldham correspondence in the Malinowski Papers, London School of Economics, Box 104.

153. G. A. Stevens, "The Future of African Art," *Africa* 3 (1930): 150–60.

154. Bronislaw Malinowski, "Practical Anthropology," *Africa* 2 (1929): 22–38; Philip E. Mitchell, "The Anthropologist and the Practical Man: A Reply and a Question," ibid., 3 (1930): 217–23; Malinowski, "The Rationalization of Anthropology and Administration," ibid., 3 (1930).

155. Edwin W. Smith, *The Christian Mission in Africa: A Study Based on the Work of the International Conference at Le Zoute, Belgium* (London: International Missionary Council, 1926).

156. David B. Barrett, *Schism and Renewal in Africa: An Analysis of Six Thousand Contemporary Religious Movements* (Nairobi: Oxford University Press, 1968), pp. 68, 243–44.

157. Oldham and Gibson, *Remaking of Man in Africa*, p. 11.

158. PP, 1924–25 [Cmd. 2387].

159. Oldham to Ormsby-Gore, Edinburgh House, 10 September 1926, CO 533/361/6539.

160. Same to same, 13 May 1925, CO 533/344/22000.

161. Same to same, 10 September 1926, CO 533/ 361/6539.

162. Oldham, Memorandum of conversations with Colonel Arthur S. Woods and Dr. Beardsley Ruml of Laura Spelman Foundation, 26 and 28 October and 5 November 1925, Grigg Papers.

163. Oldham to Grigg, 28 July 1926, ibid.

164. Same to same, 11 November 1926, ibid.

165. See Perham, *Lugard,* 2:676.

166. Jan Christian Smuts, *Africa and Some World Problems* (Oxford: Clarendon Press, 1930).

167. For the Colonial Office attitude toward African research in the early thirties see CO 323/1069/70042 (1930); CO 323/115/80018 (1931); CO 323/1166/90033 (1932). It is indicative of the changing official response that a separate series, CO 847, was begun in 1932 for African research projects and other general matters.

168. See Oldham to Charles Roberts (president of Anti-Slavery Society), and Oldham to Harris, 26 February 1929; Harris to Oldham, 28 February 1929. Anti-Slavery Society Papers, Rhodes House, MSS Brit. Emp. s. 22/G145.

169. Harris to Leys, 17 May 1928, Anti-Slavery Society Papers, Rhodes House, MSS Brit. Emp. s. 22/G144.

170. Same to same, 28 September 1927, ibid.

171. George Bennett, "Paramountcy to Partnership: J. H. Oldham and Africa," *Africa* 30 (1960): 356–60.

172. Joseph H. Oldham. *White and Black in Africa: A Critical Examination of the Rhodes*

Lectures of General Smuts (London: Longmans, 1930).

173. See the report of the Hilton Young Commission, PP, 1928–29 [Cmd. 3234].

The Leys-Oldham Correspondence

1. The "squatters" were indeed the most discon-
tented Africans in Kenya, as they were in other
settlement colonies. See Maurice P. K.
Sorrenson, *Origins of European Settlement
in Kenya* (Nairobi: Oxford University Press,
1968), pp. 150, 184–85, 236, 275. The Carter
Land Commission of 1933 estimated that some
100,000 squatters, most of them Kikuyu, lived
outside the reserves. PP, 1934 [Cmd. 4556]
10:144. As Leys maintains, many of them were
living on land which, though it had been
alienated to Europeans, they regarded as their
ancestral home.

2. The taxation system in Nyasaland was a
driving force in the unrest building up to
John Chilembwe's rising in 1915, and the
investigating commission afterward agreed
that the Africans had been ill-used. See
George S. Shepperson and Thomas Price,
*Independent African: John Chilembwe and the
Origins, Setting and Significance of the Nyasaland Native Rising of 1915* (Edinburgh:
Edinburgh University Press, 1958), pp. 216,
370. See also Stephen S. Murray, *A Handbook
of Nyasaland* (Zomba: Government Printer,
1932), pp. 289–90.

3. That the Kikuyu system of land tenure was
individual, bearing no relation whatever to the
communal concept that became the stereotyped European version of African tradition,
was recognized even before World War I by

officials who worked closely with them. See
Mervyn W. Beech, "The Kikuyu System of
Land Tenure," *Journal of the African Society*
17 (1917): 46–59, 136–44. The government's
response was to ignore the evidence and to
argue that Kikuyu who had been dispossessed
were not entitled to compensation. (Acting
Governor Sir Henry Belfield to Secretary of
State, 27 January 1913, CO 533/116/6361.)
After the war the demand for title deeds
became a persistent theme in the agitation of
Kikuyu Central Association. Even though the
additional knowledge that was acquired from
systematic investigations (by a commission of
1929 that included the anthropologist
Louis Leakey and by the Carter Land Commission of the early 1930s) made the Kikuyu
case even stronger, the government agreed to
settle only a few of the claims. (For the report
of the 1929 committee see CO 533/398/16121
[1930]. For the Carter Land Commission, see
PP, 1934 [Cmd. 4456].) As native commissioner G. V. Maxwell admitted in 1923, the
blunt truth was that a full recognition of the
"ithaka" system would have meant a confes-
sion that most of the European settlement in
Kenya had been illegal. (Report enclosed in
Acting Governor Denham to Secretary of
State, 4 July 1924, CO 533/312/37410.) Never
settled, this grievance was one of the main
causes of Mau Mau. See Sorrenson, *Origins
of European Settlement,* and *Land Reform in
the Kikuyu County: A Study in Government
Policy* (Nairobi: Oxford University Press,
1967).

4.　See Donald Savage and J. Forbes Munro,
"Carrier Corps Recruitment in the British

East African Protectorate, 1914–1918,"
Journal of African History 7 (1966): 313–42.

5. This is certainly an overstatement. The
    experiences of the Amerindian cultures in the
    Caribbean and in Latin America and that of
    the Maoris in New Zealand were surely at least
    as destructive and traumatic.

6. As has already been made clear in the intro-
    duction (see above, p. 30), Leys was mistaken
    on this point. On the predominance of
    Muslims in the King's African Rifles see
    Hubert Moyse-Bartlett, *The King's African
    Rifles: A Study in the Military History of East
    and Central Africa, 1890–1945* (Aldershot:
    Gale and Polden, 1956), pp. 105, 140.

7. Why British colonial officials should so con-
    sistently have favored Islam as a "good
    religion for natives" is strange in view of the
    long history of Islamic-inspired resistance they
    had encountered in India, the Middle East,
    Egypt, and the Sudan. On the nature of
    Islam in East Africa the leading recent
    authority concludes that Islamization "pro-
    ceeds by gradations through three main stages
    of germination, crisis, and gradual reorienta-
    tion," converts in the interior being even now
    mainly in the first stage. At this stage too
    there would have been virtually no incom-
    patibility between Islam and African tradi-
    tional religion, since nothing important had to
    be abandoned and little more than ceremony
    to be added. John S. Trimingham, *Islam in
    East Africa* (Oxford: Clarendon Press, 1964),
    p. 60 and passim.

8. For the Ethiopian movement see Bengt G.
    Sundkler, *Bantu Prophets in South Africa,* 2d

ed. (London: Oxford University Press, 1961), pp. 38-42, 53-59, and Shepperson and Price, *Independent African*, pp. 72-74, 127-85.

9. Leys here discusses some of the causes and symptoms of what he does not explicitly identify as the separatist or independent church movement, a phenomenon already well entrenched by 1918 in South Africa and Nyasaland though only in the beginning stages in Kenya. For the movement in Kenya see Frederick B. Welbourn, *East African Rebels* (London: Student Christian Movement Press, 1961), and Welbourn and Bethwell A. Ogot, *A Place to Feel at Home: A Study of Two Independent Churches in Western Kenya* (London: Oxford University Press, 1966). On the independence movement generally, see Barrett, *Schism and Renewal*.

10. This is of course John Bunyan's *Pilgrim's Progress*.

11. This was in 1911. See Huttenback, *Gandhi in South Africa*, pp. 271-73, who argues however that Hardinge bowed to London and Pretoria in an effort to achieve a compromise on this thorny question: the reverse of what Leys assumed had happened.

12. That the Kikuyu had no chiefs was common knowledge among administrators in Kenya long before Jomo Kenyatta's classic statement in *Facing Mount Kenya: The Tribal Life of the Gikuyu* (London: Secker and Warburg, 1938), a conclusion sustained by modern scholarship. See John Middleton, "Kenya: Administration and Changes in African Life, 1912-1945," in Vincent Harlow et al., eds., *History of East Africa* (Oxford: Clarendon Press, 1965) 2:333-92; Hubert E. Lambert, *Kikuyu Social and*

Political Institutions (London: Oxford University Press, 1956).

13. Leys is here referring to 2.7 million acres alienated under the settlement of Sir Harry Johnston of 1892 to the British South Africa Company. See B. S. Krishnamurthy, "Economic Policy, Land and Labour in Nyasaland, 1890-1914," in Bridglal Pachai, ed., *The Early History of Malawi*, pp. 384-404; J. Pike, *Malawi: A Political and Economic History* (London: Pall Mall Press, 1968), pp. 89-94; A. Hannah, *The Beginnings of Nyasaland and North-Eastern Rhodesia, 1859-95* (Oxford: Clarendon Press, 1956), pp. 223-45.

14. An important indication of the fact that in 1918 Leys' attitudes were still evolving. He would not have made this concession to "practicality" by 1925.

15. Shepperson observes that Leys points here toward Frantz Fanon's theory of therapeutic violence. "The Place of John Chilembwe in Malawi Historiography," in Pachai, *Early History of Malawi*, p. 423.

16. Oldham is probably referring here not only to the problem of German missionaries in the conquered German colonies but to the question of mandates to be brought before the peace conference.

17. For the finished article see Fulani bin Fulani, "Religion and Common Life: A Problem in East African Missions," *International Review of Missions* 8 (1919): 155-72.

18. The letter was in fact never registered at the Colonial Office, who were unable to find it a few years later. Minutes on Leys to C.O., 10 July 1921, CO 533/274/23713.

19. Herbert J. Read (1863-1949). Assistant private secretary to Joseph Chamberlain, 1896-97; principal clerk at the Colonial Office, 1905-16; assistant undersecretary, 1916-24. Governor of Mauritius, 1924-1930.

20. Sir Edward Percy Girouard (1867-1932). Director of railways in the Sudan, 1896-98, Egypt, 1898-99, South Africa, 1899-1904. High Commissioner, Northern Nigeria, 1907-8, Governor, 1908-9. Governor, East Africa Protectorate, 1909-12.

21. Before the war Leys had corresponded with the Colonial Office about a memorandum he had written upon the distressing effects of "culture contact" on the people of Mombasa, receiving the curt reply that the secretary of state could not undertake to revise the paper for publication. Leys to C.O., 12 February 1913, CO 533/131.

22. Lionel Curtis (1872-1955). Had been Beit lecturer on colonial history and fellow of All Souls, and a member of Milner's "kindergarten" as assistant colonial secretary of the Transvaal. Had written *The Problem of the Commonwealth* (London: Macmillan, 1916), and was editor of the *Round Table,* the principal Commonwealth journal. I have been able to find no other reference which would explain Leys' obscure report of this conversation, which may have dealt with how to implement the concept of mandates in Africa.

23. Sir Reginald Coupland (1884-1952). Beit professor of imperial history at Oxford, who wrote the classic study in three volumes of Arabic and European penetration of East Africa as well as numerous other books,

including the standard biography of William Wilberforce. Coupland was an effective "entrepreneur" in the organization and financing of research projects at Oxford, and became in the 1930s secretary of the International Institute of African Languages and Cultures, succeeding J. H. Oldham.

24.   Leys was confusing Oldham with Rev. Frank Ashcroft, of the Church of Scotland in Edinburgh.

25.   So far as I can detect there is no particular significance in the choice of this particular pseudonym, which Leys used for articles though not for letters to newspapers until the publication of *Kenya* in 1924, when he included it on the title page under his name.

26.   Sir Charles L. Temple (1871–1929). Chief secretary (1910–13) and lieutenant governor (1914–17) of Northern Nigeria. Author of *Native Races and Their Rulers: Sketches and Studies of Official Life and Administrative Problems in Nigeria* (Cape Town: Argus, 1918). One of the classics of Indirect Rule, the book is pro-Islamic and highly critical of Christian missions. For Leys' review see *International Review of Missions* 8 (1919): 263–66.

27.   Workers' Educational Association. An Oxford extension movement founded in the early 1900s by Albert Mansbridge with the encouragement of the historian John Holland Rose, its object being to educate the working class through classes given by sympathetic university dons. By the 1920s the curriculum had expanded into a general adult education program. See Alan J. Corfield, *Epoch in Workers' Education* (London: W.E.A., 1969),

and John F. C. Harrison, *Living and Learning,
1790–1960* (Toronto: University of Toronto
Press, 1961).

28. Thomas Jesse Jones (1873–1950). Director of
research department, Hampton Institute,
1902–9; U.S. Census Bureau, 1909–12; U.S.
Bureau of Education, 1912–19; educational
director, Phelps-Stokes Fund, 1913–46; and
leader of the Phelps-Stokes commissions to
Africa in the 1920s. The book here referred to
is *Negro Education in the United States,* 2
vols. (Washington, D.C.: Government Printing
Office, 1917).

29. Alexander G. Fraser (1873–1962). C.M.S.,
Uganda, 1900–1903; principal, Trinity
College, Ceylon, 1910–24; Indian Village
Education Commission, 1920–21; principal,
Achimota College, Accra, 1924–35. See
William E. F. Ward, *Fraser of Trinity and
Achimota* (Accra: Ghana Universities Press,
1965).

30. John H. Harris (1874–1940). Missionary in
Congo; parliamentary secretary of the Anti-
Slavery and Aborigines Protection Society;
Liberal M.P., 1923–24. Author of *Dawn in
Darkest Africa* (London: Smith, Elder, 1912);
Africa: Slave or Free? (London: Student
Christian Movement, 1929); *The Chartered
Millions: Rhodesia and the Challenge to the
British Commonwealth* (London: Swarthmore
Press, 1920).

31. Statement of Kenya Missionary Alliance,
enclosed in Acting Governor Bowring to C.O.,
17 May 1920, CO 533/233/30728.

32. Respectively, John J. Willis and Robert S.
Heywood, who were joined in this letter by
the Rev. John W. Arthur, head of the Church

of Scotland Kikuyu mission. The text of the
letter is printed in Leys, *Kenya,* pp. 413-20.

33. Anti-Slavery Society to Milner, 5 March 1920,
     CO 533/248/12040.

34. See Fulani bin Fulani, "Christianity and
     Labour Conditions in Africa," *IRM* 9 (1920):
     544-51.

35. John J. Willis (1872-1954). CMS missionary in
     Uganda from 1900; Archdeacon of Kavirondo,
     1909-11; Bishop of Uganda, 1912-34.

36. "Co-operation—Its Necessity and Cost." *IRM*
     8 (1919): 173-92. "The spheres of missions
     and governments are distinct. The kingdom
     which Christian missions seek to serve is not of
     this world. Their aims are religious, and not
     political. But while the spheres of missions and
     governments are distinct, and it is essential
     that the distinction should be kept in view,
     there remains a large field which is of common
     interest to both." Leys had struck an impor-
     tant point, for this idea was to be the basis
     for Oldham's whole policy during the interwar
     years.

37. William McGregor Ross (1877-1940). Assis-
     tant engineer, Uganda Railway, 1900-1904;
     director of public works, Kenya, 1905-22.
     Author of the critical work, *Kenya from
     Within: A Short Political History* (London:
     Allen and Unwin, 1927).

38. Dr. John W. Arthur (?-1952). Head of the
     Church of Scotland Mission, Kikuyu. Known
     for his part in the controversy in the late
     1920s with the Kikuyu Central Association
     over the rite of female circumcision.

39. Leonard S. Woolf (1880-1969). Colonial
     servant in Ceylon, 1904-11. Editor of the

Nation, 1923-30; *Political Quarterly*, 1931–59. Founder with his wife Virginia of the Hogarth Press, which published *Kenya*. Oldham's review is in *IRM* 9 (1920): 460-62.

40. See Evelyn Baring Cromer, *Modern Egypt*, 2 vols. (London: Macmillan, 1908), 2:406-19; Robert L. Tignor, *Modernization and British Colonial Rule in Egypt, 1892-1914* (Princeton: Princeton University Press, 1966), pp. 120-23.

41. 5 *Hansard's Parliamentary Debates*, H.C. 125: 1688-89.

42. Ibid., 128:953-54.

43. Leys would have had available David Livingstone's *Missionary Travels and Researches in South Africa* (London: J. Murray, 1857) and *Last Journals* (London: J. Murray, 1874).

44. William P. Young (1886-). Church of Scotland missionary; principal of Overtoun Institute, Livingstonia, Nyasaland; editor of several books of African folktales.

45. Johnston's books that relate to this statement are *A History of the Colonization of Africa by Alien Races* (Cambridge: Cambridge University Press, 1894); *British Central Africa* (London: Methuen, 1897); *The Uganda Protectorate*, 2 vols. (London: Hutchinson, 1902); *George Grenfell and the Congo* (London: Hutchinson, 1908).

46. Although I have not found an explicit statement of Leys' expectations, he appears by "revolution" to have meant a peaceful transition to socialist ownership of the means of production, accomplished through the ballot box.

47. Frank Weston (1871-1924). Bishop of Zanzibar, 1908-1924. Author of, among other

works, *The Black Slaves of Prussia* (London: U.M.C.A., 1918), and *The Serfs of Great Britain* (London: W. Knott, 1920).

48. That is, the Mandates committee of the League of Nations Union and the advisory committee of the Labour Party on international questions.

49. Richard H. Tawney (1880–1962). The great economic historian; a member of the Workers' Educational Association and of the Labour Party Advisory Committee.

50. William G. Ormsby-Gore (1885–1964). Fourth Baron Harlech (cr. 1938). Parliamentary undersecretary of state for the colonies, 1922–24, 1924–29; secretary of state, 1936–38; high commissioner, South Africa, 1941–44; chairman of the parliamentary commission to East Africa, 1924. Although Ormsby-Gore was a firm supporter of the mandates principle it is a little surprising to find him included in this list. By 1925 Leys considered him a bitter enemy.

51. Lord Henry Cavendish Bentinck (1863–1931). Liberal M.P. for South Nottingham, 1895, 1910–29.

52. Josiah Wedgwood (1872–1943). Labour M.P. for Newcastle-under-Lyme, 1906–42; a persistent parliamentary guardian of the interests of subject peoples of the empire.

53. Major-General Sir Edward Northey (1868–1953). Commander Nyasa-Rhodesia Field Forces in German East Africa, 1916–18; governor of British East Africa, 1918–22. Churchill removed him in large part in response to the forced labor controversy.

54. Charles Gore (1853–1932). Canon of West-

minster, 1894–1902; bishop of Worcester, 1902–4, of Birmingham, 1905–11, of Oxford, 1911–19.

55. Randall T. Davidson (1848–1930). Archbishop of Canterbury, 1903–28. The archbishop was personally very interested in the East African problem, though he faithfully followed Oldham's advice. Their valuable correspondence is mainly in the archives of the World Council of Churches in Geneva.

56. Alfred C. Hollis (1874–1961). Secretary of native affairs, East Africa Protectorate, 1907–12; colonial secretary, Sierra Leone, 1912–16; secretary to provincial administration, German East Africa, 1916–19; chief secretary, Tanganyika, 1919–24; resident, Zanzibar, 1924–30; governor, Trinidad and Tobago, 1930–36. Author of *The Masai* (Oxford: Clarendon Press, 1905), and *The Nandi* (Oxford: Clarendon Press, 1909). Played a central role in the move of the Masai: see his report of 5 July 1910 in PP, 1911 [Cmd. 5584], 52:722–29.

57. So far as I have been able to find, Leys never discussed African marriage and family systems, a curious omission in view of how crucial the issue was to missionaries; but I have no reason to think he did not mean monogamy in this case.

58. One of the ordinances passed in 1919 to implement the forced labor policy. See PP, 1920 [Cmd. 873], 33:109–11.

59. See George H. Wilson (1870–1959), "The Labour Problem in Nyasaland," *East and West* 19 (1921): 27–38.

60. That is, for the *Round Table*, of which Lionel Curtis was editor.

61. 26 October 1920; 5 *Parl. Deb.*, H.C. 133: 1589-90.

62. Thomas Jones (1870-1955). Secretary to Lloyd George and then through the interwar years to the cabinet.

63. That is, in the draft that eventually went to the Colonial Office in December 1920, CO 533/247/61543.

64. For the agitation surrounding the issue of Chinese labor in the South African gold mines in 1904-7, when Milner himself was high commissioner, see Eric A. Walker, *A History of Southern Africa* (London: Longmans, 1957), pp. 508-18, and Persia C. Campbell, *Chinese Coolie Emigration* (London: P. S. King, 1923), pp. 161-216.

65. Handley D. Hooper (1891-1966). C.M.S. missionary, Kikuyu; secretary, C.M.S., London.

66. Calhoun Colored School in Alabama.

67. Booker T. Washington remains as controversial as ever. See Louis R. Harlan, *Booker T. Washington: The Making of a Black Leader, 1856-1901* (New York: Oxford University Press, 1972), and "The Secret Life of Booker T. Washington," *Journal of Southern History* 37 (1971): 393-416; Stokeley Carmichael and Charles V. Hamilton, *Black Power: The Politics of Liberation in America* (New York: Random House, 1967).

68. This was Simbini M. Nkomo (?-1925), professor of history at Tuskegee and leader of the African Student Movement. See Kenneth J. King, *Pan-Africanism and Education: A Study of Race Philanthropy and Education in*

the Southern States of America and East Africa (Oxford: Clarendon Press, 1971), pp. 215–22.

69. Francis Peabody (1847–1936). American educational philanthropist and author of *Education for Life: The Story of Hampton Institute* (New York: Doubleday, 1918).

70. Samuel C. Armstrong (1839–1893). Founder of Hampton Institute, Hampton, Virginia.

71. Hollis B. Frissell (1851–1917). Principal of Hampton, 1893–1917.

72. Milner resigned in January 1921, effective the following month.

73. This is one of the few gaps in the correspondence, Oldham's letter having presumably been written on board ship so that he kept no copy.

74. Member of the League of Nations Union.

75. Precisely who Leys means here is unclear. The chief secretary of Kenya from 1911–23 was Charles C. Bowring. But it seems unlikely that Leys would have had much sympathy for the man who was at least the instrument for getting him dismissed in 1913. Nor is there any reason to suppose that Bowring was forced to resign, for he did so to become governor of Nyasaland. More likely Leys had in mind an assistant native commissioner, Oliver F. Watkins.

76. Commission Permanente pour la Protection des Indigènes, *Bulletin Officiel* (1920).

77. The Pan African Congress was founded by W. E. B. Du Bois in 1919 in Paris in hope of influencing the Versailles peace conference. See Elliott Rudwick, *W. E. B. Du Bois: A*

Study in Minority Group Leadership (Philadelphia: University of Pennsylvania Press,
1960), pp. 208–35; Francis Broderick,
*W. E. B. Du Bois: Negro Leader in a Time of
Crisis* (Stanford: Stanford University Press,
1959), pp. 123–49.

78. Edward Wood (1881–1959). First Earl of
Halifax (cr. 1944); parliamentary under-
secretary at the Colonial Office, 1921–22.
Later foreign secretary and ambassador to the
United States during World War II.

79. The offending sentence reads: "It is not denied
that settlers who have embarked on enterprises
calculated to assist the empire by the production of raw materials which are in urgent
demand should be helped by lawful and
reasonable means to secure the labour they
require" (Memorandum of 17 May 1921, in
CO 533/272/26127).

80. On the policy of the Government of India see
Gregory, *India and East Africa*, pp. 198–99,
and chap. 6. For the command paper see
PP, 1921 [Cmd. 1311].

81. On currency reform, which critics charged was
a conscious despoliation of holders of small
amounts of specie (i.e. the Africans), see
George Bennett, "Settlers and Politics in
Kenya," *Oxford History of East Africa,* 2:
234, and Ross, *Kenya from Within,* chap. 12.

82. See Leys to Wood, 10 July 1921, CO 533/
274/23713.

83. This is in answer to a letter of Oldham, 6 June
1921, transmitting criticisms.

84. Walter G. Owen (1879–1945). Church Missionary Society in East Africa from 1904;
Chaplain to forces in German East Africa,

1916-18; Archdeacon of Kavirondo, 1918-
45. See John M. Lonsdale's important
articles, which assess the long-term significance of this remarkable man's organizational
work among the Kavirondo: "European
Attitudes and African Pressures: Missions and
Governments in Kenya Between the Wars,"
Race 10 (1968): 141-51; "Political Associations in Western Kenya," in Robert Rotberg
and Ali Mazrui, eds., *Protest and Power in
Black Africa* (New York: Oxford University
Press, 1970), pp. 589-638.

85.   A. Ruffell Barlow. Church of Scotland
      Mission, Kikuyu. Author of *Tentative Studies
      in Kikuyu Grammar and Idiom* (Edinburgh:
      Church of Scotland Foreign Mission Com-
      mittee, 1914), and translator of the Psalms and
      gospels into Kikuyu.

86.   George H. Wilson, *A Missionary's Life in
      Nyasaland* (London: Universities Mission to
      Central Africa, 1920).

87.   On the West African Congress, see Martin
      Kilson, "The National Congress of British
      West Africa, 1918-1935," in Rotberg and
      Mazrui, *Protest and Power,* pp. 571-88.

88.   Arthur W. Wilkie (1875-1958). Church of
      Scotland, Calabar, 1901-18; in charge of Basel
      and Bremen mission, 1918-27; principal,
      Lovedale, South Africa, 1932-42.

89.   On compulsory labor in the tin mines of
      Northern Nigeria see Penelope Bower, "The
      Mining Industry," in Margery Perham, ed.,
      The Economics of a Tropical Dependency,
      2 vols. (London: Faber and Faber, 1946-48),
      2:24-25.

90.   Oldham was quite right. Although Wood
      thought the case for a commission hard to

resist, Churchill minuted shortly: "Bring up nearer the debate. I don't want a R.C." (Minute of about 15 June 1921 on John Ainsworth to C.O., 4 June, CO 533/273/ 28016). In the House of Commons Churchill defended his refusal by saying that a royal commission would merely delay the problem. 5 *Hansard,* H.C. 144 (14 July 1921): 1625.

91. Arthur Steel-Maitland (1876–1935). Conservative M.P.; parliamentary undersecretary at C.O., 1915–17; at Board of Trade, 1917–19; Minister of Labour, 1924–29.

92. This is in reference to the Phelps-Stokes commission tour of West Africa, 1920–21.

93. Although an Indian demand for a mandate in East Africa surfaced briefly as a plank of the nationalist platform during World War I, it was squelched shortly afterward by Gandhi and other leaders. See Gregory, *India and East Africa,* chap. 5.

94. A. M. Jevanjee. Wealthy Indian entrepreneur and industrialist, elected to the legislative council of the East Africa Protectorate in 1908 from which he resigned in protest. Ewart S. Grogan (1874–). Explorer, landowner, and Kenya politician.

95. As already remarked in the introduction Leys' meetings in the same week with Thomas Jesse Jones and William E. B. Du Bois were crucial in helping him to reach his logical conclusions about race.

96. See Dispatch re Native Labour, East Africa Protectorate, PP, 1920 [Cmd. 873].

97. Charles H. Robinson (1861–1925). Church Missionary Society in West Africa; lecturer in Hausa at Cambridge.

98. Thomas E. Harvey (1875-1955). Warden of Toynbee Hall, 1909-11; Labour M.P., 1910-24; Independent Progressive, Combined English Universities, 1937-45.

99. See Fulani bin Fulani, "Under a Mandate," *The New Europe* 11 (1919): 265-71, 300-306.

100. Georgiana Gollock was a secretary at Edinburgh House.

101. But see the contrary view in Winthrop D. Jordan, *White Over Black: American Attitudes Toward the Negro, 1550-1812* (Chapel Hill: University of North Carolina Press, 1968), pp. 37-38, who argues that Shakespeare's audiences would have understood Othello's blackness to be the focal point of the play.

102. This view, so strange to a southern American, was recently argued by Eliot J. Rose et al., *Colour and Citizenship: A Report on British Race Relations* (London: Oxford University Press, 1969), p. 555.

103. "Manifesto of the Second Pan-African Congress," *The Crisis* 23 (November 1921): 5-10.

104. See judgment of high court in Masai v. Attorney General, East Africa Protectorate, 26 May 1913, PP, 1913 [Cmd. 6939], 45:679-85.

105. Edward Grey (1862-1933; cr. Visc., 1916). Foreign secretary, 1905-16.

106. Marion Hunter was also a secretary at Edinburgh House.

107. That is, the approach leading to the creation in 1924 of the Colonial Office Advisory Committee on Education.

108. Charles F. Andrews (1871-1940). A missionary closer than any other Englishman of

the interwar period, save possibly Annie
Besant, to the spirit of Indian nationalism.
Edited the writings of Gandhi and Rabin-
dranath Tagore and, among other books,
wrote *India and Britain* (London: Student
Christian Mission, 1935), and *The True India*
(London: Allen and Unwin, 1935).

109. See PP, 1923 [Cmd. 1922].

110. Gordon Guggisberg (1869–1930). Surveyor,
Gold Coast, 1902, 1905–8; Surveyor-general,
Nigeria, 1910–14; governor, Gold Coast, 1919–
27. With Alexander G. Fraser, wrote *The
Future of the Negro* (London: Student
Christian Mission, 1929). The definitive
biography is by Ronald E. Wraith, *Guggisberg*
(London: Oxford University Press, 1967).

111. James H. Dillard (1856–1940). President of the
Jeanes foundation for the development of
Negro schools, 1907–31; director of the John F.
Slater Fund, 1913–31; vice-president of the
Phelps-Stokes Fund

112. Appointed in July 1924.

113. Francis J. Hopwood (1860–1947; cr. baron,
1917). Permanent secretary, Board of Trade,
1901–17; permanent undersecretary, Colonial
Office, 1907–11.

114. That is, *Christianity and the Race Problem*
(London: Student Christian Mission Press,
1925).

115. That is, the letter of 1918 to the secretary of
state.

116. Sir Hugh Clifford (1866–1941). Malay civil
service, 1883; British resident, Pahang, 1896–
99, 1901–3; colonial secretary, Trinidad and
Tobago, 1903–7, Ceylon, 1907–12; governor,

Gold Coast, 1912–19, Nigeria, 1919–25, Straits
Settlements, 1927–29.

117. The negotiations with Allen and Unwin fell
      through, and Leonard Woolf published *Kenya*
      at the Hogarth Press. To the surprise of every-
      one it was a financial success, going into three
      editions within two years.

118. Abbe L. Warnshuis (1877–1958). New York
      secretary of the International Missionary
      Council, 1925–43.

119. James Masterton–Smith (1878–1938). Admir-
      alty, 1901–19; assistant secretary, War Office
      and Air Ministry, 1919–20; joint permanent
      secretary, Ministry of Labour, 1920–21; per-
      manent undersecretary, Colonial Office, 1921–
      24.

120. Leopold Amery was the new secretary of state
      for the colonies.

121. Philip H. Kerr (1882–1940; eleventh Marquess
      of Lothian, cr. 1930). One of Sir Alfred Mil-
      ner's "kindergarten" in South Africa during
      the Boer War; a founder in 1910 of *Round
      Table;* private secretary to David Lloyd George
      1916–21. Secretary of Rhodes Trust. Under-
      secretary for India, 1930–32; ambassador to
      the United States, 1938–40. His review of
      Kenya is in the *Times Literary Supplement,* 4
      December 1924.

122. Donald Cameron (1872–1948). Colonial secre-
      tary, Southern Nigeria, 1912; central secretary,
      Nigeria, from 1914, and chief secretary, 1921–
      24. Governor, Tanganyika Territory, 1925–31;
      of Nigeria, 1931–35. See *My Tanganyika Ser-
      vice and Some Nigeria* (London: Allen and
      Unwin, 1939).

123. From his investigative tour of East Africa.

124. The White Paper asserting "African paramountcy": PP, 1923 [Cmd. 1922].

125. Robert T. Coryndon (1870–1925). Born in South Africa, went into the British South Africa Company and was with the pioneer column into Mashonaland, 1890. Made the first survey and drawings of Great Zimbabwe. Private secretary to Cecil Rhodes; resident with Lewanika of the Lozi. Administrator, North West Rhodesia, 1900–1907; of Swaziland, 1907–16; of Basutoland, 1916; governor of Uganda, 1917–22; and of Kenya, 1922–25.

126. See report of the East Africa Commission, PP, 1924–25 [Cmd. 2387].

127. Garfield H. Williams (1881–1960). Secretary of the Student Christian Mission, 1907; foreign secretary, Church Missionary Society, 1921–24; secretary of Missionary Council of the National Church Assembly, 1924–29.

128. Sydney H. Olivier (1859–1943; cr. baron, 1924). Entered C.O., 1882; colonial secretary, British Honduras, 1890–91; auditor-general, Leeward Islands, 1895–96; colonial secretary, Jamaica, 1900–1904; Governor, Jamaica, 1907–13; Secretary of state for India, 1924. Member of the Fabian Society. Wrote several books, including *White Capital and Coloured Labour* (London: Independent Labour Party, 1906), and *The Anatomy of African Misery* (London: Hogarth Press, 1927).

129. Thomas Jesse Jones, *Education in East Africa: A Study of East, Central and South Africa* (New York: Phelps-Stokes Fund, 1925).

130. Sir William Ormsby-Gore, Frederick C. Linfield, and Archibald G. Church.

131. Ormsby-Gore's speech, 28 January 1925, is in

the *Journal of the African Society* 24 (1924–25): 165–77.

132. This is a common error. Abolition was finally carried in 1806, after the death of Charles James Fox, by Lord William W. Grenville (1759–1834). See Roger Anstey, "A Re-interpretation of the Abolition of the British Slave Trade: 1806–1807," *English Historical Review* 87 (1972): 304–32.

133. Oldham's review of *Kenya* appeared in the *International Review of Missions* 15 (1925): 277–80.

134. George E. Schuster (1881–). Financial secretary, Sudan, 1922–27; chairman, advisory committee to the C.O. on East African loans, 1926–28; on East African Commission on Closer Union, 1928; financial member, Executive Council of Viceroy of India, 1928–34; Colonial Development Advisory Committee, 1936–38.

135. Graeme Thomson (1875–1933). Colonial secretary, Ceylon, 1919–22; governor, British Guiana, 1922–25, of Nigeria, 1925–31.

136. Richard Feetham (1874–1965). Legislative Assembly, South Africa, 1915–23; chairman, Irish Boundary Commission, 1924–25; chairman, Local Government Commission, Kenya, 1926; judge in Natal, 1931–39, and in Supreme Court of South Africa, 1939–44; vice-chancellor, University of Witwatersrand, 1938–48; chancellor, 1949–61.

137. See *The Times*, 23 April 1925.

138. Sir James Currie (1868–1937). Principal, Gordon College, Khartoum, and director of education, Sudan, 1900–1914; director, Empire Cotton Growing Corporation.

139. George Geoffrey Dawson (1874-1944). Editor of *The Times*, 1912-19, 1923-41.

140. Waldorf Astor (1895-1952; cr. second viscount, 1919). Owner and publisher of *The Observer*.

141. Ian D. Colvin (1877-1938). Biographer of Cecil Rhodes, his lieutenant, Leander Starr Jameson, and General Reginald E. Dyer, the commander of the force at the Amritsar massacre.

142. Herbert A. L. Fisher (1865-1940). M.P. (National Liberal), 1916-26; president, Board of Education, 1916-22; warden, New College Oxford, 1925-40. Well-known historian of Europe.

143. That is, Stanley Baldwin.

144. James E. H. Gascoyne-Cecil (1861-1947; fourth marquess, cr. 1903).

145. Winston Churchill.

146. 5 *Hansard* (Lords), 61 (20 May 1925): 385-96.

147. Ibid., 404-14.

148. Delivered by Olivier, ibid., 415-17.

149. Dr. Abraham Flexner (1866-1959). Carnegie Foundation: committee on advancement of teaching, 1908-25; director, division of medical education, 1925-28. Director, Institute of Advanced Study, 1939-40. Author of the seminal reports: *Medical Education in the United States and Canada* (New York: Carnegie, 1907), *The American College* (New York: Century, 1908), and *Medical Education: A Comparative Study* (New York: Macmillan, 1925).

150. Edward W. Grigg (1879-1955; Baron Altrincham, cr. 1945). With *The Times*, 1903, 1908-13; secretary to the Prince of Wales,

1919, to Lloyd George, 1921–22; M.P. (National Liberal), 1922–25; governor, Kenya, 1925–31; M.P. (National Conservative), Altrincham, 1933–45. Author of *The British Commonwealth* (London: Hutchinson, 1943), and *Kenya's Opportunity* (London: Faber and Faber, 1955).

151. For Lugard's proposal for administrative segregation in Kenya, see Margery Perham, *Lugard*, 2 vols. (London: Collins, 1956–60), 2:678–80. Oldham came to Brailsford on 19 June 1925.

152. Kenneth Leys, a lecturer at Oxford.

153. On the strain in their relationship see Leys to Jones, 23 January and 16 October 1925, Thomas Jones Papers, National Library of Wales, Aberystwyth.

154. The sentence in question is presumably the following: "The beginnings of a revolt against the rigidity of education are apparent in America and Europe" (*Education in East Africa*, p. 9).

155. "A Note on the Report of the East African Commission" (privately printed by W. H. Smith), encl. in Oldham to Ormsby-Gore, 6 May 1925, CO 533/344/20779. (See above, Appendix.)

156. Charles Roden Buxton, *The Black Man's Rights* (London: Independent Labour Party, 1925).

157. The proofs of his article on "Christianity and Native Labour," *Brotherhood Magazine*, 1925, enclosed in Leys to Oldham, 18 July 1925.

158. Gerald V. Maxwell (1877–1965). Chairman, Native Lands Commission, Fiji, 1912–21; chief native commissioner, Kenya, 1921–31.

159. Thomas Jesse Jones.

160. On the important Le Zoute conference see Edwin W. Smith, *The Christian Mission in Africa* (London: International Missionary Council, 1926).

161. John L. Dube (1871–1946). Founded in 1906 the Zulu newspaper *Ilanga Lase Natal* and led deputation to Britain in 1914 to protest against South African Native Land Act. Author of *The Zulu's Appeal for Light and England's Duty* (London: Unwin, 1909).

162. Zaccheus R. Mahabane. President of South African Native Congress.

163. John Hope (1868–1936). President, Morehouse College, Atlanta, 1906–31; president, Atlanta University, 1929–36.

164. Thomas Jesse Jones, *Four Essentials of Education* (New York: Scribners, 1926).

165. Michael Sadler (1861–1943). Royal commission on education, 1893–95; department of education, 1895–1903; vice-chancellor, Leeds University, 1911–23; master, University College Oxford, 1923–24. Author of *Our Public Elementary Schools* (London: Butterworth, 1926).

166. Makerere College in Kampala, Uganda, was founded in 1922, became a university college (attached to the University of London) in 1949, and a university in 1970.

167. James W. C. Dougall. Secretary to the Phelps-Stokes Commission in East Africa, director of the Jeanes program in Kenya, and later successor to Oldham in the African section of the work of the Conference of British Missionary Societies at Edinburgh House.

168. R. G. M. Calderwood. A young missionary in
      Kenya, whose letter defending the missionaries
      appeared in the *Scots Observer*, 11 December
      1926.

Index

Index

Achimota College: founding, 64–67, 224, 279, 292–93, 335 n.135. *See also* Education; Fraser, Alexander G.

Africa: traditional culture, 152; British ignorance of, 143; last test for Christianity, 57–58; last problem of human race, 139; a world problem, 313; not Oldham's ultimate objective, 87. *See also* Africans

Africa, Central: weakness of white interests, 4. *See also* Nyasaland; Rhodesia, Northern

Africa, East: coming of colonialism to, 24; select committee on, 51, 225–26, 229–30, 236, 237–38, 239, 248; Ormsby-Gore report on economic development, 79–80, 233, 234, 235, 256, 257, 260, 261, 337 n.158; Oldham memorandum on, 295–316; closer union movement, 7, 34, 35, 82, 319 n.14; Hilton Young commission, 86. *See also* Kenya; Tanganyika; Uganda

Africa, South. *See* South Africa

Africa, West: number of settlers, 3, 282; missionary attitudes, 57–61; cocoa in, 133; free labor system, 170, 185. *See also* Gold Coast; Nigeria; West African Congress

Africans: Leys on capability for resistance, 95, 123, 135–36, 175; no distinctive features, 146, 276; idleness a myth, 157, 171, 173, 184; educated, 134; political rights of, 190, 194–97, 217, 281. *See also* Education; Labor; Race; Resistance, African

African Students Association

(U.S.). *See* Pan-Africanism

Aggrey, James E. K.: and Achimota College, 64–67, 224, 279, 334 n.129. *See also* Achimota College; Phelps-Stokes Commission

Agriculture, African peasant: Colonial Office attitude, 5; Oldham wants research on, 80, 163, 259, 302–3, 308; Leys on difficulty and need to stimulate, 133, 171, 184. *See also* Development, economic; Industry, African native; Labor

Ainsworth, John: Leys on, 329 n.90; and forced-labor campaign in Kenya, 39, 42, 155, 156, 164, 275, 330 n.92. *See also* Labor

Amani Institute, 314 n.3. *See also* Germany; Research, African

America. *See* United States

Amery, Leopold S., 261, 358 n.120; and colonial investment, 45; Oldham and, 79, 233, 234; and forced labor, 149, 150, 159; and education, 230, 231; on African research, 264, 265

Amritsar massacre, 48

Andrews, Charles F., 49, 220, 356 n.108

Ankylostomiasis, 174. *See also* Disease

Anthropology: before Malinowski, 19, 324 n.48; functional, 20, 325 n.60; Leys' attitude toward, 22; impact on racial attitudes, 54–56; Oldham wants in Africa, 302, 307; and International Institute of African Languages and Cultures, 72–75

Anti-Corn Law League, 170